Mastering Linux - Fundamentals

A catalogue record for this book is available from the Hong Kong Public Libraries.

Published in Hong Kong by Samurai Media Limited.

Email: info@samuraimedia.org

ISBN 978-988-8406-16-6

Background Cover Image by https://www.flickr.com/people/webtreatsetc/

Table of Contents

List of Tables

Part I. introduction to Linux

Table of Contents

Chapter 1. Linux history

This chapter briefly tells the history of Unix and where Linux fits in.

If you are eager to start working with Linux without this blah, blah, blah over history, distributions, and licensing then jump straight to **Part II - Chapter 8. Working with Directories** page 73.

1.1. 1969

All modern operating systems have their roots in 1969 when **Dennis Ritchie** and **Ken Thompson** developed the C language and the **Unix** operating system at AT&T Bell Labs. They shared their source code (yes, there was open source back in the Seventies) with the rest of the world, including the hippies in Berkeley California. By 1975, when AT&T started selling Unix commercially, about half of the source code was written by others. The hippies were not happy that a commercial company sold software that they had written; the resulting (legal) battle ended in there being two versions of **Unix**: the official AT&T Unix, and the free **BSD** Unix.

Development of BSD descendants like FreeBSD, OpenBSD, NetBSD, DragonFly BSD and PC-BSD is still active today.

```
https://en.wikipedia.org/wiki/Dennis_Ritchie
https://en.wikipedia.org/wiki/Ken_Thompson
https://en.wikipedia.org/wiki/BSD
https://en.wikipedia.org/wiki/Comparison_of_BSD_operating_systems
```

1.2. 1980s

In the Eighties many companies started developing their own Unix: IBM created AIX, Sun SunOS (later Solaris), HP HP-UX and about a dozen other companies did the same. The result was a mess of Unix dialects and a dozen different ways to do the same thing. And here is the first real root of **Linux**, when **Richard Stallman** aimed to end this era of Unix separation and everybody re-inventing the wheel by starting the **GNU** project (GNU is Not Unix). His goal was to make an operating system that was freely available to everyone, and where everyone could work together (like in the Seventies). Many of the command line tools that you use today on **Linux** are GNU tools.

```
https://en.wikipedia.org/wiki/Richard_Stallman
https://en.wikipedia.org/wiki/IBM_AIX
https://en.wikipedia.org/wiki/HP-UX
```

1.3. 1990s

The Nineties started with **Linus Torvalds**, a Swedish speaking Finnish student, buying a 386 computer and writing a brand new POSIX compliant kernel. He put the source code online, thinking it would never support anything but 386 hardware. Many people embraced the combination of this kernel with the GNU tools, and the rest, as they say, is history.

```
http://en.wikipedia.org/wiki/Linus_Torvalds
https://en.wikipedia.org/wiki/History_of_Linux
https://en.wikipedia.org/wiki/Linux
https://lwn.net
http://www.levenez.com/unix/    (a huge Unix history poster)
```

1.4. 2015

Today more than 97 percent of the world's supercomputers (including the complete top 10), more than 80 percent of all smartphones, many millions of desktop computers, around 70 percent of all web servers, a large chunk of tablet computers, and several appliances (dvd-players, washing machines, dsl modems, routers, self-driving cars, space station laptops...) run **Linux**. Linux is by far the most commonly used operating system in the world.

Linux kernel version 4.0 was released in April 2015. Its source code grew by several hundred thousand lines (compared to version 3.19 from February 2015) thanks to contributions of thousands of developers paid by hundreds of commercial companies including Red Hat, Intel, Samsung, Broadcom, Texas Instruments, IBM, Novell, Qualcomm, Nokia, Oracle, Google, AMD and even Microsoft (and many more).

```
http://kernelnewbies.org/DevelopmentStatistics
http://kernel.org
http://www.top500.org
```

Chapter 2. distributions

This chapter gives a short overview of current Linux distributions.

A Linux **distribution** is a collection of (usually open source) software on top of a Linux kernel. A distribution (or short, distro) can bundle server software, system management tools, documentation and many desktop applications in a **central secure software repository**. A distro aims to provide a common look and feel, secure and easy software management and often a specific operational purpose.

Let's take a look at some popular distributions.

2.1. Red Hat

Red Hat is a billion dollar commercial Linux company that puts a lot of effort in developing Linux. They have hundreds of Linux specialists and are known for their excellent support. They give their products (Red Hat Enterprise Linux and Fedora) away for free. While **Red Hat Enterprise Linux** (RHEL) is well tested before release and supported for up to seven years after release, **Fedora** is a distro with faster updates but without support.

2.2. Ubuntu

Canonical started sending out free compact discs with **Ubuntu** Linux in 2004 and quickly became popular for home users (many switching from Microsoft Windows). Canonical wants Ubuntu to be an easy to use graphical Linux desktop without need to ever see a command line. Of course they also want to make a profit by selling support for Ubuntu.

2.3. Debian

There is no company behind **Debian**. Instead there are thousands of well organised developers that elect a **Debian Project Leader** every two years. Debian is seen as one of the most stable Linux distributions. It is also the basis of every release of Ubuntu. Debian comes in three versions: stable, testing and unstable. Every Debian release is named after a character in the movie Toy Story.

2.4. Other

Distributions like CentOS, Oracle Enterprise Linux and Scientific Linux are based on Red Hat Enterprise Linux and share many of the same principles, directories and system administration techniques. **Linux Mint**, Edubuntu and many other *buntu named distributions are based on Ubuntu and thus share a lot with Debian. There are hundreds of other Linux distributions.

2.5. Which to choose ?

Below are some very personal opinions on some of the most popular Linux Distributions. Keep in mind that any of the below Linux distributions can be a stable server and a nice graphical desktop client.

Table 2.1. choosing a Linux distro

distribution name	reason(s) for using
Red Hat Enterprise (RHEL)	You are a manager and you want a good support contract.
CentOS	You want Red Hat without the support contract from Red Hat.
Fedora	You want Red Hat on your laptop/desktop.
Linux Mint	You want a personal graphical desktop to play movies, music and games.
Debian	My personal favorite for servers, laptops, and any other device.
Ubuntu	Very popular, based on Debian, not my favorite.
Kali	You want a pointy-clicky hacking interface.
others	Advanced users may prefer Arch, Gentoo, OpenSUSE, Scientific, ...

When you are new to Linux in 2015, go for the latest Mint or Fedora. If you only want to practice the Linux command line then install one Debian server and/or one CentOS server (without graphical interface).

Here are some links to help you choose:

```
distrowatch.com
redhat.com
centos.org
debian.org
www.linuxmint.com
ubuntu.com
```

Chapter 3. licensing

This chapter briefly explains the different licenses used for distributing operating systems software.

Many thanks go to **Ywein Van den Brande** for writing most of this chapter.

Ywein is an attorney at law, co-author of **The International FOSS Law Book** and author of **Praktijkboek Informaticarecht** (in Dutch).

http://ifosslawbook.org
http://www.crealaw.eu

3.1. about software licenses

There are two predominant software paradigms: **Free and Open Source Software** (FOSS) and **proprietary software**. The criteria for differentiation between these two approaches is based on control over the software. With **proprietary software**, control tends to lie more with the vendor, while with **Free and Open Source Software** it tends to be more weighted towards the end user. But even though the paradigms differ, they use the same **copyright laws** to reach and enforce their goals. From a legal perspective, **Free and Open Source Software** can be considered as software to which users generally receive more rights via their license agreement than they would have with a **proprietary software license**, yet the underlying license mechanisms are the same.

Legal theory states that the author of FOSS, contrary to the author of **public domain** software, has in no way whatsoever given up his rights on his work. FOSS supports on the rights of the author (the **copyright**) to impose FOSS license conditions. The FOSS license conditions need to be respected by the user in the same way as proprietary license conditions. Always check your license carefully before you use third party software.

Examples of proprietary software are **AIX** from IBM, **HP-UX** from HP and **Oracle Database 11g**. You are not authorised to install or use this software without paying a licensing fee. You are not authorised to distribute copies and you are not authorised to modify the closed source code.

3.2. public domain software and freeware

Software that is original in the sense that it is an intellectual creation of the author benefits **copyright** protection. Non-original software does not come into consideration for **copyright** protection and can, in principle, be used freely.

Public domain software is considered as software to which the author has given up all rights and on which nobody is able to enforce any rights. This software can be used, reproduced or executed freely, without permission or the payment of a fee. Public domain software can in certain cases even be presented by third parties as own work, and by modifying the original work, third parties can take certain versions of the public domain software out of the public domain again.

Freeware is not public domain software or FOSS. It is proprietary software that you can use without paying a license cost. However, the often strict license terms need to be respected.

Examples of freeware are **Adobe Reader**, **Skype** and **Command and Conquer: Tiberian Sun** (this game was sold as proprietary in 1999 and is since 2011 available as freeware).

3.3. Free Software or Open Source Software

Both the **Free Software** (translates to **vrije software** in Dutch and to **Logiciel Libre** in French) and the **Open Source Software** movement largely pursue similar goals and endorse similar software licenses. But historically, there has been some perception of differentiation due to different emphases. Where the **Free Software** movement focuses on the rights (the four freedoms) which Free Software provides to its users, the **Open Source Software** movement points to its Open Source Definition and the advantages of peer-to-peer software development.

Recently, the term free and open source software or FOSS has arisen as a neutral alternative. A lesser-used variant is free/libre/open source software (FLOSS), which uses **libre** to clarify the meaning of free as in **freedom** rather than as in **at no charge**.

Examples of **free software** are **gcc**, **MySQL** and **gimp**.

Detailed information about the **four freedoms** can be found here:

`http://www.gnu.org/philosophy/free-sw.html`

The **open source definition** can be found at:

`http://www.opensource.org/docs/osd`

The above definition is based on the **Debian Free Software Guidelines** available here:

`http://www.debian.org/social_contract#guidelines`

3.4. GNU General Public License

More and more software is being released under the **GNU GPL** (in 2006 Java was released under the GPL). This license (v2 and v3) is the main license endorsed by the Free Software Foundation. It's main characteristic is the **copyleft** principle. This means that everyone in the chain of consecutive users, in return for the right of use that is assigned, needs to distribute the improvements he makes to the software and his derivative works under the same conditions to other users, if he chooses to distribute such improvements or derivative works. In other words, software which incorporates GNU GPL software, needs to be distributed in turn as GNU GPL software (or compatible, see below). It is not possible to incorporate copyright protected parts of GNU GPL software in a proprietary licensed work. The GPL has been upheld in court.

3.5. using GPLv3 software

You can use **GPLv3 software** almost without any conditions. If you solely run the software you even don't have to accept the terms of the GPLv3. However, any other use - such as modifying or distributing the software - implies acceptance.

In case you use the software internally (including over a network), you may modify the software without being obliged to distribute your modification. You may hire third parties to work on the software exclusively for you and under your direction and control. But if you modify the software and use it otherwise than merely internally, this will be considered as distribution. You must distribute your modifications under GPLv3 (the copyleft principle). Several more obligations apply if you distribute GPLv3 software. Check the GPLv3 license carefully.

You create output with GPLv3 software: The GPLv3 does not automatically apply to the output.

3.6. BSD license

There are several versions of the original Berkeley Distribution License. The most common one is the 3-clause license ("New BSD License" or "Modified BSD License").

This is a permissive free software license. The license places minimal restrictions on how the software can be redistributed. This is in contrast to copyleft licenses such as the GPLv. 3 discussed above, which have a copyleft mechanism.

This difference is of less importance when you merely use the software, but kicks in when you start redistributing verbatim copies of the software or your own modified versions.

3.7. other licenses

FOSS or not, there are many kind of licenses on software. You should read and understand them before using any software.

3.8. combination of software licenses

When you use several sources or wishes to redistribute your software under a different license, you need to verify whether all licenses are compatible. Some FOSS licenses (such as BSD) are compatible with proprietary licenses, but most are not. If you detect a license incompatibility, you must contact the author to negotiate different license conditions or refrain from using the incompatible software.

Part II. installing Linux

Table of Contents

Chapter 4. installing Debian 8

This module is a step by step demonstration of an actual installation of **Debian 8** (also known as **Jessie**).

We start by downloading an image from the internet and install **Debian 8** as a virtual machine in **Virtualbox**. We will also do some basic configuration of this new machine like setting an **ip address** and fixing a **hostname**.

This procedure should be very similar for other versions of **Debian**, and also for distributions like **Linux Mint, xubuntu/ubuntu/kubuntu** or **Mepis**. This procedure can also be helpful if you are using another virtualization solution.

Go to the next chapter if you want to install **CentOS, Fedora, Red Hat Enterprise Linux, ...**

4.1. Debian

Debian is one of the oldest Linux distributions. I use Debian myself on almost every computer that I own (including **raspbian** on the **Raspberry Pi**).

Debian comes in **releases** named after characters in the movie **Toy Story**. The **Jessie** release contains about 36000 packages.

Table 4.1. Debian releases

name	number	year
Woody	3.0	2002
Sarge	3.1	2005
Etch	4.0	2007
Lenny	5.0	2009
Squeeze	6.0	2011
Wheezy	7	2013
Jessie	8	2015

There is never a fixed date for the next **Debian** release. The next version is released when it is ready.

4.2. Downloading

All these screenshots were made in November 2014, which means **Debian 8** was still in 'testing' (but in 'freeze', so there will be no major changes when it is released).

Download Debian here:

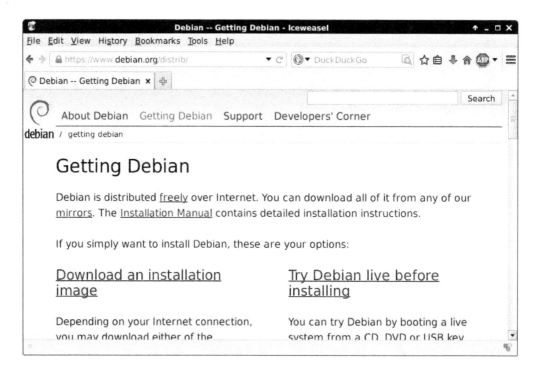

After a couple of clicks on that website, I ended up downloading **Debian 8** (testing) here. It should be only one click once **Debian 8** is released (somewhere in 2015).

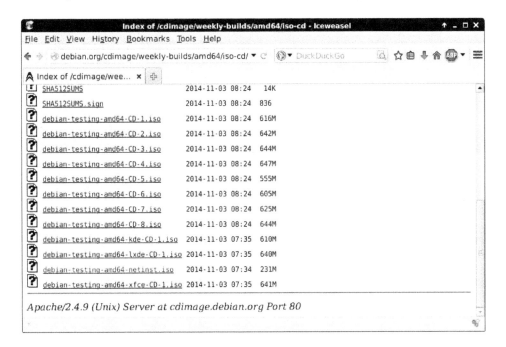

You have many other options to download and install **Debian**. We will discuss them much later.

This small screenshot shows the downloading of a **netinst** .iso file. Most of the software will be downloaded during the installation. This also means that you will have the most recent version of all packages when the install is finished.

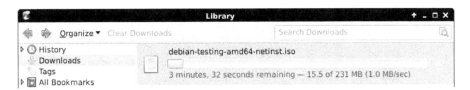

I already have Debian 8 installed on my laptop (hence the **paul@debian8** prompt). Anyway, this is the downloaded file just before starting the installation.

```
paul@debian8:~$ ls -hl debian-testing-amd64-netinst.iso
-rw-r--r-- 1 paul paul 231M Nov 10 17:59 debian-testing-amd64-netinst.iso
```

Create a new virtualbox machine (I already have five, you might have zero for now). Click the **New** button to start a wizard that will help you create a virtual machine.

The machine needs a name, this screenshot shows that I named it **server42**.

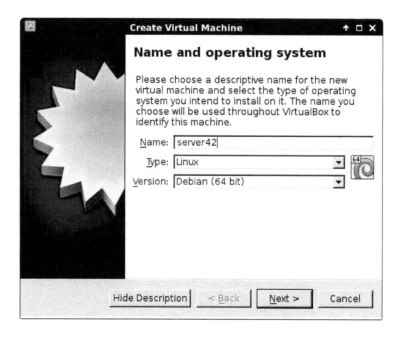

Most of the defaults in Virtualbox are ok.

512MB of RAM is enough to practice all the topics in this book.

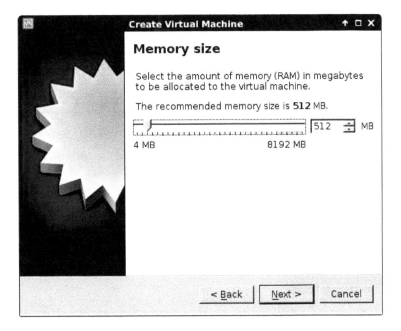

We do not care about the virtual disk format.

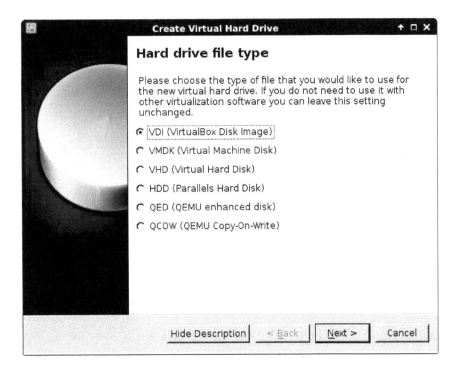

Choosing **dynamically allocated** will save you some disk space (for a small performance hit).

8GB should be plenty for learning about Linux servers.

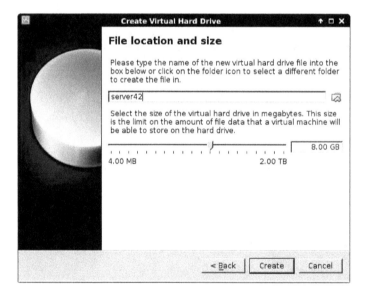

This finishes the wizard. You virtual machine is almost ready to begin the installation.

First, make sure that you attach the downloaded .iso image to the virtual CD drive. (by opening **Settings**, **Storage** followed by a mouse click on the round CD icon)

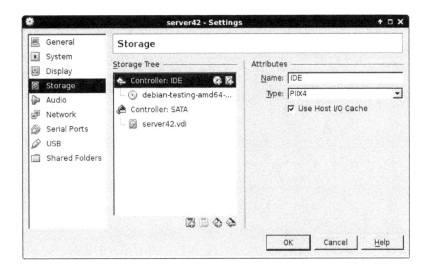

Personally I also disable sound and usb, because I never use these features. I also remove the floppy disk and use a PS/2 mouse pointer. This is probably not very important, but I like the idea that it saves some resources.

Now boot the virtual machine and begin the actual installation. After a couple of seconds you should see a screen similar to this. Choose **Install** to begin the installation of Debian.

First select the language you want to use.

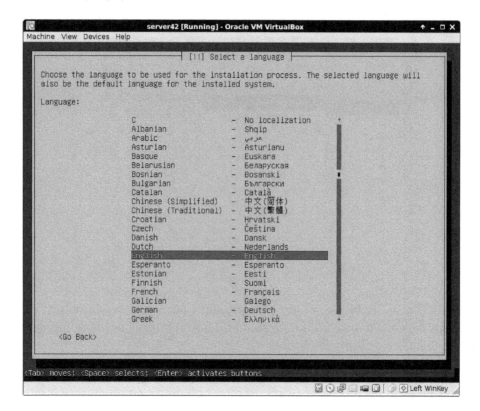

Choose your country. This information will be used to suggest a download mirror.

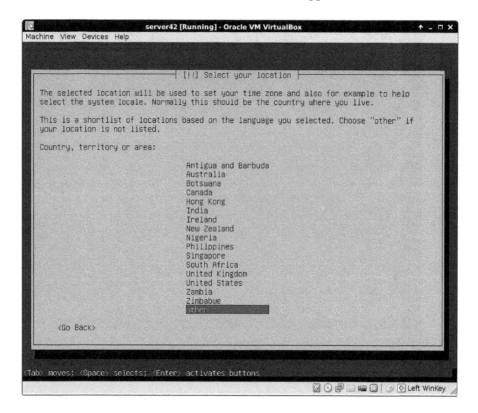

Choose the correct keyboard. On servers this is of no importance since most servers are remotely managed via **ssh**.

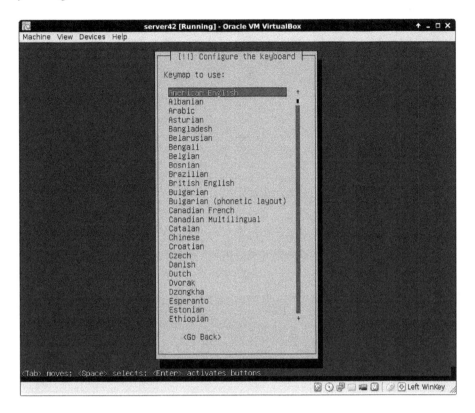

Enter a **hostname** (with **fqdn** to set a **dnsdomainname**).

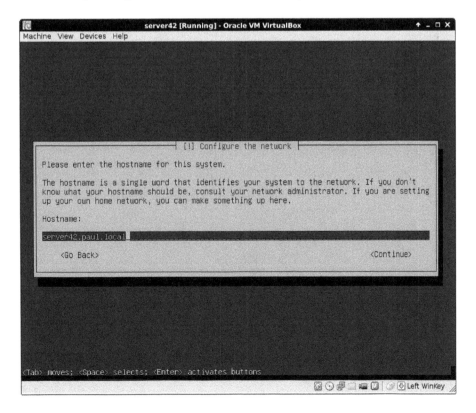

Give the **root** user a password. Remember this password (or use **hunter2**).

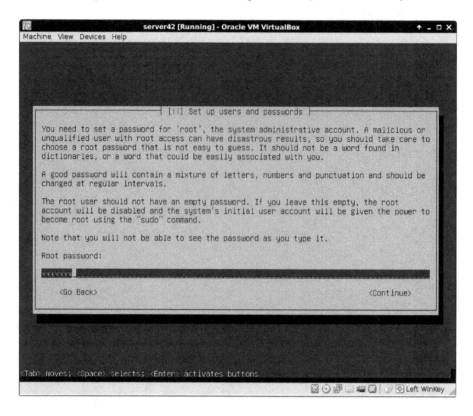

It is adviced to also create a normal user account. I don't give my full name, Debian 8 accepts an identical username and full name **paul**.

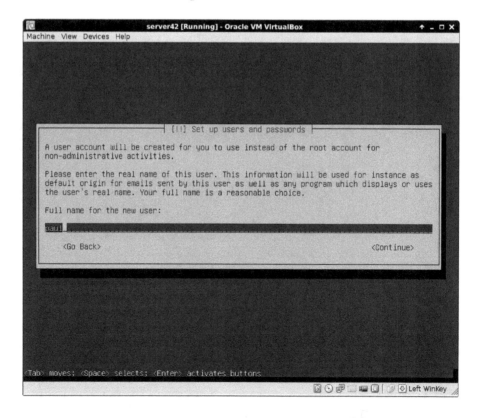

The **use entire disk** refers to the **virtual disk** that you created before in **Virtualbox**..

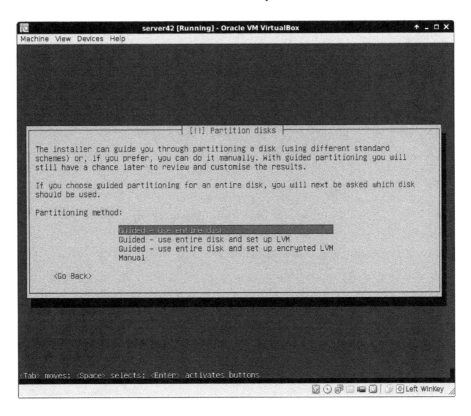

Again the default is probably what you want. Only change partitioning if you really know what you are doing.

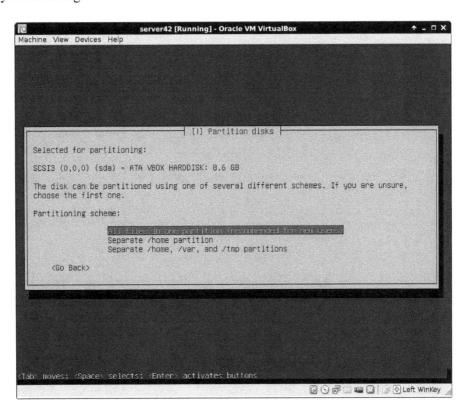

Accept the partition layout (again only change if you really know what you are doing).

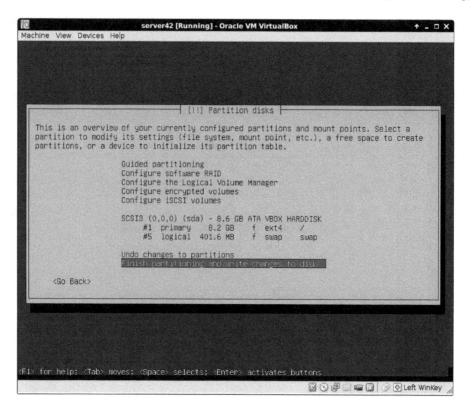

This is the point of no return, the magical moment where pressing **yes** will forever erase data on the (virtual) computer.

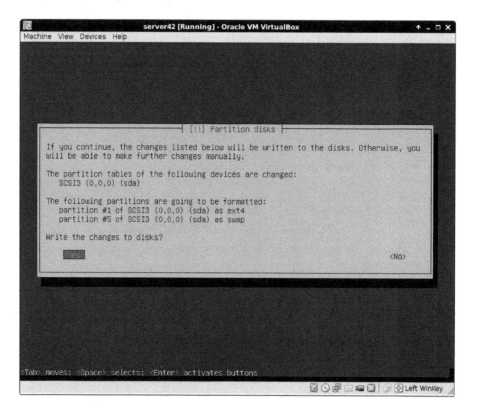

Software is downloaded from a mirror repository, preferably choose one that is close by (as in the same country).

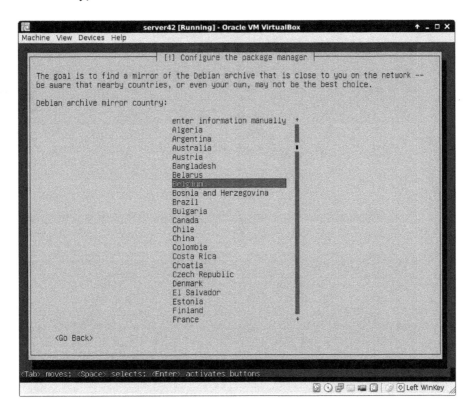

This setup was done in Belgium.

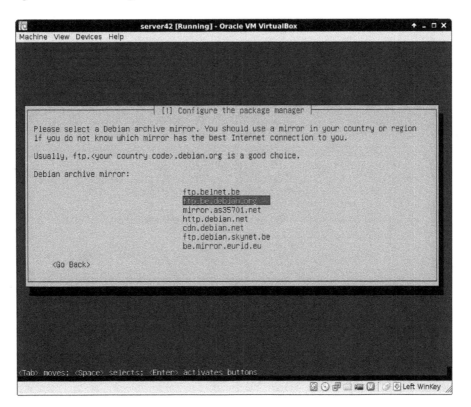

Leave the proxy field empty (unless you are sure that you are behind a proxy server).

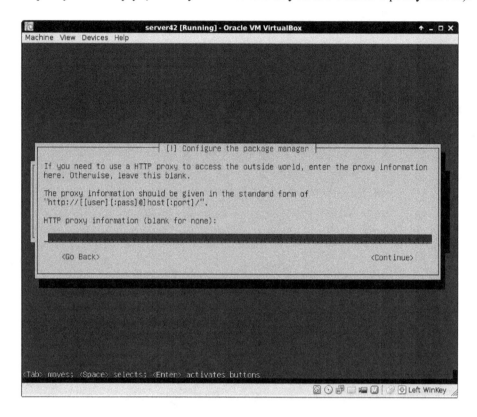

Choose whether you want to send anonymous statistics to the Debian project (it gathers data about installed packages). You can view the statistics here **http://popcon.debian.org/**.

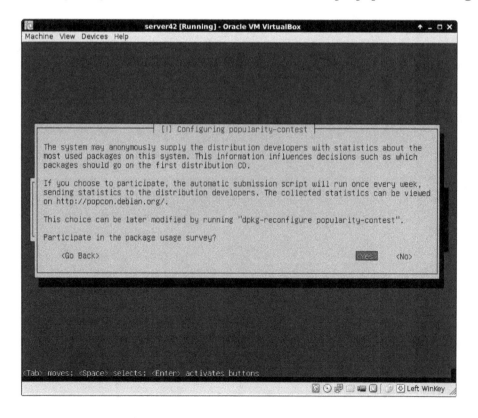

Choose what software to install, we do not need any graphical stuff for this training.

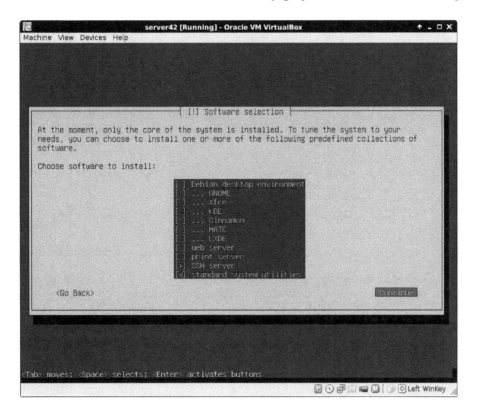

The latest versions are being downloaded.

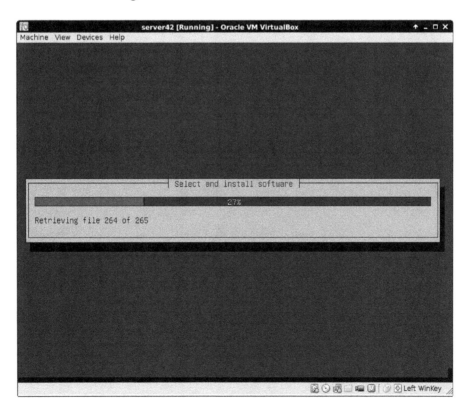

Say yes to install the bootloader on the virtual machine.

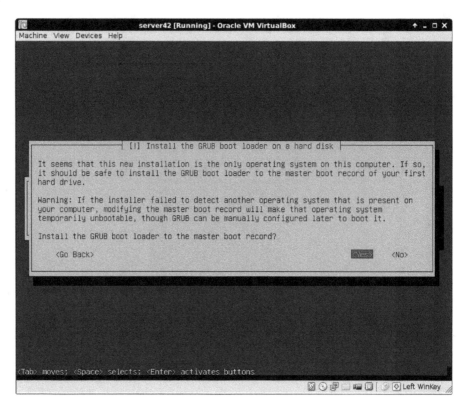

Booting for the first time shows the grub screen

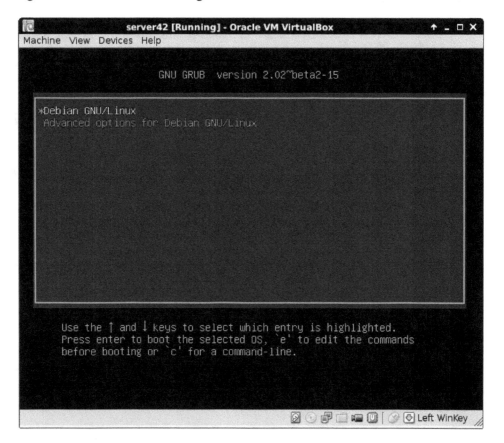

A couple seconds later you should see a lot of text scrolling of the screen (**dmesg**). After which you are presented with this **getty** and are allowed your first logon.

You should now be able to log on to your virtual machine with the **root** account. Do you remember the password ? Was it **hunter2** ?

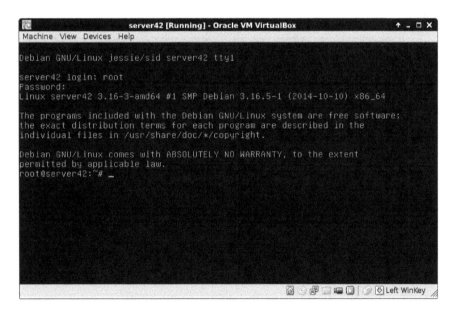

The screenshots in this book will look like this from now on. You can just type those commands in the terminal (after you logged on).

```
root@server42:~# who am i
root     tty1         2014-11-10 18:21
root@server42:~# hostname
server42
root@server42:~# date
Mon Nov 10 18:21:56 CET 2014
```

4.3. virtualbox networking

You can also log on from remote (or from your Windows/Mac/Linux host computer) using **ssh** or **putty**. Change the **network** settings in the virtual machine to **bridge**. This will enable your virtual machine to receive an ip address from your local dhcp server.

The default virtualbox networking is to attach virtual network cards to **nat**. This screenshiot shows the ip address **10.0.2.15** when on **nat**:

```
root@server42:~# ifconfig
eth0      Link encap:Ethernet  HWaddr 08:00:27:f5:74:cf
          inet addr:10.0.2.15  Bcast:10.0.2.255  Mask:255.255.255.0
          inet6 addr: fe80::a00:27ff:fef5:74cf/64 Scope:Link
          UP BROADCAST RUNNING MULTICAST  MTU:1500  Metric:1
          RX packets:11 errors:0 dropped:0 overruns:0 frame:0
          TX packets:19 errors:0 dropped:0 overruns:0 carrier:0
          collisions:0 txqueuelen:1000
          RX bytes:2352 (2.2 KiB)  TX bytes:1988 (1.9 KiB)

lo        Link encap:Local Loopback
          inet addr:127.0.0.1  Mask:255.0.0.0
          inet6 addr: ::1/128 Scope:Host
          UP LOOPBACK RUNNING  MTU:65536  Metric:1
          RX packets:0 errors:0 dropped:0 overruns:0 frame:0
          TX packets:0 errors:0 dropped:0 overruns:0 carrier:0
          collisions:0 txqueuelen:0
          RX bytes:0 (0.0 B)  TX bytes:0 (0.0 B)
```

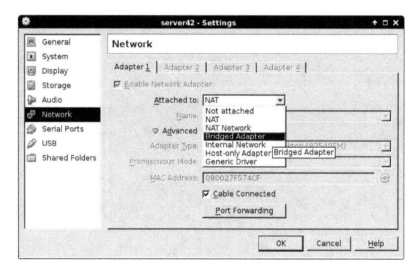

By shutting down the network interface and enabling it again, we force Debian to renew an ip address from the bridged network.

```
root@server42:~# # do not run ifdown while connected over ssh!
root@server42:~# ifdown eth0
Killed old client process
Internet Systems Consortium DHCP Client 4.3.1
Copyright 2004-2014 Internet Systems Consortium.
All rights reserved.
For info, please visit https://www.isc.org/software/dhcp/

Listening on LPF/eth0/08:00:27:f5:74:cf
Sending on   LPF/eth0/08:00:27:f5:74:cf
```

```
Sending on   Socket/fallback
DHCPRELEASE on eth0 to 10.0.2.2 port 67
root@server42:~# # now enable bridge in virtualbox settings
root@server42:~# ifup eth0
Internet Systems Consortium DHCP Client 4.3.1
Copyright 2004-2014 Internet Systems Consortium.
All rights reserved.
For info, please visit https://www.isc.org/software/dhcp/

Listening on LPF/eth0/08:00:27:f5:74:cf
Sending on   LPF/eth0/08:00:27:f5:74:cf
Sending on   Socket/fallback
DHCPDISCOVER on eth0 to 255.255.255.255 port 67 interval 8
DHCPDISCOVER on eth0 to 255.255.255.255 port 67 interval 8
DHCPREQUEST on eth0 to 255.255.255.255 port 67
DHCPOFFER from 192.168.1.42
DHCPACK from 192.168.1.42
bound to 192.168.1.111 -- renewal in 2938 seconds.
root@server42:~# ifconfig eth0
eth0      Link encap:Ethernet  HWaddr 08:00:27:f5:74:cf
          inet addr:192.168.1.111  Bcast:192.168.1.255  Mask:255.255.255.0
          inet6 addr: fe80::a00:27ff:fef5:74cf/64 Scope:Link
          UP BROADCAST RUNNING MULTICAST  MTU:1500  Metric:1
          RX packets:15 errors:0 dropped:0 overruns:0 frame:0
          TX packets:31 errors:0 dropped:0 overruns:0 carrier:0
          collisions:0 txqueuelen:1000
          RX bytes:3156 (3.0 KiB)  TX bytes:3722 (3.6 KiB)
root@server42:~#
```

Here is an example of **ssh** to this freshly installed computer. Note that **Debian 8** has disabled remote root access, so i need to use the normal user account.

```
paul@debian8:~$ ssh paul@192.168.1.111
paul@192.168.1.111's password:

The programs included with the Debian GNU/Linux system are free software;
the exact distribution terms for each program are described in the
individual files in /usr/share/doc/*/copyright.

Debian GNU/Linux comes with ABSOLUTELY NO WARRANTY, to the extent
permitted by applicable law.
paul@server42:~$
paul@server42:~$ su -
Password:
root@server42:~#
```

TODO: putty screenshot here...

4.4. setting the hostname

The hostname of the server is asked during installation, so there is no need to configure this manually.

```
root@server42:~# hostname
server42
root@server42:~# cat /etc/hostname
server42
root@server42:~# dnsdomainname
paul.local
root@server42:~# grep server42 /etc/hosts
127.0.1.1        server42.paul.local        server42
root@server42:~#
```

4.5. adding a static ip address

This example shows how to add a static ip address to your server.

You can use **ifconfig** to set a static address that is active until the next **reboot** (or until the next **ifdown**).
a

```
root@server42:~# ifconfig eth0:0 10.104.33.39
```

Adding a couple of lines to the **/etc/network/interfaces** file to enable an extra ip address forever.

```
root@server42:~# vi /etc/network/interfaces
root@server42:~# tail -4 /etc/network/interfaces
auto eth0:0
iface eth0:0 inet static
address 10.104.33.39
netmask 255.255.0.0
root@server42:~# ifconfig
eth0      Link encap:Ethernet  HWaddr 08:00:27:f5:74:cf
          inet addr:192.168.1.111  Bcast:192.168.1.255  Mask:255.255.255.0
          inet6 addr: fe80::a00:27ff:fef5:74cf/64 Scope:Link
          UP BROADCAST RUNNING MULTICAST  MTU:1500  Metric:1
          RX packets:528 errors:0 dropped:0 overruns:0 frame:0
          TX packets:333 errors:0 dropped:0 overruns:0 carrier:0
          collisions:0 txqueuelen:1000
          RX bytes:45429 (44.3 KiB)  TX bytes:48763 (47.6 KiB)

eth0:0    Link encap:Ethernet  HWaddr 08:00:27:f5:74:cf
          inet addr:10.104.33.39  Bcast:10.255.255.255  Mask:255.0.0.0
          UP BROADCAST RUNNING MULTICAST  MTU:1500  Metric:1

lo        Link encap:Local Loopback
          inet addr:127.0.0.1  Mask:255.0.0.0
          inet6 addr: ::1/128 Scope:Host
          UP LOOPBACK RUNNING  MTU:65536  Metric:1
          RX packets:0 errors:0 dropped:0 overruns:0 frame:0
          TX packets:0 errors:0 dropped:0 overruns:0 carrier:0
          collisions:0 txqueuelen:0
          RX bytes:0 (0.0 B)  TX bytes:0 (0.0 B)

root@server42:~#
```

4.6. Debian package management

To get all information about the newest packages form the online repository:

```
root@server42:~# aptitude update
Get: 1 http://ftp.be.debian.org jessie InRelease [191 kB]
Get: 2 http://security.debian.org jessie/updates InRelease [84.1 kB]
Get: 3 http://ftp.be.debian.org jessie-updates InRelease [117 kB]
Get: 4 http://ftp.be.debian.org jessie-backports InRelease [118 kB]
Get: 5 http://security.debian.org jessie/updates/main Sources [14 B]
Get: 6 http://ftp.be.debian.org jessie/main Sources/DiffIndex [7,876 B]
... (output truncated)
```

To download and apply all updates for all installed packages:

```
root@server42:~# aptitude upgrade
Resolving dependencies...
The following NEW packages will be installed:
  firmware-linux-free{a} irqbalance{a} libnuma1{a} linux-image-3.16.0-4-amd64{a}
The following packages will be upgraded:
  busybox file libc-bin libc6 libexpat1 libmagic1 libpaper-utils libpaper1 libsqlite3-0
  linux-image-amd64 locales multiarch-support
12 packages upgraded, 4 newly installed, 0 to remove and 0 not upgraded.
Need to get 44.9 MB of archives. After unpacking 161 MB will be used.
Do you want to continue? [Y/n/?]
... (output truncated)
```

To install new software (**vim** and **tmux** in this example):

```
root@server42:~# aptitude install vim tmux
The following NEW packages will be installed:
  tmux vim vim-runtime{a}
0 packages upgraded, 3 newly installed, 0 to remove and 0 not upgraded.
Need to get 6,243 kB of archives. After unpacking 29.0 MB will be used.
Do you want to continue? [Y/n/?]
Get: 1 http://ftp.be.debian.org/debian/ jessie/main tmux amd64 1.9-6 [245 kB]
Get: 2 http://ftp.be.debian.org/debian/ jessie/main vim-runtime all 2:7.4.488-1 [5,046 kB]
Get: 3 http://ftp.be.debian.org/debian/ jessie/main vim amd64 2:7.4.488-1 [952 kB]
```

Refer to the **package management** chapter in LinuxAdm.pdf for more information.

Chapter 5. installing CentOS 7

This module is a step by step demonstration of an actual installation of **CentOS 7**.

We start by downloading an image from the internet and install **CentOS 7** as a virtual machine in **Virtualbox**. We will also do some basic configuration of this new machine like setting an **ip address** and fixing a **hostname**.

This procedure should be very similar for other versions of **CentOS**, and also for distributions like **RHEL** (Red Hat Enterprise Linux) or **Fedora**. This procedure can also be helpful if you are using another virtualization solution.

5.1. download a CentOS 7 image

This demonstration uses a laptop computer with **Virtualbox** to install **CentOS 7** as a virtual machine. The first task is to download an **.iso** image of **CentOS 7**.

The **CentOS 7** website looks like this today (November 2014). They change the look regularly, so it may look different when you visit it.

You can download a full DVD, which allows for an off line installation of a graphical **CentOS 7** desktop. You can select this because it should be easy and complete, and should get you started with a working **CentOS 7** virtual machine.

But I clicked instead on 'alternative downloads', selected **CentOS 7** and **x86_64** and ended up on a **mirror list**. Each mirror is a server that contains copies of **CentOS 7** media. I selected a Belgian mirror because I currently am in Belgium.

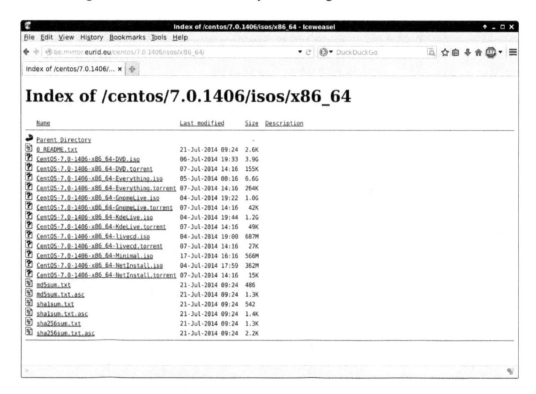

There is again the option for full DVD's and more. This demonstration will use the **minimal** .iso file, because it is much smaller in size. The download takes a couple of minutes.

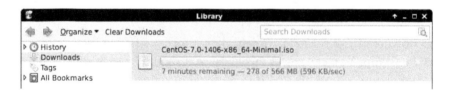

Verify the size of the file after download to make sure it is complete. Probably a right click on the file and selecting 'properties' (if you use Windows or Mac OSX).

I use Linux on the laptop already:

```
paul@debian8:~$ ls -lh CentOS-7.0-1406-x86_64-Minimal.iso
-rw-r--r-- 1 paul paul 566M Nov  1 14:45 CentOS-7.0-1406-x86_64-Minimal.iso
```

Do not worry if you do no understand the above command. Just try to make sure that the size of this file is the same as the size that is mentioned on the **CentOS 7** website.

5.2. Virtualbox

This screenshot shows up when I start Virtualbox. I already have four virtual machines, you might have none.

Below are the steps for creating a new virtual machine. Start by clicking **New** and give your machine a name (I chose **server33**). Click **Next**.

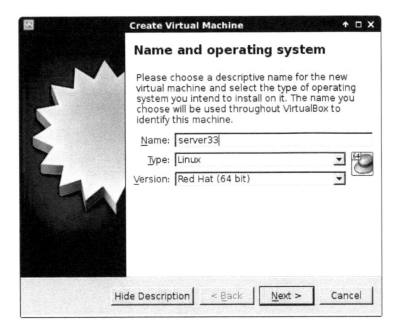

A Linux computer without graphical interface will run fine on **half a gigabyte** of RAM.

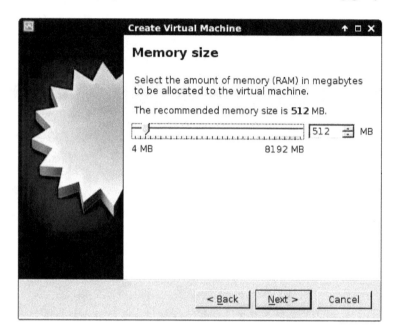

A Linux virtual machine will need a **virtual hard drive**.

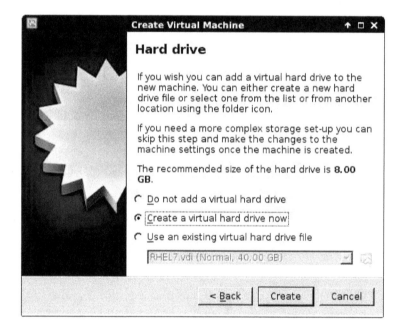

Any format will do for our purpose, so I left the default **vdi**.

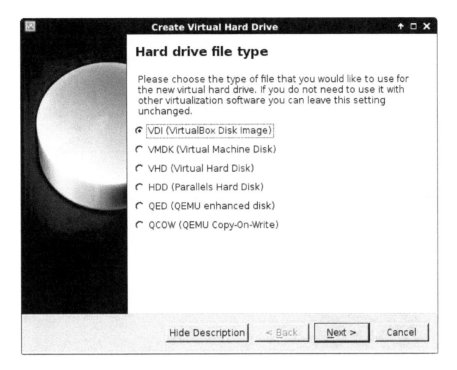

The default **dynamically allocated** type will save disk space (until we fill the virtual disk up to 100 percent). It makes the virtual machine a bit slower than **fixed size**, but the **fixed size** speed improvement is not worth it for our purpose.

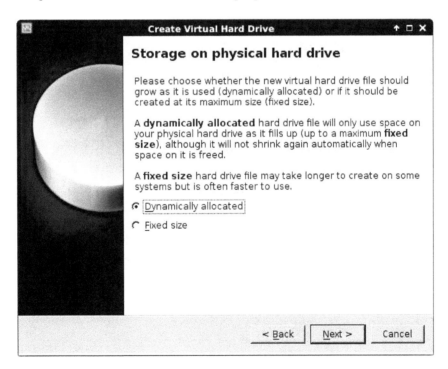

The name of the virtual disk file on the host computer will be **server33.vdi** in my case (I left it default and it uses the vm name). Also 16 GB should be enough to practice Linux. The file will stay much smaller than 16GB, unless you copy a lot of files to the virtual machine.

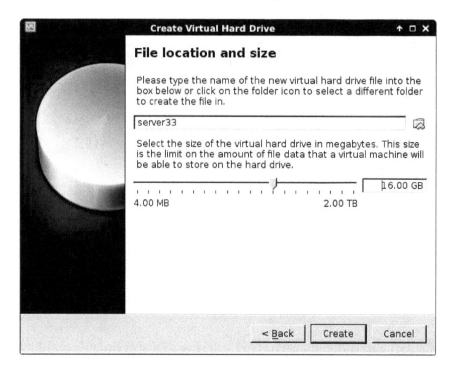

You should now be back to the start screen of **Virtualbox**. If all went well, then you should see the machine you just created in the list.

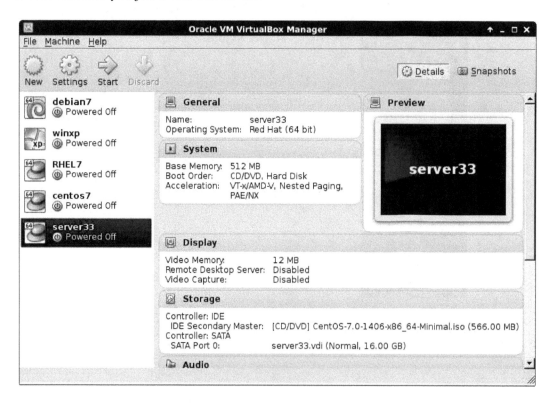

After finishing the setup, we go into the **Settings** of our virtual machine and attach the **.iso** file we downloaded before. Below is the default screenshot.

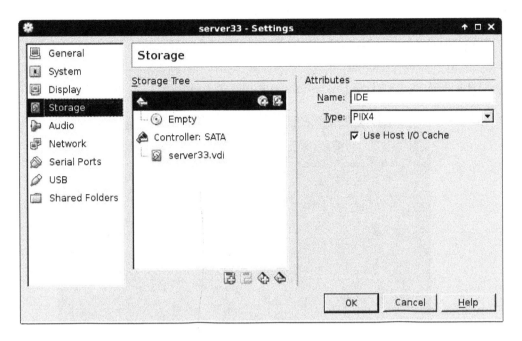

This is a screenshot with the **.iso** file properly attached.

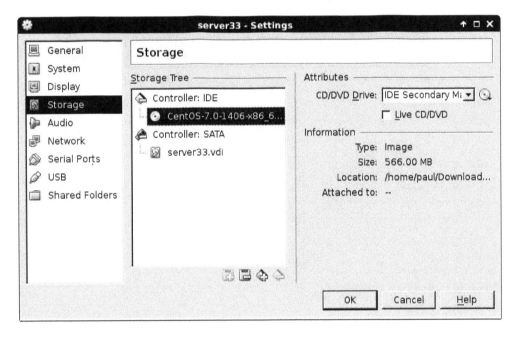

5.3. CentOS 7 installing

The screenshots below will show every step from starting the virtual machine for the first time (with the .iso file attached) until the first logon.

You should see this when booting, otherwise verify the attachment of the .iso file form the previous steps. Select **Test this media and install CentOS 7**.

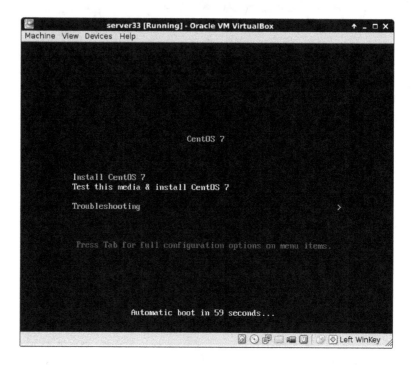

Carefully select the language in which you want your **CentOS**. I always install operating systems in English, even though my native language is not English.

Also select the right keyboard, mine is a US qwerty, but yours may be different.

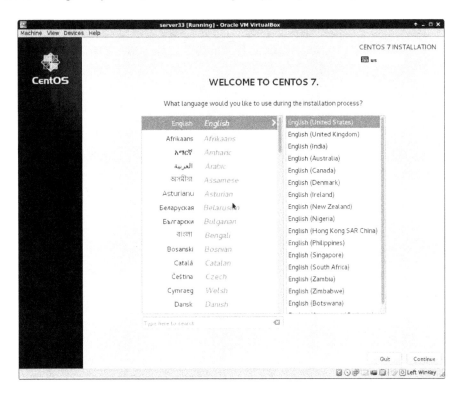

You should arrive at a summary page (with one or more warnings).

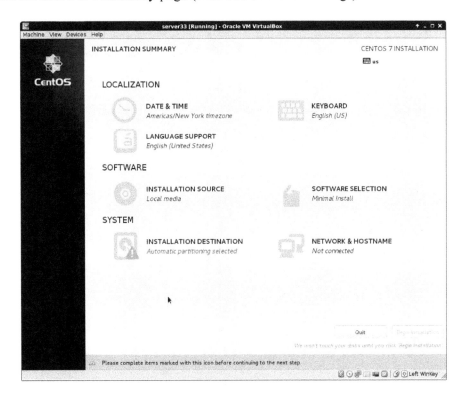

Start by configuring the network. During this demonstration I had a DHCP server running at 192.168.1.42, yours is probably different. Ask someone (a network administator ?) for help if this step fails.

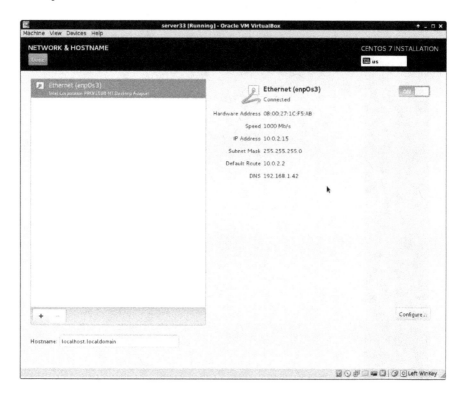

Select your time zone, and activate **ntp**.

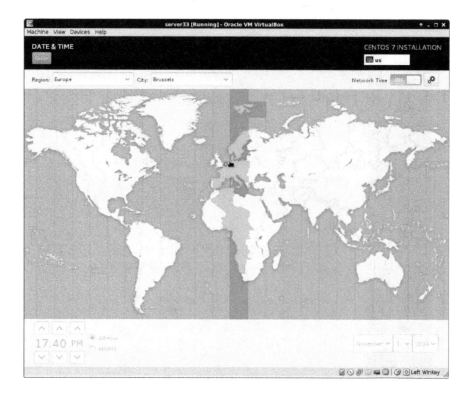

Choose a mirror that is close to you. If you can't find a local mirror, then you can copy the one from this screenshot (it is a general **CentOS** mirror).

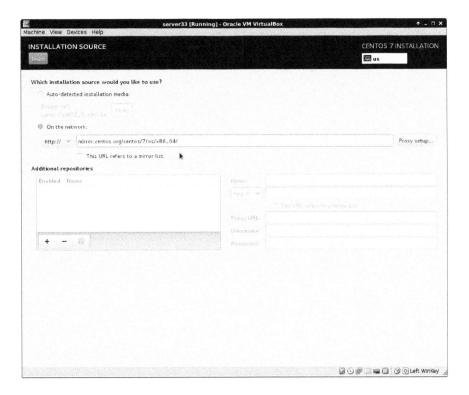

It can take a couple of seconds before the mirror is verified.

I did not select any software here (because I want to show it all in this training).

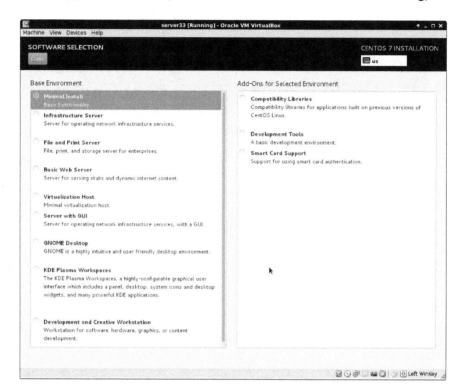

After configuring network, location, software and all, you should be back on this page. Make sure there are no warnings anymore (and that you made the correct choice everywhere).

You can enter a **root password** and create a **user account** while the installation is downloading from the internet. This is the longest step, it can take several minutes (or up to an hour if you have a slow internet connection).

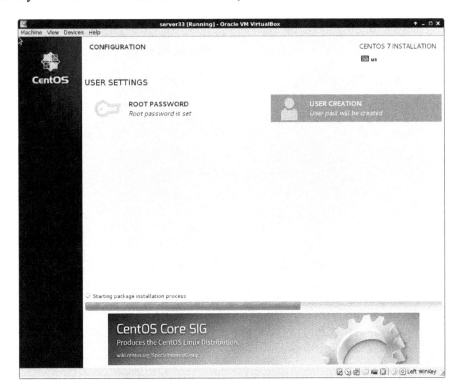

If you see this, then the installation was successful.

Time to reboot the computer and start **CentOS 7** for the first time.

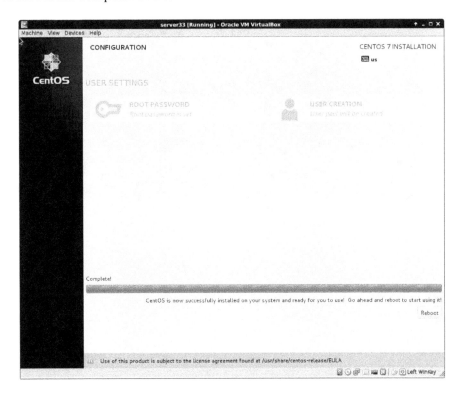

This screen will appear briefly when the virtual machines starts. You don't have to do anything.

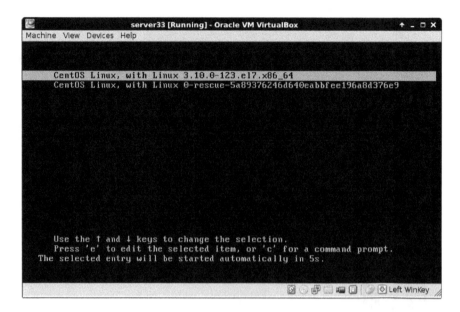

After a couple of seconds, you should see a logon screen. This is called a **tty** or a **getty**. Here you can type **root** as username. The **login process** will then ask your password (nothing will appear on screen when you type your password).

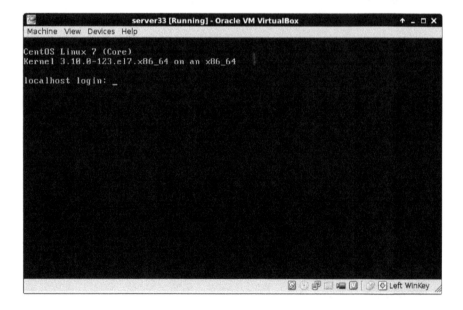

And this is what it looks like after logon. You are logged on to your own Linux machine, very good.

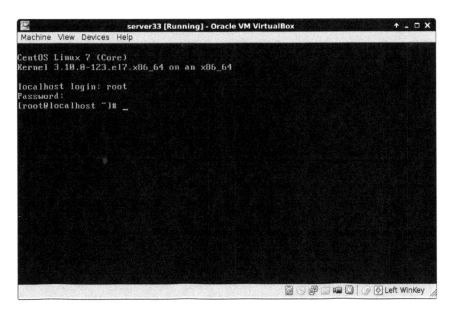

All subsequent screenshots will be text only, no images anymore.

For example this screenshot shows three commands being typed on my new CentOS 7 install.

```
[root@localhost ~]# who am i
root     pts/0        2014-11-01 22:14
[root@localhost ~]# hostname
localhost.localdomain
[root@localhost ~]# date
Sat Nov  1 22:14:37 CET 2014
```

When using **ssh** the same commands will give this screenshot:

```
[root@localhost ~]# who am i
root     pts/0        2014-11-01 21:00 (192.168.1.35)
[root@localhost ~]# hostname
localhost.localdomain
[root@localhost ~]# date
Sat Nov  1 22:10:04 CET 2014
[root@localhost ~]#
```

If the last part is a bit too fast, take a look at the next topic **CentOS 7 first logon**.

5.4. CentOS 7 first logon

All you have to log on, after finishing the installation, is this screen in Virtualbox.

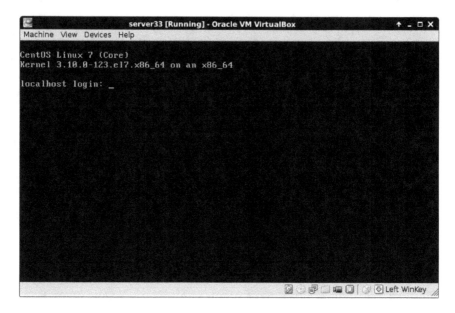

This is workable to learn Linux, and you will be able to practice a lot. But there are more ways to access your virtual machine, the next chapters discuss some of these and will also introduce some basic system configuration.

5.4.1. setting the hostname

Setting the hostname is a simple as changing the **/etc/hostname** file. As you can see here, it is set to **localhost.localdomain** by default.

```
[root@localhost ~]# cat /etc/hostname
localhost.localdomain
```

You could do **echo server33.netsec.local > /etc/hostname** followed by a **reboot**. But there is also the new **CentOS 7** way of setting a new hostname.

```
[root@localhost ~]# nmtui
```

The above command will give you a menu to choose from with a **set system hostname** option. Using this **nmtui** option will edit the **/etc/hostname** file for you.

```
[root@localhost ~]# cat /etc/hostname
server33.netsec.local
[root@localhost ~]# hostname
server33.netsec.local
[root@localhost ~]# dnsdomainname
netsec.local
```

For some reason the documentation on the **centos.org** and **docs.redhat.com** websites tell you to also execute this command:

```
[root@localhost ~]# systemctl restart systemd-hostnamed
```

5.5. Virtualbox network interface

By default **Virtualbox** will connect your virtual machine over a **nat** interface. This will show up as a 10.0.2.15 (or similar).

```
[root@server33 ~]# ip a
1: lo: <LOOPBACK,UP,LOWER_UP> mtu 65536 qdisc noqueue state UNKNOWN
    link/loopback 00:00:00:00:00:00 brd 00:00:00:00:00:00
    inet 127.0.0.1/8 scope host lo
       valid_lft forever preferred_lft forever
    inet6 ::1/128 scope host
       valid_lft forever preferred_lft forever
2: enp0s3: <BROADCAST,MULTICAST,UP,LOWER_UP> mtu 1500 qdisc pfifo_fast s\
tate UP qlen 1000
    link/ether 08:00:27:1c:f5:ab brd ff:ff:ff:ff:ff:ff
    inet 10.0.2.15/24 brd 10.0.2.255 scope global dynamic enp0s3
       valid_lft 86399sec preferred_lft 86399sec
    inet6 fe80::a00:27ff:fe1c:f5ab/64 scope link
       valid_lft forever preferred_lft forever
```

You can change this to **bridge** (over your wi-fi or over the ethernet cable) and thus make it appear as if your virtual machine is directly on your local network (receiving an ip address from your real dhcp server).

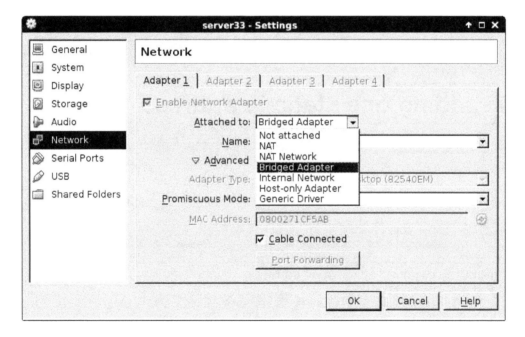

You can make this change while the vm is running, provided that you execute this command:

```
[root@server33 ~]# systemctl restart network
[root@server33 ~]# ip a s dev enp0s3
2: enp0s3: <BROADCAST,MULTICAST,UP,LOWER_UP> mtu 1500 qdisc pfifo_fast s\
tate UP qlen 1000
    link/ether 08:00:27:1c:f5:ab brd ff:ff:ff:ff:ff:ff
    inet 192.168.1.110/24 brd 192.168.1.255 scope global dynamic enp0s3
       valid_lft 7199sec preferred_lft 7199sec
    inet6 fe80::a00:27ff:fe1c:f5ab/64 scope link
       valid_lft forever preferred_lft forever
[root@server33 ~]#
```

5.6. configuring the network

The new way of changing network configuration is through the **nmtui** tool. If you want to manually play with the files in **/etc/sysconfig/network-scripts** then you will first need to verify (and disable) **NetworkManager** on that interface.

Verify whether an interface is controlled by **NetworkManager** using the **nmcli** command (connected means managed bu NM).

```
[root@server33 ~]# nmcli dev status
DEVICE   TYPE       STATE       CONNECTION
enp0s3   ethernet   connected   enp0s3
lo       loopback   unmanaged   --
```

Disable **NetworkManager** on an interface (enp0s3 in this case):

```
echo 'NM_CONTROLLED=no' >> /etc/sysconfig/network-scripts/ifcfg-enp0s3
```

You can restart the network without a reboot like this:

```
[root@server33 ~]# systemctl restart network
```

Also, forget **ifconfig** and instead use **ip a**.

```
[root@server33 ~]# ip a s dev enp0s3 | grep inet
    inet 192.168.1.110/24 brd 192.168.1.255 scope global dynamic enp0s3
    inet6 fe80::a00:27ff:fe1c:f5ab/64 scope link
[root@server33 ~]#
```

5.7. adding one static ip address

This example shows how to add one static ip address to your computer.

```
[root@server33 ~]# nmtui edit enp0s3
```

In this interface leave the IPv4 configuration to automatic, and add an ip address just below.

```
        IPv4 CONFIGURATION <Automatic>                        <Hide>
        Addresses 10.104.33.32/16_____   <Remove>
```

Execute this command after exiting **nmtui**.

```
[root@server33 ~]# systemctl restart network
```

And verify with **ip** (not with **ifconfig**):

```
[root@server33 ~]# ip a s dev enp0s3 | grep inet
    inet 192.168.1.110/24 brd 192.168.1.255 scope global dynamic enp0s3
    inet 10.104.33.32/16 brd 10.104.255.255 scope global enp0s3
    inet6 fe80::a00:27ff:fe1c:f5ab/64 scope link
[root@server33 ~]#
```

5.8. package management

Even with a network install, **CentOS 7** did not install the latest version of some packages. Luckily there is only one command to run (as root). This can take a while.

```
[root@server33 ~]# yum update
Loaded plugins: fastestmirror
Loading mirror speeds from cached hostfile
 * base: centos.weepeetelecom.be
 * extras: centos.weepeetelecom.be
 * updates: centos.weepeetelecom.be
Resolving Dependencies
--> Running transaction check
---> Package NetworkManager.x86_64 1:0.9.9.1-13.git20140326.4dba720.el7 \
will be updated
... (output truncated)
```

You can also use **yum** to install one or more packages. Do not forget to run **yum update** from time to time.

```
[root@server33 ~]# yum update -y && yum install vim -y
Loaded plugins: fastestmirror
Loading mirror speeds from cached hostfile
 * base: centos.weepeetelecom.be
... (output truncated)
```

Refer to the package management chapter for more information on installing and removing packages.

5.9. logon from Linux and MacOSX

You can now open a terminal on Linux or MacOSX and use **ssh** to log on to your virtual machine.

```
paul@debian8:~$ ssh root@192.168.1.110
root@192.168.1.110's password:
Last login: Sun Nov  2 11:53:57 2014
[root@server33 ~]# hostname
server33.netsec.local
[root@server33 ~]#
```

5.10. logon from MS Windows

There is no **ssh** installed on MS Windows, but you can download **putty.exe** from **http://www.chiark.greenend.org.uk/~sgtatham/putty/download.html** (just Google it).

Use **putty.exe** as shown in this screenshot (I saved the ip address by giving it a name 'server33' and presing the 'save' button).

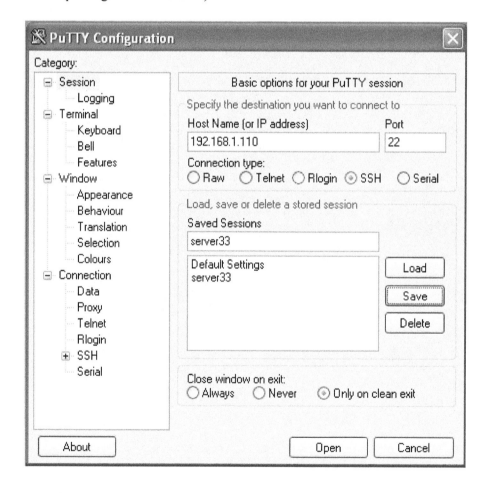

The first time you will get a message about keys, accept this (this is explained in the ssh chapter).

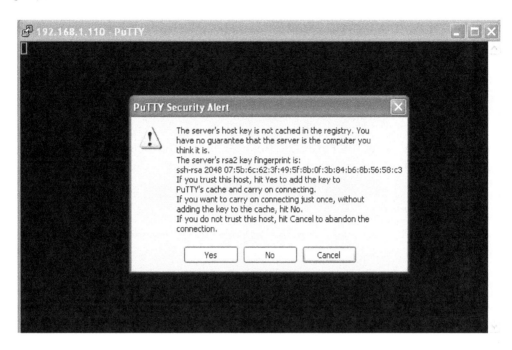

Enter your userid (or root) and the correct password (nothing will appear on the screen when typing a password).

```
login as: root
root@192.168.1.110's password:
Last login: Sun Nov  2 12:07:49 2014 from 192.168.1.35
[root@server33 ~]#
[root@server33 ~]# hostname
server33.netsec.local
[root@server33 ~]#
```

Chapter 6. getting Linux at home

This chapter shows a Ubuntu install in Virtualbox. Consider it legacy and use CentOS7 or Debian8 instead (each have their own chapter now).

This book assumes you have access to a working Linux computer. Most companies have one or more Linux servers, if you have already logged on to it, then you 're all set (skip this chapter and go to the next).

Another option is to insert a Ubuntu Linux CD in a computer with (or without) Microsoft Windows and follow the installation. Ubuntu will resize (or create) partitions and setup a menu at boot time to choose Windows or Linux.

If you do not have access to a Linux computer at the moment, and if you are unable or unsure about installing Linux on your computer, then this chapter proposes a third option: installing Linux in a virtual machine.

Installation in a virtual machine (provided by **Virtualbox**) is easy and safe. Even when you make mistakes and crash everything on the virtual Linux machine, then nothing on the real computer is touched.

This chapter gives easy steps and screenshots to get a working Ubuntu server in a Virtualbox virtual machine. The steps are very similar to installing Fedora or CentOS or even Debian, and if you like you can also use VMWare instead of Virtualbox.

6.1. download a Linux CD image

Start by downloading a Linux CD image (an .ISO file) from the distribution of your choice from the Internet. Take care selecting the correct cpu architecture of your computer; choose **i386** if unsure. Choosing the wrong cpu type (like x86_64 when you have an old Pentium) will almost immediately fail to boot the CD.

6.2. download Virtualbox

Step two (when the .ISO file has finished downloading) is to download Virtualbox. If you are currently running Microsoft Windows, then download and install Virtualbox for Windows!

6.3. create a virtual machine

Now start Virtualbox. Contrary to the screenshot below, your left pane should be empty.

Click **New** to create a new virtual machine. We will walk together through the wizard. The screenshots below are taken on Mac OSX; they will be slightly different if you are running Microsoft Windows.

Name your virtual machine (and maybe select 32-bit or 64-bit).

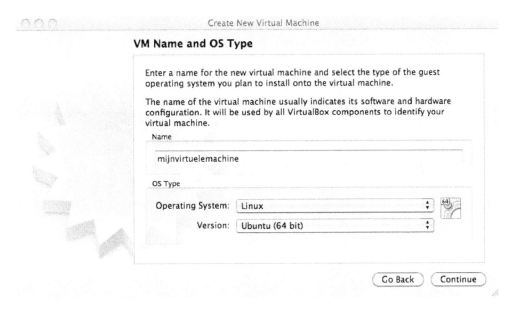

Give the virtual machine some memory (512MB if you have 2GB or more, otherwise select 256MB).

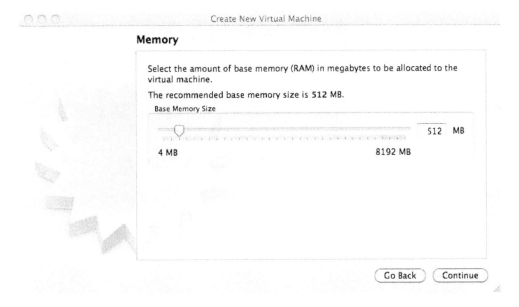

Select to create a new disk (remember, this will be a virtual disk).

If you get the question below, choose vdi.

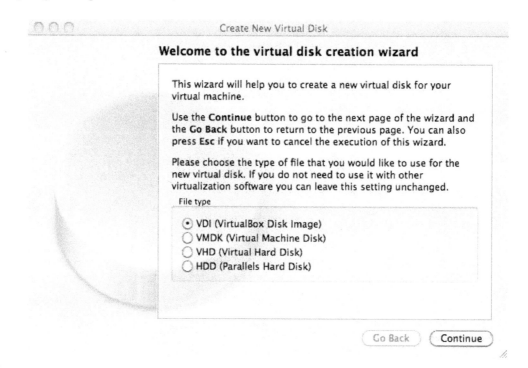

Choose **dynamically allocated** (fixed size is only useful in production or on really old, slow hardware).

Choose between 10GB and 16GB as the disk size.

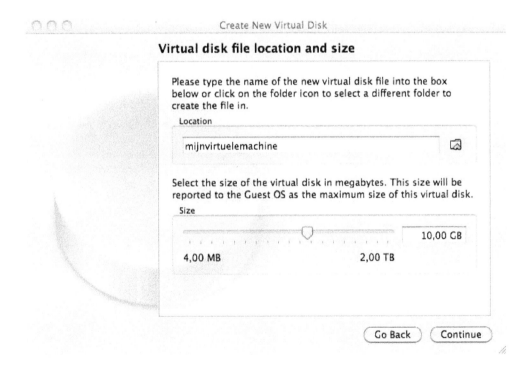

Click **create** to create the virtual disk.

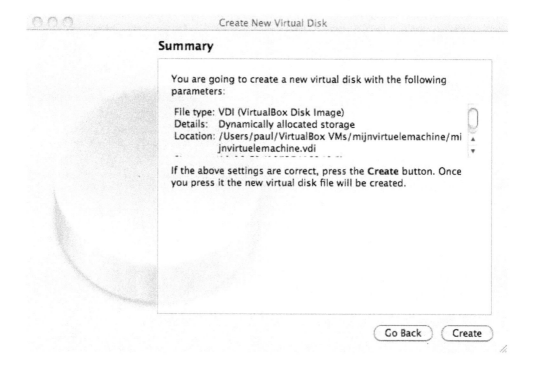

Click **create** to create the virtual machine.

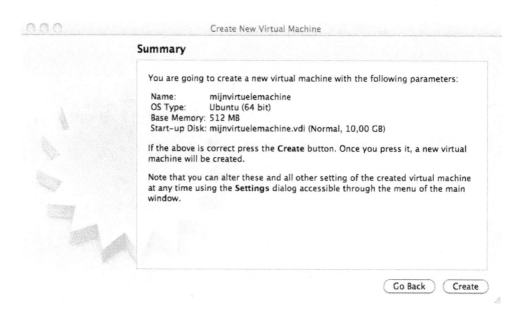

6.4. attach the CD image

Before we start the virtual computer, let us take a look at some settings (click **Settings**).

Do not worry if your screen looks different, just find the button named **storage**.

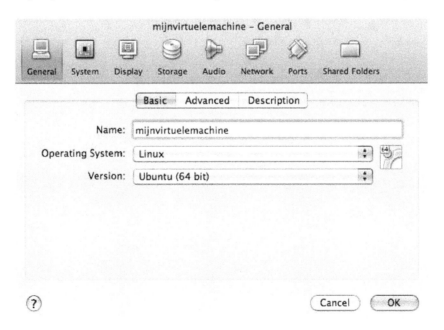

Remember the .ISO file you downloaded? Connect this .ISO file to this virtual machine by clicking on the CD icon next to **Empty**.

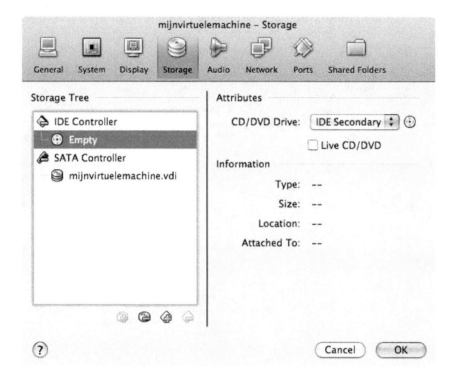

Now click on the other CD icon and attach your ISO file to this virtual CD drive.

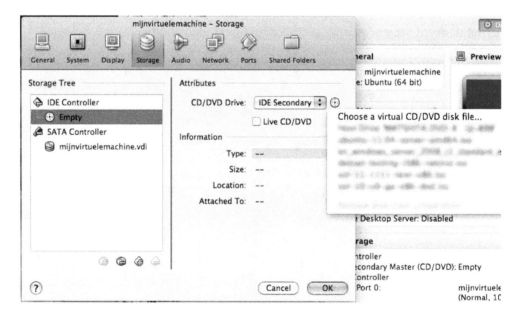

Verify that your download is accepted. If Virtualbox complains at this point, then you probably did not finish the download of the CD (try downloading it again).

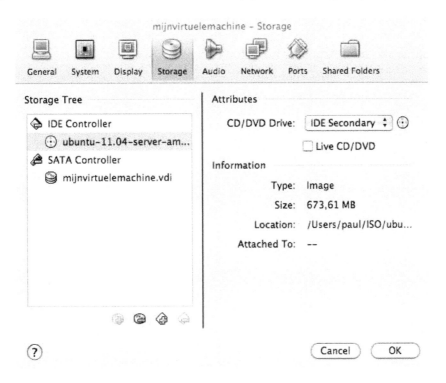

It could be useful to set the network adapter to bridge instead of NAT. Bridged usually will connect your virtual computer to the Internet.

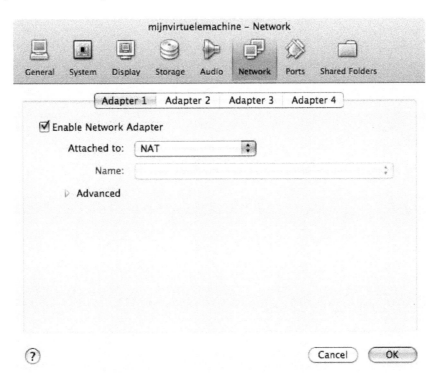

6.5. install Linux

The virtual machine is now ready to start. When given a choice at boot, select **install** and follow the instructions on the screen. When the installation is finished, you can log on to the machine and start practising Linux!

Part III. first steps on the command line

Table of Contents

Chapter 7. man pages

This chapter will explain the use of **man** pages (also called **manual pages**) on your Unix or Linux computer.

You will learn the **man** command together with related commands like **whereis**, **whatis** and **mandb**.

Most Unix files and commands have pretty good man pages to explain their use. Man pages also come in handy when you are using multiple flavours of Unix or several Linux distributions since options and parameters sometimes vary.

7.1. man $command

Type **man** followed by a command (for which you want help) and start reading. Press **q** to quit the manpage. Some man pages contain examples (near the end).

```
paul@laika:~$ man whois
Reformatting whois(1), please wait...
```

7.2. man $configfile

Most **configuration files** have their own manual.

```
paul@laika:~$ man syslog.conf
Reformatting syslog.conf(5), please wait...
```

7.3. man $daemon

This is also true for most **daemons** (background programs) on your system..

```
paul@laika:~$ man syslogd
Reformatting syslogd(8), please wait...
```

7.4. man -k (apropos)

man -k (or **apropos**) shows a list of man pages containing a string.

```
paul@laika:~$ man -k syslog
lm-syslog-setup (8)   - configure laptop mode to switch syslog.conf ...
logger (1)            - a shell command interface to the syslog(3) ...
syslog-facility (8)   - Setup and remove LOCALx facility for sysklogd
syslog.conf (5)       - syslogd(8) configuration file
syslogd (8)           - Linux system logging utilities.
syslogd-listfiles (8) - list system logfiles
```

7.5. whatis

To see just the description of a manual page, use **whatis** followed by a string.

```
paul@u810:~$ whatis route
route (8)               - show / manipulate the IP routing table
```

7.6. whereis

The location of a manpage can be revealed with **whereis**.

```
paul@laika:~$ whereis -m whois
whois: /usr/share/man/man1/whois.1.gz
```

This file is directly readable by **man**.

```
paul@laika:~$ man /usr/share/man/man1/whois.1.gz
```

7.7. man sections

By now you will have noticed the numbers between the round brackets. **man man** will explain to you that these are section numbers. Executable programs and shell commands reside in section one.

```
1 Executable programs or shell commands
2 System calls (functions provided by the kernel)
3 Library calls (functions within program libraries)
4 Special files (usually found in /dev)
5 File formats and conventions eg /etc/passwd
6 Games
7 Miscellaneous (including macro packages and conventions), e.g. man(7)
8 System administration commands (usually only for root)
9 Kernel routines [Non standard]
```

7.8. man $section $file

Therefor, when referring to the man page of the passwd command, you will see it written as **passwd(1)**; when referring to the **passwd file**, you will see it written as **passwd(5)**. The screenshot explains how to open the man page in the correct section.

```
[paul@RHEL52 ~]$ man passwd       # opens the first manual found
[paul@RHEL52 ~]$ man 5 passwd     # opens a page from section 5
```

7.9. man man

If you want to know more about **man**, then Read The Fantastic Manual (RTFM).

Unfortunately, manual pages do not have the answer to everything...

```
paul@laika:~$ man woman
No manual entry for woman
```

7.10. mandb

Should you be convinced that a man page exists, but you can't access it, then try running **mandb** on Debian/Mint.

```
root@laika:~# mandb
0 man subdirectories contained newer manual pages.
0 manual pages were added.
0 stray cats were added.
0 old database entries were purged.
```

Or run **makewhatis** on CentOS/Redhat.

```
[root@centos65 ~]# apropos scsi
scsi: nothing appropriate
[root@centos65 ~]# makewhatis
[root@centos65 ~]# apropos scsi
hpsa              (4)  - HP Smart Array SCSI driver
lsscsi            (8)  - list SCSI devices (or hosts) and their attributes
sd                (4)  - Driver for SCSI Disk Drives
st                (4)  - SCSI tape device
```

Chapter 8. working with directories

This module is a brief overview of the most common commands to work with directories: **pwd**, **cd**, **ls**, **mkdir** and **rmdir**. These commands are available on any Linux (or Unix) system.

This module also discusses **absolute** and **relative paths** and **path completion** in the **bash** shell.

8.1. pwd

The **you are here** sign can be displayed with the **pwd** command (Print Working Directory). Go ahead, try it: Open a command line interface (also called a terminal, console or xterm) and type **pwd**. The tool displays your **current directory**.

```
paul@debian8:~$ pwd
/home/paul
```

8.2. cd

You can change your current directory with the **cd** command (Change Directory).

```
paul@debian8$ cd /etc
paul@debian8$ pwd
/etc
paul@debian8$ cd /bin
paul@debian8$ pwd
/bin
paul@debian8$ cd /home/paul/
paul@debian8$ pwd
/home/paul
```

8.2.1. cd ~

The **cd** is also a shortcut to get back into your home directory. Just typing **cd** without a target directory, will put you in your home directory. Typing **cd** ~ has the same effect.

```
paul@debian8$ cd /etc
paul@debian8$ pwd
/etc
paul@debian8$ cd
paul@debian8$ pwd
/home/paul
paul@debian8$ cd ~
paul@debian8$ pwd
/home/paul
```

8.2.2. cd ..

To go to the **parent directory** (the one just above your current directory in the directory tree), type **cd ..** .

```
paul@debian8$ pwd
/usr/share/games
paul@debian8$ cd ..
paul@debian8$ pwd
/usr/share
```

*To stay in the current directory, type **cd .** ;-)* We will see useful use of the **.** character representing the current directory later.

8.2.3. cd -

Another useful shortcut with **cd** is to just type **cd -** to go to the previous directory.

```
paul@debian8$ pwd
/home/paul
paul@debian8$ cd /etc
paul@debian8$ pwd
/etc
paul@debian8$ cd -
/home/paul
paul@debian8$ cd -
/etc
```

8.3. absolute and relative paths

You should be aware of **absolute and relative paths** in the file tree. When you type a path starting with a **slash (/)**, then the **root** of the file tree is assumed. If you don't start your path with a slash, then the current directory is the assumed starting point.

The screenshot below first shows the current directory **/home/paul**. From within this directory, you have to type **cd /home** instead of **cd home** to go to the **/home** directory.

```
paul@debian8$ pwd
/home/paul
paul@debian8$ cd home
bash: cd: home: No such file or directory
paul@debian8$ cd /home
paul@debian8$ pwd
/home
```

When inside **/home**, you have to type **cd paul** instead of **cd /paul** to enter the subdirectory **paul** of the current directory **/home**.

```
paul@debian8$ pwd
/home
paul@debian8$ cd /paul
bash: cd: /paul: No such file or directory
paul@debian8$ cd paul
paul@debian8$ pwd
/home/paul
```

In case your current directory is the **root directory /**, then both **cd /home** and **cd home** will get you in the **/home** directory.

```
paul@debian8$ pwd
/
paul@debian8$ cd home
paul@debian8$ pwd
/home
paul@debian8$ cd /
paul@debian8$ cd /home
paul@debian8$ pwd
/home
```

This was the last screenshot with **pwd** statements. From now on, the current directory will often be displayed in the prompt. Later in this book we will explain how the shell variable **$PS1** can be configured to show this.

8.4. path completion

The **tab key** can help you in typing a path without errors. Typing **cd /et** followed by the **tab key** will expand the command line to **cd /etc/**. When typing **cd /Et** followed by the **tab key**, nothing will happen because you typed the wrong **path** (upper case E).

You will need fewer key strokes when using the **tab key**, and you will be sure your typed **path** is correct!

8.5. ls

You can list the contents of a directory with **ls**.

```
paul@debian8:~$ ls
allfiles.txt  dmesg.txt  services  stuff  summer.txt
paul@debian8:~$
```

8.5.1. ls -a

A frequently used option with ls is **-a** to show all files. Showing all files means including the **hidden files**. When a file name on a Linux file system starts with a dot, it is considered a **hidden file** and it doesn't show up in regular file listings.

```
paul@debian8:~$ ls
allfiles.txt  dmesg.txt  services  stuff  summer.txt
paul@debian8:~$ ls -a
.   allfiles.txt  .bash_profile  dmesg.txt  .lesshst  stuff
..  .bash_history  .bashrc       services   .ssh      summer.txt
paul@debian8:~$
```

8.5.2. ls -l

Many times you will be using options with **ls** to display the contents of the directory in different formats or to display different parts of the directory. Typing just **ls** gives you a list of files in the directory. Typing **ls -l** (that is a letter L, not the number 1) gives you a long listing.

```
paul@debian8:~$ ls -l
total 17296
-rw-r--r-- 1 paul paul 17584442 Sep 17 00:03 allfiles.txt
-rw-r--r-- 1 paul paul    96650 Sep 17 00:03 dmesg.txt
-rw-r--r-- 1 paul paul    19558 Sep 17 00:04 services
drwxr-xr-x 2 paul paul     4096 Sep 17 00:04 stuff
-rw-r--r-- 1 paul paul        0 Sep 17 00:04 summer.txt
```

8.5.3. ls -lh

Another frequently used ls option is **-h**. It shows the numbers (file sizes) in a more human readable format. Also shown below is some variation in the way you can give the options to **ls**. We will explain the details of the output later in this book.

Note that we use the letter L as an option in this screenshot, not the number 1.

```
paul@debian8:~$ ls -l -h
total 17M
-rw-r--r-- 1 paul paul  17M Sep 17 00:03 allfiles.txt
-rw-r--r-- 1 paul paul  95K Sep 17 00:03 dmesg.txt
-rw-r--r-- 1 paul paul  20K Sep 17 00:04 services
drwxr-xr-x 2 paul paul 4.0K Sep 17 00:04 stuff
-rw-r--r-- 1 paul paul    0 Sep 17 00:04 summer.txt
paul@debian8:~$ ls -lh
total 17M
-rw-r--r-- 1 paul paul  17M Sep 17 00:03 allfiles.txt
-rw-r--r-- 1 paul paul  95K Sep 17 00:03 dmesg.txt
-rw-r--r-- 1 paul paul  20K Sep 17 00:04 services
drwxr-xr-x 2 paul paul 4.0K Sep 17 00:04 stuff
-rw-r--r-- 1 paul paul    0 Sep 17 00:04 summer.txt
paul@debian8:~$ ls -hl
total 17M
-rw-r--r-- 1 paul paul  17M Sep 17 00:03 allfiles.txt
-rw-r--r-- 1 paul paul  95K Sep 17 00:03 dmesg.txt
-rw-r--r-- 1 paul paul  20K Sep 17 00:04 services
drwxr-xr-x 2 paul paul 4.0K Sep 17 00:04 stuff
-rw-r--r-- 1 paul paul    0 Sep 17 00:04 summer.txt
paul@debian8:~$ ls -h -l
total 17M
-rw-r--r-- 1 paul paul  17M Sep 17 00:03 allfiles.txt
-rw-r--r-- 1 paul paul  95K Sep 17 00:03 dmesg.txt
-rw-r--r-- 1 paul paul  20K Sep 17 00:04 services
drwxr-xr-x 2 paul paul 4.0K Sep 17 00:04 stuff
-rw-r--r-- 1 paul paul    0 Sep 17 00:04 summer.txt
paul@debian8:~$
```

8.6. mkdir

Walking around the Unix file tree is fun, but it is even more fun to create your own directories with **mkdir**. You have to give at least one parameter to **mkdir**, the name of the new directory to be created. Think before you type a leading / .

```
paul@debian8:~$ mkdir mydir
paul@debian8:~$ cd mydir
paul@debian8:~/mydir$ ls -al
total 8
drwxr-xr-x  2 paul paul 4096 Sep 17 00:07 .
drwxr-xr-x 48 paul paul 4096 Sep 17 00:07 ..
paul@debian8:~/mydir$ mkdir stuff
paul@debian8:~/mydir$ mkdir otherstuff
paul@debian8:~/mydir$ ls -l
total 8
drwxr-xr-x 2 paul paul 4096 Sep 17 00:08 otherstuff
drwxr-xr-x 2 paul paul 4096 Sep 17 00:08 stuff
paul@debian8:~/mydir$
```

8.6.1. mkdir -p

The following command will fail, because the **parent directory** of **threedirsdeep** does not exist.

```
paul@debian8:~$ mkdir mydir2/mysubdir2/threedirsdeep
mkdir: cannot create directory 'mydir2/mysubdir2/threedirsdeep': No such fi\
le or directory
```

When given the option **-p**, then **mkdir** will create **parent directories** as needed.

```
paul@debian8:~$ mkdir -p mydir2/mysubdir2/threedirsdeep
paul@debian8:~$ cd mydir2
paul@debian8:~/mydir2$ ls -l
total 4
drwxr-xr-x 3 paul paul 4096 Sep 17 00:11 mysubdir2
paul@debian8:~/mydir2$ cd mysubdir2
paul@debian8:~/mydir2/mysubdir2$ ls -l
total 4
drwxr-xr-x 2 paul paul 4096 Sep 17 00:11 threedirsdeep
paul@debian8:~/mydir2/mysubdir2$ cd threedirsdeep/
paul@debian8:~/mydir2/mysubdir2/threedirsdeep$ pwd
/home/paul/mydir2/mysubdir2/threedirsdeep
```

8.7. rmdir

When a directory is empty, you can use **rmdir** to remove the directory.

```
paul@debian8:~/mydir$ ls -l
total 8
drwxr-xr-x 2 paul paul 4096 Sep 17 00:08 otherstuff
drwxr-xr-x 2 paul paul 4096 Sep 17 00:08 stuff
paul@debian8:~/mydir$ rmdir otherstuff
paul@debian8:~/mydir$ cd ..
paul@debian8:~$ rmdir mydir
rmdir: failed to remove 'mydir': Directory not empty
paul@debian8:~$ rmdir mydir/stuff
paul@debian8:~$ rmdir mydir
paul@debian8:~$
```

8.7.1. rmdir -p

And similar to the **mkdir -p** option, you can also use **rmdir** to recursively remove directories.

```
paul@debian8:~$ mkdir -p test42/subdir
paul@debian8:~$ rmdir -p test42/subdir
paul@debian8:~$
```

8.8. practice: working with directories

1. Display your current directory.

2. Change to the /etc directory.

3. Now change to your home directory using only three key presses.

4. Change to the /boot/grub directory using only eleven key presses.

5. Go to the parent directory of the current directory.

6. Go to the root directory.

7. List the contents of the root directory.

8. List a long listing of the root directory.

9. Stay where you are, and list the contents of /etc.

10. Stay where you are, and list the contents of /bin and /sbin.

11. Stay where you are, and list the contents of ~.

12. List all the files (including hidden files) in your home directory.

13. List the files in /boot in a human readable format.

14. Create a directory testdir in your home directory.

15. Change to the /etc directory, stay here and create a directory newdir in your home directory.

16. Create in one command the directories ~/dir1/dir2/dir3 (dir3 is a subdirectory from dir2, and dir2 is a subdirectory from dir1).

17. Remove the directory testdir.

18. If time permits (or if you are waiting for other students to finish this practice), use and understand **pushd** and **popd**. Use the man page of **bash** to find information about these commands.

8.9. solution: working with directories

1. Display your current directory.

```
pwd
```

2. Change to the /etc directory.

```
cd /etc
```

3. Now change to your home directory using only three key presses.

```
cd (and the enter key)
```

4. Change to the /boot/grub directory using only eleven key presses.

```
cd /boot/grub (use the tab key)
```

5. Go to the parent directory of the current directory.

```
cd .. (with space between cd and ..)
```

6. Go to the root directory.

```
cd /
```

7. List the contents of the root directory.

```
ls
```

8. List a long listing of the root directory.

```
ls -l
```

9. Stay where you are, and list the contents of /etc.

```
ls /etc
```

10. Stay where you are, and list the contents of /bin and /sbin.

```
ls /bin /sbin
```

11. Stay where you are, and list the contents of ~.

```
ls ~
```

12. List all the files (including hidden files) in your home directory.

```
ls -al ~
```

13. List the files in /boot in a human readable format.

```
ls -lh /boot
```

14. Create a directory testdir in your home directory.

```
mkdir ~/testdir
```

15. Change to the /etc directory, stay here and create a directory newdir in your home directory.

```
cd /etc ; mkdir ~/newdir
```

16. Create in one command the directories ~/dir1/dir2/dir3 (dir3 is a subdirectory from dir2, and dir2 is a subdirectory from dir1).

```
mkdir -p ~/dir1/dir2/dir3
```

17. Remove the directory testdir.

```
rmdir testdir
```

18. If time permits (or if you are waiting for other students to finish this practice), use and understand **pushd** and **popd**. Use the man page of **bash** to find information about these commands.

```
man bash          # opens the manual
/pushd            # searches for pushd
n                 # next (do this two/three times)
```

The Bash shell has two built-in commands called **pushd** and **popd**. Both commands work with a common stack of previous directories. Pushd adds a directory to the stack and changes to a new current directory, popd removes a directory from the stack and sets the current directory.

```
paul@debian7:/etc$ cd /bin
paul@debian7:/bin$ pushd /lib
/lib /bin
paul@debian7:/lib$ pushd /proc
/proc /lib /bin
paul@debian7:/proc$ popd
/lib /bin
paul@debian7:/lib$ popd
/bin
```

Chapter 9. working with files

In this chapter we learn how to recognise, create, remove, copy and move files using commands like **file, touch, rm, cp, mv** and **rename**.

9.1. all files are case sensitive

Files on Linux (or any Unix) are **case sensitive**. This means that **FILE1** is different from **file1**, and **/etc/hosts** is different from **/etc/Hosts** (the latter one does not exist on a typical Linux computer).

This screenshot shows the difference between two files, one with upper case **W**, the other with lower case **w**.

```
paul@laika:~/Linux$ ls
winter.txt  Winter.txt
paul@laika:~/Linux$ cat winter.txt
It is cold.
paul@laika:~/Linux$ cat Winter.txt
It is very cold!
```

9.2. everything is a file

A **directory** is a special kind of **file**, but it is still a (case sensitive!) **file**. Each terminal window (for example **/dev/pts/4**), any hard disk or partition (for example **/dev/sdb1**) and any process are all represented somewhere in the **file system** as a **file**. It will become clear throughout this course that everything on Linux is a **file**.

9.3. file

The **file** utility determines the file type. Linux does not use extensions to determine the file type. The command line does not care whether a file ends in .txt or .pdf. As a system administrator, you should use the **file** command to determine the file type. Here are some examples on a typical Linux system.

```
paul@laika:~$ file pic33.png
pic33.png: PNG image data, 3840 x 1200, 8-bit/color RGBA, non-interlaced
paul@laika:~$ file /etc/passwd
/etc/passwd: ASCII text
paul@laika:~$ file HelloWorld.c
HelloWorld.c: ASCII C program text
```

The file command uses a magic file that contains patterns to recognise file types. The magic file is located in **/usr/share/file/magic**. Type **man 5 magic** for more information.

It is interesting to point out **file -s** for special files like those in **/dev** and **/proc**.

```
root@debian6~# file /dev/sda
/dev/sda: block special
root@debian6~# file -s /dev/sda
/dev/sda: x86 boot sector; partition 1: ID=0x83, active, starthead...
root@debian6~# file /proc/cpuinfo
/proc/cpuinfo: empty
root@debian6~# file -s /proc/cpuinfo
/proc/cpuinfo: ASCII C++ program text
```

9.4. touch

9.4.1. create an empty file

One easy way to create an empty file is with **touch**. (We will see many other ways for creating files later in this book.)

This screenshot starts with an empty directory, creates two files with **touch** and the lists those files.

```
paul@debian7:~$ ls -l
total 0
paul@debian7:~$ touch file42
paul@debian7:~$ touch file33
paul@debian7:~$ ls -l
total 0
-rw-r--r-- 1 paul paul 0 Oct 15 08:57 file33
-rw-r--r-- 1 paul paul 0 Oct 15 08:56 file42
paul@debian7:~$
```

9.4.2. touch -t

The **touch** command can set some properties while creating empty files. Can you determine what is set by looking at the next screenshot? If not, check the manual for **touch**.

```
paul@debian7:~$ touch -t 200505050000 SinkoDeMayo
paul@debian7:~$ touch -t 130207111630 BigBattle.txt
paul@debian7:~$ ls -l
total 0
-rw-r--r-- 1 paul paul 0 Jul 11  1302 BigBattle.txt
-rw-r--r-- 1 paul paul 0 Oct 15 08:57 file33
-rw-r--r-- 1 paul paul 0 Oct 15 08:56 file42
-rw-r--r-- 1 paul paul 0 May  5  2005 SinkoDeMayo
paul@debian7:~$
```

9.5. rm

9.5.1. remove forever

When you no longer need a file, use **rm** to remove it. Unlike some graphical user interfaces, the command line in general does not have a **waste bin** or **trash can** to recover files. When you use **rm** to remove a file, the file is gone. Therefore, be careful when removing files!

```
paul@debian7:~$ ls
BigBattle.txt  file33  file42  SinkoDeMayo
paul@debian7:~$ rm BigBattle.txt
paul@debian7:~$ ls
file33  file42  SinkoDeMayo
paul@debian7:~$
```

9.5.2. rm -i

To prevent yourself from accidentally removing a file, you can type **rm -i**.

```
paul@debian7:~$ ls
file33  file42  SinkoDeMayo
paul@debian7:~$ rm -i file33
rm: remove regular empty file `file33'? yes
paul@debian7:~$ rm -i SinkoDeMayo
rm: remove regular empty file `SinkoDeMayo'? n
paul@debian7:~$ ls
file42  SinkoDeMayo
paul@debian7:~$
```

9.5.3. rm -rf

By default, **rm -r** will not remove non-empty directories. However **rm** accepts several options that will allow you to remove any directory. The **rm -rf** statement is famous because it will erase anything (providing that you have the permissions to do so). When you are logged on as root, be very careful with **rm -rf** (the **f** means **force** and the **r** means **recursive**) since being root implies that permissions don't apply to you. You can literally erase your entire file system by accident.

```
paul@debian7:~$ mkdir test
paul@debian7:~$ rm test
rm: cannot remove `test': Is a directory
paul@debian7:~$ rm -rf test
paul@debian7:~$ ls test
ls: cannot access test: No such file or directory
paul@debian7:~$
```

9.6. cp

9.6.1. copy one file

To copy a file, use **cp** with a source and a target argument.

```
paul@debian7:~$ ls
file42  SinkoDeMayo
paul@debian7:~$ cp file42 file42.copy
paul@debian7:~$ ls
file42  file42.copy  SinkoDeMayo
```

9.6.2. copy to another directory

If the target is a directory, then the source files are copied to that target directory.

```
paul@debian7:~$ mkdir dir42
paul@debian7:~$ cp SinkoDeMayo dir42
paul@debian7:~$ ls dir42/
SinkoDeMayo
```

9.6.3. cp -r

To copy complete directories, use **cp -r** (the **-r** option forces **recursive** copying of all files in all subdirectories).

```
paul@debian7:~$ ls
dir42  file42  file42.copy  SinkoDeMayo
paul@debian7:~$ cp -r dir42/ dir33
paul@debian7:~$ ls
dir33  dir42  file42  file42.copy  SinkoDeMayo
paul@debian7:~$ ls dir33/
SinkoDeMayo
```

9.6.4. copy multiple files to directory

You can also use cp to copy multiple files into a directory. In this case, the last argument (a.k.a. the target) must be a directory.

```
paul@debian7:~$ cp file42 file42.copy SinkoDeMayo dir42/
paul@debian7:~$ ls dir42/
file42  file42.copy  SinkoDeMayo
```

9.6.5. cp -i

To prevent **cp** from overwriting existing files, use the **-i** (for interactive) option.

```
paul@debian7:~$ cp SinkoDeMayo file42
paul@debian7:~$ cp SinkoDeMayo file42
paul@debian7:~$ cp -i SinkoDeMayo file42
cp: overwrite `file42'? n
paul@debian7:~$
```

9.7. mv

9.7.1. rename files with mv

Use **mv** to rename a file or to move the file to another directory.

```
paul@debian7:~$ ls
dir33  dir42  file42  file42.copy  SinkoDeMayo
paul@debian7:~$ mv file42 file33
paul@debian7:~$ ls
dir33  dir42  file33  file42.copy  SinkoDeMayo
paul@debian7:~$
```

When you need to rename only one file then **mv** is the preferred command to use.

9.7.2. rename directories with mv

The same **mv** command can be used to rename directories.

```
paul@debian7:~$ ls -l
total 8
drwxr-xr-x 2 paul paul 4096 Oct 15 09:36 dir33
drwxr-xr-x 2 paul paul 4096 Oct 15 09:36 dir42
-rw-r--r-- 1 paul paul    0 Oct 15 09:38 file33
-rw-r--r-- 1 paul paul    0 Oct 15 09:16 file42.copy
-rw-r--r-- 1 paul paul    0 May  5  2005 SinkoDeMayo
paul@debian7:~$ mv dir33 backup
paul@debian7:~$ ls -l
total 8
drwxr-xr-x 2 paul paul 4096 Oct 15 09:36 backup
drwxr-xr-x 2 paul paul 4096 Oct 15 09:36 dir42
-rw-r--r-- 1 paul paul    0 Oct 15 09:38 file33
-rw-r--r-- 1 paul paul    0 Oct 15 09:16 file42.copy
-rw-r--r-- 1 paul paul    0 May  5  2005 SinkoDeMayo
paul@debian7:~$
```

9.7.3. mv -i

The **mv** also has a **-i** switch similar to **cp** and **rm**.

this screenshot shows that **mv -i** will ask permission to overwrite an existing file.

```
paul@debian7:~$ mv -i file33 SinkoDeMayo
mv: overwrite `SinkoDeMayo'? no
paul@debian7:~$
```

9.8. rename

9.8.1. about rename

The **rename** command is one of the rare occasions where the Linux Fundamentals book has to make a distinction between Linux distributions. Almost every command in the **Fundamentals** part of this book works on almost every Linux computer. But **rename** is different.

Try to use **mv** whenever you need to rename only a couple of files.

9.8.2. rename on Debian/Ubuntu

The **rename** command on Debian uses regular expressions (regular expression or shor regex are explained in a later chapter) to rename many files at once.

Below a **rename** example that switches all occurrences of txt to png for all file names ending in .txt.

```
paul@debian7:~/test42$ ls
abc.txt   file33.txt   file42.txt
paul@debian7:~/test42$ rename 's/\.txt/\.png/' *.txt
paul@debian7:~/test42$ ls
abc.png   file33.png   file42.png
```

This second example switches all (first) occurrences of **file** into **document** for all file names ending in .png.

```
paul@debian7:~/test42$ ls
abc.png   file33.png   file42.png
paul@debian7:~/test42$ rename 's/file/document/' *.png
paul@debian7:~/test42$ ls
abc.png   document33.png   document42.png
paul@debian7:~/test42$
```

9.8.3. rename on CentOS/RHEL/Fedora

On Red Hat Enterprise Linux, the syntax of **rename** is a bit different. The first example below renames all *.conf files replacing any occurrence of .conf with .backup.

```
[paul@centos7 ~]$ touch one.conf two.conf three.conf
[paul@centos7 ~]$ rename .conf .backup *.conf
[paul@centos7 ~]$ ls
one.backup   three.backup   two.backup
[paul@centos7 ~]$
```

The second example renames all (*) files replacing one with ONE.

```
[paul@centos7 ~]$ ls
one.backup   three.backup   two.backup
[paul@centos7 ~]$ rename one ONE *
[paul@centos7 ~]$ ls
ONE.backup   three.backup   two.backup
[paul@centos7 ~]$
```

9.9. practice: working with files

1. List the files in the /bin directory

2. Display the type of file of /bin/cat, /etc/passwd and /usr/bin/passwd.

3a. Download wolf.jpg and LinuxFun.pdf from http://linux-training.be (wget http://linux-training.be/files/studentfiles/wolf.jpg and wget http://linux-training.be/files/books/LinuxFun.pdf)

```
wget http://linux-training.be/files/studentfiles/wolf.jpg
wget http://linux-training.be/files/studentfiles/wolf.png
wget http://linux-training.be/files/books/LinuxFun.pdf
```

3b. Display the type of file of wolf.jpg and LinuxFun.pdf

3c. Rename wolf.jpg to wolf.pdf (use mv).

3d. Display the type of file of wolf.pdf and LinuxFun.pdf.

4. Create a directory ~/touched and enter it.

5. Create the files today.txt and yesterday.txt in touched.

6. Change the date on yesterday.txt to match yesterday's date.

7. Copy yesterday.txt to copy.yesterday.txt

8. Rename copy.yesterday.txt to kim

9. Create a directory called ~/testbackup and copy all files from ~/touched into it.

10. Use one command to remove the directory ~/testbackup and all files into it.

11. Create a directory ~/etcbackup and copy all *.conf files from /etc into it. Did you include all subdirectories of /etc ?

12. Use rename to rename all *.conf files to *.backup . (if you have more than one distro available, try it on all!)

9.10. solution: working with files

1. List the files in the /bin directory

```
ls /bin
```

2. Display the type of file of /bin/cat, /etc/passwd and /usr/bin/passwd.

```
file /bin/cat /etc/passwd /usr/bin/passwd
```

3a. Download wolf.jpg and LinuxFun.pdf from http://linux-training.be (wget http://linux-training.be/files/studentfiles/wolf.jpg and wget http://linux-training.be/files/books/LinuxFun.pdf)

```
wget http://linux-training.be/files/studentfiles/wolf.jpg
wget http://linux-training.be/files/studentfiles/wolf.png
wget http://linux-training.be/files/books/LinuxFun.pdf
```

3b. Display the type of file of wolf.jpg and LinuxFun.pdf

```
file wolf.jpg LinuxFun.pdf
```

3c. Rename wolf.jpg to wolf.pdf (use mv).

```
mv wolf.jpg wolf.pdf
```

3d. Display the type of file of wolf.pdf and LinuxFun.pdf.

```
file wolf.pdf LinuxFun.pdf
```

4. Create a directory ~/touched and enter it.

```
mkdir ~/touched ; cd ~/touched
```

5. Create the files today.txt and yesterday.txt in touched.

```
touch today.txt yesterday.txt
```

6. Change the date on yesterday.txt to match yesterday's date.

```
touch -t 200810251405 yesterday.txt (substitute 20081025 with yesterday)
```

7. Copy yesterday.txt to copy.yesterday.txt

```
cp yesterday.txt copy.yesterday.txt
```

8. Rename copy.yesterday.txt to kim

```
mv copy.yesterday.txt kim
```

9. Create a directory called ~/testbackup and copy all files from ~/touched into it.

```
mkdir ~/testbackup ; cp -r ~/touched ~/testbackup/
```

10. Use one command to remove the directory ~/testbackup and all files into it.

```
rm -rf ~/testbackup
```

11. Create a directory ~/etcbackup and copy all *.conf files from /etc into it. Did you include all subdirectories of /etc ?

```
cp -r /etc/*.conf ~/etcbackup
```

Only *.conf files that are directly in /etc/ are copied.

12. Use rename to rename all *.conf files to *.backup . (if you have more than one distro available, try it on all!)

On RHEL: touch 1.conf 2.conf ; rename conf backup *.conf

On Debian: touch 1.conf 2.conf ; rename 's/conf/backup/' *.conf

Chapter 10. working with file contents

In this chapter we will look at the contents of **text files** with **head, tail, cat, tac, more, less** and **strings**.

We will also get a glimpse of the possibilities of tools like **cat** on the command line.

10.1. head

You can use **head** to display the first ten lines of a file.

```
paul@debian7~$ head /etc/passwd
root:x:0:0:root:/root:/bin/bash
daemon:x:1:1:daemon:/usr/sbin:/bin/sh
bin:x:2:2:bin:/bin:/bin/sh
sys:x:3:3:sys:/dev:/bin/sh
sync:x:4:65534:sync:/bin:/bin/sync
games:x:5:60:games:/usr/games:/bin/sh
man:x:6:12:man:/var/cache/man:/bin/sh
lp:x:7:7:lp:/var/spool/lpd:/bin/sh
mail:x:8:8:mail:/var/mail:/bin/sh
news:x:9:9:news:/var/spool/news:/bin/sh
root@debian7~#
```

The **head** command can also display the first **n** lines of a file.

```
paul@debian7~$ head -4 /etc/passwd
root:x:0:0:root:/root:/bin/bash
daemon:x:1:1:daemon:/usr/sbin:/bin/sh
bin:x:2:2:bin:/bin:/bin/sh
sys:x:3:3:sys:/dev:/bin/sh
paul@debian7~$
```

And **head** can also display the first **n bytes**.

```
paul@debian7~$ head -c14 /etc/passwd
root:x:0:0:roopaul@debian7~$
```

10.2. tail

Similar to **head**, the **tail** command will display the last ten lines of a file.

```
paul@debian7~$ tail /etc/services
vboxd           20012/udp
binkp           24554/tcp              # binkp fidonet protocol
asp             27374/tcp              # Address Search Protocol
asp             27374/udp
csync2          30865/tcp              # cluster synchronization tool
dircproxy       57000/tcp              # Detachable IRC Proxy
tfido           60177/tcp              # fidonet EMSI over telnet
fido            60179/tcp              # fidonet EMSI over TCP

# Local services
paul@debian7~$
```

You can give **tail** the number of lines you want to see.

```
paul@debian7~$ tail -3 /etc/services
fido            60179/tcp              # fidonet EMSI over TCP

# Local services
paul@debian7~$
```

The **tail** command has other useful options, some of which we will use during this course.

10.3. cat

The **cat** command is one of the most universal tools, yet all it does is copy **standard input** to **standard output**. In combination with the shell this can be very powerful and diverse. Some examples will give a glimpse into the possibilities. The first example is simple, you can use cat to display a file on the screen. If the file is longer than the screen, it will scroll to the end.

```
paul@debian8:~$ cat /etc/resolv.conf
domain linux-training.be
search linux-training.be
nameserver 192.168.1.42
```

10.3.1. concatenate

cat is short for **concatenate**. One of the basic uses of **cat** is to concatenate files into a bigger (or complete) file.

```
paul@debian8:~$ echo one >part1
paul@debian8:~$ echo two >part2
paul@debian8:~$ echo three >part3
paul@debian8:~$ cat part1
one
paul@debian8:~$ cat part2
two
paul@debian8:~$ cat part3
three
paul@debian8:~$ cat part1 part2 part3
one
two
three
paul@debian8:~$ cat part1 part2 part3 >all
paul@debian8:~$ cat all
one
two
three
paul@debian8:~$
```

10.3.2. create files

You can use **cat** to create flat text files. Type the **cat > winter.txt** command as shown in the screenshot below. Then type one or more lines, finishing each line with the enter key. After the last line, type and hold the Control (Ctrl) key and press d.

```
paul@debian8:~$ cat > winter.txt
It is very cold today!
paul@debian8:~$ cat winter.txt
It is very cold today!
paul@debian8:~$
```

The **Ctrl d** key combination will send an **EOF** (End of File) to the running process ending the **cat** command.

10.3.3. custom end marker

You can choose an end marker for **cat** with << as is shown in this screenshot. This construction is called a **here directive** and will end the **cat** command.

```
paul@debian8:~$ cat > hot.txt <<stop
> It is hot today!
> Yes it is summer.
> stop
paul@debian8:~$ cat hot.txt
It is hot today!
Yes it is summer.
paul@debian8:~$
```

10.3.4. copy files

In the third example you will see that cat can be used to copy files. We will explain in detail what happens here in the bash shell chapter.

```
paul@debian8:~$ cat winter.txt
It is very cold today!
paul@debian8:~$ cat winter.txt > cold.txt
paul@debian8:~$ cat cold.txt
It is very cold today!
paul@debian8:~$
```

10.4. tac

Just one example will show you the purpose of **tac** (cat backwards).

```
paul@debian8:~$ cat count
one
two
three
four
paul@debian8:~$ tac count
four
three
two
one
```

10.5. more and less

The **more** command is useful for displaying files that take up more than one screen. More will allow you to see the contents of the file page by page. Use the space bar to see the next page, or **q** to quit. Some people prefer the **less** command to **more**.

10.6. strings

With the **strings** command you can display readable ascii strings found in (binary) files. This example locates the **ls** binary then displays readable strings in the binary file (output is truncated).

```
paul@laika:~$ which ls
/bin/ls
paul@laika:~$ strings /bin/ls
/lib/ld-linux.so.2
librt.so.1
__gmon_start__
_Jv_RegisterClasses
clock_gettime
libacl.so.1
...
```

10.7. practice: file contents

1. Display the first 12 lines of **/etc/services**.

2. Display the last line of **/etc/passwd**.

3. Use cat to create a file named **count.txt** that looks like this:

```
One
Two
Three
Four
Five
```

4. Use **cp** to make a backup of this file to **cnt.txt**.

5. Use **cat** to make a backup of this file to **catcnt.txt**.

6. Display **catcnt.txt**, but with all lines in reverse order (the last line first).

7. Use more to display **/etc/services**.

8. Display the readable character strings from the **/usr/bin/passwd** command.

9. Use **ls** to find the biggest file in **/etc**.

10. Open two terminal windows (or tabs) and make sure you are in the same directory in both. Type **echo this is the first line > tailing.txt** in the first terminal, then issue **tail -f tailing.txt** in the second terminal. Now go back to the first terminal and type **echo This is another line >> tailing.txt** (note the double >>), verify that the **tail -f** in the second terminal shows both lines. Stop the **tail -f** with **Ctrl-C**.

11. Use **cat** to create a file named **tailing.txt** that contains the contents of **tailing.txt** followed by the contents of **/etc/passwd**.

12. Use **cat** to create a file named **tailing.txt** that contains the contents of **tailing.txt** preceded by the contents of **/etc/passwd**.

10.8. solution: file contents

1. Display the first 12 lines of **/etc/services**.

```
head -12 /etc/services
```

2. Display the last line of **/etc/passwd**.

```
tail -1 /etc/passwd
```

3. Use cat to create a file named **count.txt** that looks like this:

```
cat > count.txt
One
Two
Three
Four
Five (followed by Ctrl-d)
```

4. Use **cp** to make a backup of this file to **cnt.txt**.

```
cp count.txt cnt.txt
```

5. Use **cat** to make a backup of this file to **catcnt.txt**.

```
cat count.txt > catcnt.txt
```

6. Display **catcnt.txt**, but with all lines in reverse order (the last line first).

```
tac catcnt.txt
```

7. Use more to display **/etc/services**.

```
more /etc/services
```

8. Display the readable character strings from the **/usr/bin/passwd** command.

```
strings /usr/bin/passwd
```

9. Use **ls** to find the biggest file in **/etc**.

```
ls -lrS /etc
```

10. Open two terminal windows (or tabs) and make sure you are in the same directory in both. Type **echo this is the first line > tailing.txt** in the first terminal, then issue **tail -f tailing.txt** in the second terminal. Now go back to the first terminal and type **echo This is another line >> tailing.txt** (note the double >>), verify that the **tail -f** in the second terminal shows both lines. Stop the **tail -f** with **Ctrl-C**.

11. Use **cat** to create a file named **tailing.txt** that contains the contents of **tailing.txt** followed by the contents of **/etc/passwd**.

```
cat /etc/passwd >> tailing.txt
```

12. Use **cat** to create a file named **tailing.txt** that contains the contents of **tailing.txt** preceded by the contents of **/etc/passwd**.

```
mv tailing.txt tmp.txt ; cat /etc/passwd tmp.txt > tailing.txt
```

Chapter 11. the Linux file tree

This chapter takes a look at the most common directories in the **Linux file tree**. It also shows that on Unix everything is a file.

11.1. filesystem hierarchy standard

Many Linux distributions partially follow the **Filesystem Hierarchy Standard**. The **FHS** may help make more Unix/Linux file system trees conform better in the future. The **FHS** is available online at **http://www.pathname.com/fhs/** where we read: "The filesystem hierarchy standard has been designed to be used by Unix distribution developers, package developers, and system implementers. However, it is primarily intended to be a reference and is not a tutorial on how to manage a Unix filesystem or directory hierarchy."

11.2. man hier

There are some differences in the filesystems between **Linux distributions**. For help about your machine, enter **man hier** to find information about the file system hierarchy. This manual will explain the directory structure on your computer.

11.3. the root directory /

All Linux systems have a directory structure that starts at the **root directory**. The root directory is represented by a **forward slash**, like this: /. Everything that exists on your Linux system can be found below this root directory. Let's take a brief look at the contents of the root directory.

```
[paul@RHELv4u3 ~]$ ls /
bin   dev   home   media   mnt   proc   sbin     srv   tftpboot   usr
boot  etc   lib    misc    opt   root   selinux  sys   tmp        var
```

11.4. binary directories

Binaries are files that contain compiled source code (or machine code). Binaries can be **executed** on the computer. Sometimes binaries are called **executables**.

11.4.1. /bin

The **/bin** directory contains **binaries** for use by all users. According to the FHS the **/bin** directory should contain **/bin/cat** and **/bin/date** (among others).

In the screenshot below you see common Unix/Linux commands like cat, cp, cpio, date, dd, echo, grep, and so on. Many of these will be covered in this book.

```
paul@laika:~$ ls /bin
archdetect       egrep            mt               setupcon
autopartition    false            mt-gnu           sh
bash             fgconsole        mv               sh.distrib
bunzip2          fgrep            nano             sleep
bzcat            fuser            nc               stralign
bzcmp            fusermount       nc.traditional   stty
bzdiff           get_mountoptions netcat           su
bzegrep          grep             netstat          sync
bzexe            gunzip           ntfs-3g          sysfs
bzfgrep          gzexe            ntfs-3g.probe    tailf
bzgrep           gzip             parted_devices   tar
bzip2            hostname         parted_server    tempfile
bzip2recover     hw-detect        partman          touch
bzless           ip               partman-commit   true
bzmore           kbd_mode         perform_recipe   ulockmgr
cat              kill             pidof            umount
...
```

11.4.2. other /bin directories

You can find a **/bin subdirectory** in many other directories. A user named **serena** could put her own programs in **/home/serena/bin**.

Some applications, often when installed directly from source will put themselves in **/opt**. A **samba server** installation can use **/opt/samba/bin** to store its binaries.

11.4.3. /sbin

/sbin contains binaries to configure the operating system. Many of the **system binaries** require **root** privilege to perform certain tasks.

Below a screenshot containing **system binaries** to change the ip address, partition a disk and create an ext4 file system.

```
paul@ubu1010:~$ ls -l /sbin/ifconfig /sbin/fdisk /sbin/mkfs.ext4
-rwxr-xr-x 1 root root 97172 2011-02-02 09:56 /sbin/fdisk
-rwxr-xr-x 1 root root 65708 2010-07-02 09:27 /sbin/ifconfig
-rwxr-xr-x 5 root root 55140 2010-08-18 18:01 /sbin/mkfs.ext4
```

11.4.4. /lib

Binaries found in **/bin** and **/sbin** often use **shared libraries** located in **/lib**. Below is a screenshot of the partial contents of **/lib**.

```
paul@laika:~$ ls /lib/libc*
/lib/libc-2.5.so      /lib/libcfont.so.0.0.0   /lib/libcom_err.so.2.1
/lib/libcap.so.1      /lib/libcidn-2.5.so      /lib/libconsole.so.0
/lib/libcap.so.1.10   /lib/libcidn.so.1        /lib/libconsole.so.0.0.0
/lib/libcfont.so.0    /lib/libcom_err.so.2     /lib/libcrypt-2.5.so
```

/lib/modules

Typically, the **Linux kernel** loads kernel modules from **/lib/modules/$kernel-version/**. This directory is discussed in detail in the Linux kernel chapter.

/lib32 and /lib64

We currently are in a transition between **32-bit** and **64-bit** systems. Therefore, you may encounter directories named **/lib32** and **/lib64** which clarify the register size used during compilation time of the libraries. A 64-bit computer may have some 32-bit binaries and libraries for compatibility with legacy applications. This screenshot uses the **file** utility to demonstrate the difference.

```
paul@laika:~$ file /lib32/libc-2.5.so
/lib32/libc-2.5.so: ELF 32-bit LSB shared object, Intel 80386, \
version 1 (SYSV), for GNU/Linux 2.6.0, stripped
paul@laika:~$ file /lib64/libcap.so.1.10
/lib64/libcap.so.1.10: ELF 64-bit LSB shared object, AMD x86-64, \
version 1 (SYSV), stripped
```

The ELF **(Executable and Linkable Format)** is used in almost every Unix-like operating system since **System V**.

11.4.5. /opt

The purpose of **/opt** is to store **optional** software. In many cases this is software from outside the distribution repository. You may find an empty **/opt** directory on many systems.

A large package can install all its files in **/bin**, **/lib**, **/etc** subdirectories within **/opt/$packagename/**. If for example the package is called wp, then it installs in **/opt/wp**, putting binaries in **/opt/wp/bin** and manpages in **/opt/wp/man**.

11.5. configuration directories

11.5.1. /boot

The **/boot** directory contains all files needed to boot the computer. These files don't change very often. On Linux systems you typically find the **/boot/grub** directory here. **/boot/grub** contains **/boot/grub/grub.cfg** (older systems may still have **/boot/grub/grub.conf**) which defines the boot menu that is displayed before the kernel starts.

11.5.2. /etc

All of the machine-specific **configuration files** should be located in **/etc**. Historically **/etc** stood for **etcetera**, today people often use the **Editable Text Configuration** backronym.

Many times the name of a configuration files is the same as the application, daemon, or protocol with **.conf** added as the extension.

```
paul@laika:~$ ls /etc/*.conf
/etc/adduser.conf          /etc/ld.so.conf          /etc/scrollkeeper.conf
/etc/brltty.conf           /etc/lftp.conf           /etc/sysctl.conf
/etc/ccertificates.conf    /etc/libao.conf          /etc/syslog.conf
/etc/cvs-cron.conf         /etc/logrotate.conf      /etc/ucf.conf
/etc/ddclient.conf         /etc/ltrace.conf         /etc/uniconf.conf
/etc/debconf.conf          /etc/mke2fs.conf         /etc/updatedb.conf
/etc/deluser.conf          /etc/netscsid.conf       /etc/usplash.conf
/etc/fdmount.conf          /etc/nsswitch.conf       /etc/uswsusp.conf
/etc/hdparm.conf           /etc/pam.conf            /etc/vnc.conf
/etc/host.conf             /etc/pnm2ppa.conf        /etc/wodim.conf
/etc/inetd.conf            /etc/povray.conf         /etc/wvdial.conf
/etc/kernel-img.conf       /etc/resolv.conf
paul@laika:~$
```

There is much more to be found in **/etc**.

/etc/init.d/

A lot of Unix/Linux distributions have an **/etc/init.d** directory that contains scripts to start and stop **daemons**. This directory could disappear as Linux migrates to systems that replace the old **init** way of starting all **daemons**.

/etc/X11/

The graphical display (aka **X Window System** or just **X**) is driven by software from the X.org foundation. The configuration file for your graphical display is **/etc/X11/xorg.conf**.

/etc/skel/

The **skeleton** directory **/etc/skel** is copied to the home directory of a newly created user. It usually contains hidden files like a **.bashrc** script.

/etc/sysconfig/

This directory, which is not mentioned in the FHS, contains a lot of **Red Hat Enterprise Linux** configuration files. We will discuss some of them in greater detail. The screenshot below is the **/etc/sysconfig** directory from RHELv4u4 with everything installed.

```
paul@RHELv4u4:~$ ls /etc/sysconfig/
apmd          firstboot      irda              network         saslauthd
apm-scripts   grub           irqbalance        networking      selinux
authconfig    hidd           keyboard          ntpd            spamassassin
autofs        httpd          kudzu             openib.conf     squid
bluetooth     hwconf         lm_sensors        pand            syslog
clock         i18n           mouse             pcmcia          sys-config-sec
console       init           mouse.B           pgsql           sys-config-users
crond         installinfo    named             prelink         sys-logviewer
desktop       ipmi           netdump           rawdevices      tux
diskdump      iptables       netdump_id_dsa    rhn             vncservers
dund          iptables-cfg   netdump_id_dsa.p  samba           xinetd
paul@RHELv4u4:~$
```

The file **/etc/sysconfig/firstboot** tells the Red Hat Setup Agent not to run at boot time. If you want to run the Red Hat Setup Agent at the next reboot, then simply remove this file, and run **chkconfig --level 5 firstboot on**. The Red Hat Setup Agent allows you to install the latest updates, create a user account, join the Red Hat Network and more. It will then create the /etc/sysconfig/firstboot file again.

```
paul@RHELv4u4:~$ cat /etc/sysconfig/firstboot
RUN_FIRSTBOOT=NO
```

The **/etc/sysconfig/harddisks** file contains some parameters to tune the hard disks. The file explains itself.

You can see hardware detected by **kudzu** in **/etc/sysconfig/hwconf**. Kudzu is software from Red Hat for automatic discovery and configuration of hardware.

The keyboard type and keymap table are set in the **/etc/sysconfig/keyboard** file. For more console keyboard information, check the manual pages of **keymaps(5)**, **dumpkeys(1)**, **loadkeys(1)** and the directory **/lib/kbd/keymaps/**.

```
root@RHELv4u4:/etc/sysconfig# cat keyboard
KEYBOARDTYPE="pc"
KEYTABLE="us"
```

We will discuss networking files in this directory in the networking chapter.

11.6. data directories

11.6.1. /home

Users can store personal or project data under **/home**. It is common (but not mandatory by the fhs) practice to name the users home directory after the user name in the format **/home/ $USERNAME**. For example:

```
paul@ubu606:~$ ls /home
geert  annik  sandra  paul  tom
```

Besides giving every user (or every project or group) a location to store personal files, the home directory of a user also serves as a location to store the user profile. A typical Unix user profile contains many hidden files (files whose file name starts with a dot). The hidden files of the Unix user profiles contain settings specific for that user.

```
paul@ubu606:~$ ls -d /home/paul/.*
/home/paul/.                /home/paul/.bash_profile  /home/paul/.ssh
/home/paul/..               /home/paul/.bashrc        /home/paul/.viminfo
/home/paul/.bash_history    /home/paul/.lesshst
```

11.6.2. /root

On many systems **/root** is the default location for personal data and profile of the **root user**. If it does not exist by default, then some administrators create it.

11.6.3. /srv

You may use **/srv** for data that is **served by your system**. The FHS allows locating cvs, rsync, ftp and www data in this location. The FHS also approves administrative naming in / srv, like /srv/project55/ftp and /srv/sales/www.

On Sun Solaris (or Oracle Solaris) **/export** is used for this purpose.

11.6.4. /media

The **/media** directory serves as a mount point for **removable media devices** such as CD-ROM's, digital cameras, and various usb-attached devices. Since **/media** is rather new in the Unix world, you could very well encounter systems running without this directory. Solaris 9 does not have it, Solaris 10 does. Most Linux distributions today mount all removable media in **/media**.

```
paul@debian5:~$ ls /media/
cdrom  cdrom0  usbdisk
```

11.6.5. /mnt

The **/mnt** directory should be empty and should only be used for temporary mount points (according to the FHS).

Unix and Linux administrators used to create many directories here, like /mnt/something/. You likely will encounter many systems with more than one directory created and/or mounted inside **/mnt** to be used for various local and remote filesystems.

11.6.6. /tmp

Applications and users should use **/tmp** to store temporary data when needed. Data stored in **/tmp** may use either disk space or RAM. Both of which are managed by the operating system. Never use **/tmp** to store data that is important or which you wish to archive.

11.7. in memory directories

11.7.1. /dev

Device files in **/dev** appear to be ordinary files, but are not actually located on the hard disk. The **/dev** directory is populated with files as the kernel is recognising hardware.

common physical devices

Common hardware such as hard disk devices are represented by device files in **/dev**. Below a screenshot of SATA device files on a laptop and then IDE attached drives on a desktop. (The detailed meaning of these devices will be discussed later.)

```
#
# SATA or SCSI or USB
#
paul@laika:~$ ls /dev/sd*
/dev/sda  /dev/sda1  /dev/sda2  /dev/sda3  /dev/sdb  /dev/sdb1  /dev/sdb2

#
# IDE or ATAPI
#
paul@barry:~$ ls /dev/hd*
/dev/hda  /dev/hda1  /dev/hda2  /dev/hdb  /dev/hdb1  /dev/hdb2  /dev/hdc
```

Besides representing physical hardware, some device files are special. These special devices can be very useful.

/dev/tty and /dev/pts

For example, **/dev/tty1** represents a terminal or console attached to the system. (Don't break your head on the exact terminology of 'terminal' or 'console', what we mean here is a command line interface.) When typing commands in a terminal that is part of a graphical interface like Gnome or KDE, then your terminal will be represented as **/dev/pts/1** (1 can be another number).

/dev/null

On Linux you will find other special devices such as **/dev/null** which can be considered a black hole; it has unlimited storage, but nothing can be retrieved from it. Technically speaking, anything written to /dev/null will be discarded. /dev/null can be useful to discard unwanted output from commands. *dev/null is not a good location to store your backups ;-)*.

11.7.2. /proc conversation with the kernel

/proc is another special directory, appearing to be ordinary files, but not taking up disk space. It is actually a view of the kernel, or better, what the kernel manages, and is a means to interact with it directly. **/proc** is a proc filesystem.

```
paul@RHELv4u4:~$ mount -t proc
```

```
none on /proc type proc (rw)
```

When listing the /proc directory you will see many numbers (on any Unix) and some interesting files (on Linux)

```
mul@laika:~$ ls /proc
1        2339    4724    5418    6587    7201    cmdline         mounts
10175    2523    4729    5421    6596    7204    cpuinfo         mtrr
10211    2783    4741    5658    6599    7206    crypto          net
10239    2975    4873    5661    6638    7214    devices         pagetypeinfo
141      29775   4874    5665    6652    7216    diskstats       partitions
15045    29792   4878    5927    6719    7218    dma             sched_debug
1519     2997    4879    6       6736    7223    driver          scsi
1548     3       4881    6032    6737    7224    execdomains     self
1551     30228   4882    6033    6755    7227    fb              slabinfo
1554     3069    5       6145    6762    7260    filesystems     stat
1557     31422   5073    6298    6774    7267    fs              swaps
1606     3149    5147    6414    6816    7275    ide             sys
180      31507   5203    6418    6991    7282    interrupts      sysrq-trigger
181      3189    5206    6419    6993    7298    iomem           sysvipc
182      3193    5228    6420    6996    7319    ioports         timer_list
18898    3246    5272    6421    7157    7330    irq             timer_stats
19799    3248    5291    6422    7163    7345    kallsyms        tty
19803    3253    5294    6423    7164    7513    kcore           uptime
19804    3372    5356    6424    7171    7525    key-users       version
1987     4       5370    6425    7175    7529    kmsg            version_signature
1989     42      5379    6426    7188    9964    loadavg         vmcore
2        45      5380    6430    7189    acpi    locks           vmnet
20845    4542    5412    6450    7191    asound  meminfo         vmstat
221      46      5414    6551    7192    buddyinfo  misc         zoneinfo
2338     4704    5416    6568    7199    bus     modules
```

Let's investigate the file properties inside **/proc**. Looking at the date and time will display the current date and time showing the files are constantly updated (a view on the kernel).

```
paul@RHELv4u4:~$ date
Mon Jan 29 18:06:32 EST 2007
paul@RHELv4u4:~$ ls -al /proc/cpuinfo
-r--r--r--  1 root root 0 Jan 29 18:06 /proc/cpuinfo
paul@RHELv4u4:~$
paul@RHELv4u4:~$  ...time passes...
paul@RHELv4u4:~$
paul@RHELv4u4:~$ date
Mon Jan 29 18:10:00 EST 2007
paul@RHELv4u4:~$ ls -al /proc/cpuinfo
-r--r--r--  1 root root 0 Jan 29 18:10 /proc/cpuinfo
```

Most files in /proc are 0 bytes, yet they contain data--sometimes a lot of data. You can see this by executing cat on files like **/proc/cpuinfo**, which contains information about the CPU.

```
paul@RHELv4u4:~$ file /proc/cpuinfo
/proc/cpuinfo: empty
paul@RHELv4u4:~$ cat /proc/cpuinfo
processor       : 0
vendor_id       : AuthenticAMD
cpu family      : 15
model           : 43
```

```
model name      : AMD Athlon(tm) 64 X2 Dual Core Processor 4600+
stepping        : 1
cpu MHz         : 2398.628
cache size      : 512 KB
fdiv_bug        : no
hlt_bug         : no
f00f_bug        : no
coma_bug        : no
fpu             : yes
fpu_exception   : yes
cpuid level     : 1
wp              : yes
flags           : fpu vme de pse tsc msr pae mce cx8 apic mtrr pge...
bogomips        : 4803.54
```

Just for fun, here is /proc/cpuinfo on a Sun Sunblade 1000...

```
paul@pasha:~$ cat /proc/cpuinfo
cpu : TI UltraSparc III (Cheetah)
fpu : UltraSparc III integrated FPU
promlib : Version 3 Revision 2
prom : 4.2.2
type : sun4u
ncpus probed : 2
ncpus active : 2
Cpu0Bogo : 498.68
Cpu0ClkTck : 000000002cb41780
Cpu1Bogo : 498.68
Cpu1ClkTck : 000000002cb41780
MMU Type : Cheetah
State:
CPU0: online
CPU1: online
```

Most of the files in /proc are read only, some require root privileges, some files are writable, and many files in **/proc/sys** are writable. Let's discuss some of the files in /proc.

/proc/interrupts

On the x86 architecture, **/proc/interrupts** displays the interrupts.

```
paul@RHELv4u4:~$ cat /proc/interrupts
           CPU0
   0:    13876877      IO-APIC-edge   timer
   1:          15      IO-APIC-edge   i8042
   8:           1      IO-APIC-edge   rtc
   9:           0     IO-APIC-level   acpi
  12:          67      IO-APIC-edge   i8042
  14:         128      IO-APIC-edge   ide0
  15:      124320      IO-APIC-edge   ide1
 169:      111993     IO-APIC-level   ioc0
 177:        2428     IO-APIC-level   eth0
NMI:           0
LOC:    13878037
ERR:           0
MIS:           0
```

On a machine with two CPU's, the file looks like this.

```
paul@laika:~$ cat /proc/interrupts
           CPU0       CPU1
   0:     860013          0   IO-APIC-edge      timer
   1:       4533          0   IO-APIC-edge      i8042
   7:          0          0   IO-APIC-edge      parport0
   8:    6588227          0   IO-APIC-edge      rtc
  10:       2314          0   IO-APIC-fasteoi   acpi
  12:        133          0   IO-APIC-edge      i8042
  14:          0          0   IO-APIC-edge      libata
  15:      72269          0   IO-APIC-edge      libata
  18:          1          0   IO-APIC-fasteoi   yenta
  19:     115036          0   IO-APIC-fasteoi   eth0
  20:     126871          0   IO-APIC-fasteoi   libata, ohci1394
  21:      30204          0   IO-APIC-fasteoi   ehci_hcd:usb1, uhci_hcd:usb2
  22:       1334          0   IO-APIC-fasteoi   saa7133[0], saa7133[0]
  24:     234739          0   IO-APIC-fasteoi   nvidia
NMI:         72         42
LOC:     860000     859994
ERR:          0
```

/proc/kcore

The physical memory is represented in **/proc/kcore**. Do not try to cat this file, instead use a debugger. The size of /proc/kcore is the same as your physical memory, plus four bytes.

```
paul@laika:~$ ls -lh /proc/kcore
-r-------- 1 root root 2.0G 2007-01-30 08:57 /proc/kcore
paul@laika:~$
```

11.7.3. /sys Linux 2.6 hot plugging

The **/sys** directory was created for the Linux 2.6 kernel. Since 2.6, Linux uses **sysfs** to support **usb** and **IEEE 1394 (FireWire)** hot plug devices. See the manual pages of udev(8) (the successor of **devfs**) and hotplug(8) for more info (or visit http://linux-hotplug.sourceforge.net/).

Basically the **/sys** directory contains kernel information about hardware.

11.8. /usr Unix System Resources

Although **/usr** is pronounced like user, remember that it stands for **Unix System Resources**. The **/usr** hierarchy should contain **shareable, read only** data. Some people choose to mount **/usr** as read only. This can be done from its own partition or from a read only NFS share (NFS is discussed later).

11.8.1. /usr/bin

The **/usr/bin** directory contains a lot of commands.

```
paul@deb508:~$ ls /usr/bin | wc -l
1395
```

(On Solaris the **/bin** directory is a symbolic link to **/usr/bin**.)

11.8.2. /usr/include

The **/usr/include** directory contains general use include files for C.

```
paul@ubu1010:~$ ls /usr/include/
aalib.h        expat_config.h      math.h        search.h
af_vfs.h       expat_external.h    mcheck.h      semaphore.h
aio.h          expat.h             memory.h      setjmp.h
AL             fcntl.h             menu.h        sgtty.h
aliases.h      features.h          mntent.h      shadow.h
...
```

11.8.3. /usr/lib

The **/usr/lib** directory contains libraries that are not directly executed by users or scripts.

```
paul@deb508:~$ ls /usr/lib | head -7
4Suite
ao
apt
arj
aspell
avahi
bonobo
```

11.8.4. /usr/local

The **/usr/local** directory can be used by an administrator to install software locally.

```
paul@deb508:~$ ls /usr/local/
bin  etc games  include  lib  man  sbin  share  src
paul@deb508:~$ du -sh /usr/local/
128K /usr/local/
```

11.8.5. /usr/share

The **/usr/share** directory contains architecture independent data. As you can see, this is a fairly large directory.

```
paul@deb508:~$ ls /usr/share/ | wc -l
```

```
263
paul@deb508:~$ du -sh /usr/share/
1.3G /usr/share/
```

This directory typically contains **/usr/share/man** for manual pages.

```
paul@deb508:~$ ls /usr/share/man
cs  fr      hu   it.UTF-8   man2 man6  pl.ISO8859-2  sv
de  fr.ISO8859-1 id   ja    man3 man7  pl.UTF-8      tr
es  fr.UTF-8  it   ko    man4 man8  pt_BR         zh_CN
fi  gl      it.ISO8859-1 man1   man5 pl    ru            zh_TW
```

And it contains **/usr/share/games** for all static game data (so no high-scores or play logs).

```
paul@ubu1010:~$ ls /usr/share/games/
openttd  wesnoth
```

11.8.6. /usr/src

The **/usr/src** directory is the recommended location for kernel source files.

```
paul@deb508:~$ ls -l /usr/src/
total 12
drwxr-xr-x  4 root root 4096 2011-02-01 14:43 linux-headers-2.6.26-2-686
drwxr-xr-x 18 root root 4096 2011-02-01 14:43 linux-headers-2.6.26-2-common
drwxr-xr-x  3 root root 4096 2009-10-28 16:01 linux-kbuild-2.6.26
```

11.9. /var variable data

Files that are unpredictable in size, such as log, cache and spool files, should be located in **/var**.

11.9.1. /var/log

The **/var/log** directory serves as a central point to contain all log files.

```
[paul@RHEL4b ~]$ ls /var/log
acpid           cron.2      maillog.2    quagga            secure.4
amanda          cron.3      maillog.3    radius            spooler
anaconda.log    cron.4      maillog.4    rpmpkgs           spooler.1
anaconda.syslog cups        mailman      rpmpkgs.1         spooler.2
anaconda.xlog   dmesg       messages     rpmpkgs.2         spooler.3
audit           exim        messages.1   rpmpkgs.3         spooler.4
boot.log        gdm         messages.2   rpmpkgs.4         squid
boot.log.1      httpd       messages.3   sa                uucp
boot.log.2      iiim        messages.4   samba             vbox
boot.log.3      iptraf      mysqld.log   scrollkeeper.log  vmware-tools-guestd
boot.log.4      lastlog     news         secure            wtmp
canna           mail        pgsql        secure.1          wtmp.1
cron            maillog     ppp          secure.2          Xorg.0.log
cron.1          maillog.1   prelink.log  secure.3          Xorg.0.log.old
```

11.9.2. /var/log/messages

A typical first file to check when troubleshooting on Red Hat (and derivatives) is the **/var/log/messages** file. By default this file will contain information on what just happened to the system. The file is called **/var/log/syslog** on Debian and Ubuntu.

```
[root@RHEL4b ~]# tail /var/log/messages
Jul 30 05:13:56 anacron: anacron startup succeeded
Jul 30 05:13:56 atd: atd startup succeeded
Jul 30 05:13:57 messagebus: messagebus startup succeeded
Jul 30 05:13:57 cups-config-daemon: cups-config-daemon startup succeeded
Jul 30 05:13:58 haldaemon: haldaemon startup succeeded
Jul 30 05:14:00 fstab-sync[3560]: removed all generated mount points
Jul 30 05:14:01 fstab-sync[3628]: added mount point /media/cdrom for...
Jul 30 05:14:01 fstab-sync[3646]: added mount point /media/floppy for...
Jul 30 05:16:46 sshd(pam_unix)[3662]: session opened for user paul by...
Jul 30 06:06:37 su(pam_unix)[3904]: session opened for user root by paul
```

11.9.3. /var/cache

The **/var/cache** directory can contain **cache data** for several applications.

```
paul@ubu1010:~$ ls /var/cache/
apt       dictionaries-common      gdm      man        software-center
binfmts   flashplugin-installer    hald     pm-utils
cups      fontconfig               jockey   pppconfig
debconf   fonts                    ldconfig samba
```

11.9.4. /var/spool

The **/var/spool** directory typically contains spool directories for **mail** and **cron**, but also serves as a parent directory for other spool files (for example print spool files).

11.9.5. /var/lib

The **/var/lib** directory contains application state information.

Red Hat Enterprise Linux for example keeps files pertaining to **rpm** in **/var/lib/rpm/**.

11.9.6. /var/...

/var also contains Process ID files in **/var/run** (soon to be replaced with **/run**) and temporary files that survive a reboot in **/var/tmp** and information about file locks in **/var/lock**. There will be more examples of **/var** usage further in this book.

11.10. practice: file system tree

1. Does the file **/bin/cat** exist ? What about **/bin/dd** and **/bin/echo**. What is the type of these files ?

2. What is the size of the Linux kernel file(s) (vmlinu*) in **/boot** ?

3. Create a directory ~/test. Then issue the following commands:

```
cd ~/test

dd if=/dev/zero of=zeroes.txt count=1 bs=100

od zeroes.txt
```

dd will copy one times (count=1) a block of size 100 bytes (bs=100) from the file **/dev/zero** to ~/test/zeroes.txt. Can you describe the functionality of **/dev/zero** ?

4. Now issue the following command:

```
dd if=/dev/random of=random.txt count=1 bs=100 ; od random.txt
```

dd will copy one times (count=1) a block of size 100 bytes (bs=100) from the file **/dev/random** to ~/test/random.txt. Can you describe the functionality of **/dev/random** ?

5. Issue the following two commands, and look at the first character of each output line.

```
ls -l /dev/sd* /dev/hd*

ls -l /dev/tty* /dev/input/mou*
```

The first ls will show block(b) devices, the second ls shows character(c) devices. Can you tell the difference between block and character devices ?

6. Use cat to display **/etc/hosts** and **/etc/resolv.conf**. What is your idea about the purpose of these files ?

7. Are there any files in **/etc/skel/** ? Check also for hidden files.

8. Display **/proc/cpuinfo**. On what architecture is your Linux running ?

9. Display **/proc/interrupts**. What is the size of this file ? Where is this file stored ?

10. Can you enter the **/root** directory ? Are there (hidden) files ?

11. Are ifconfig, fdisk, parted, shutdown and grub-install present in **/sbin** ? Why are these binaries in **/sbin** and not in **/bin** ?

12. Is **/var/log** a file or a directory ? What about **/var/spool** ?

13. Open two command prompts (Ctrl-Shift-T in gnome-terminal) or terminals (Ctrl-Alt-F1, Ctrl-Alt-F2, ...) and issue the **who am i** in both. Then try to echo a word from one terminal to the other.

14. Read the man page of **random** and explain the difference between **/dev/random** and **/dev/urandom**.

11.11. solution: file system tree

1. Does the file **/bin/cat** exist ? What about **/bin/dd** and **/bin/echo**. What is the type of these files ?

```
ls /bin/cat ; file /bin/cat

ls /bin/dd ; file /bin/dd

ls /bin/echo ; file /bin/echo
```

2. What is the size of the Linux kernel file(s) (vmlinu*) in **/boot** ?

```
ls -lh /boot/vm*
```

3. Create a directory ~/test. Then issue the following commands:

```
cd ~/test

dd if=/dev/zero of=zeroes.txt count=1 bs=100

od zeroes.txt
```

dd will copy one times (count=1) a block of size 100 bytes (bs=100) from the file **/dev/zero** to ~/test/zeroes.txt. Can you describe the functionality of **/dev/zero** ?

/dev/zero is a Linux special device. It can be considered a source of zeroes. You cannot send something to **/dev/zero**, but you can read zeroes from it.

4. Now issue the following command:

```
dd if=/dev/random of=random.txt count=1 bs=100 ; od random.txt
```

dd will copy one times (count=1) a block of size 100 bytes (bs=100) from the file **/dev/random** to ~/test/random.txt. Can you describe the functionality of **/dev/random** ?

/dev/random acts as a **random number generator** on your Linux machine.

5. Issue the following two commands, and look at the first character of each output line.

```
ls -l /dev/sd* /dev/hd*

ls -l /dev/tty* /dev/input/mou*
```

The first ls will show block(b) devices, the second ls shows character(c) devices. Can you tell the difference between block and character devices ?

Block devices are always written to (or read from) in blocks. For hard disks, blocks of 512 bytes are common. Character devices act as a stream of characters (or bytes). Mouse and keyboard are typical character devices.

6. Use cat to display **/etc/hosts** and **/etc/resolv.conf**. What is your idea about the purpose of these files ?

```
/etc/hosts contains hostnames with their ip address

/etc/resolv.conf should contain the ip address of a DNS name server.
```

7. Are there any files in **/etc/skel/** ? Check also for hidden files.

```
Issue "ls -al /etc/skel/". Yes, there should be hidden files there.
```

8. Display **/proc/cpuinfo**. On what architecture is your Linux running ?

```
The file should contain at least one line with Intel or other cpu.
```

9. Display **/proc/interrupts**. What is the size of this file ? Where is this file stored ?

The size is zero, yet the file contains data. It is not stored anywhere because /proc is a virtual file system that allows you to talk with the kernel. (If you answered "stored in RAM-memory, that is also correct...).

10. Can you enter the **/root** directory ? Are there (hidden) files ?

```
Try "cd /root". The /root directory is not accessible for normal users on most modern Linux sy
```

11. Are ifconfig, fdisk, parted, shutdown and grub-install present in **/sbin** ? Why are these binaries in **/sbin** and not in /bin ?

```
Because those files are only meant for system administrators.
```

12. Is **/var/log** a file or a directory ? What about **/var/spool** ?

```
Both are directories.
```

13. Open two command prompts (Ctrl-Shift-T in gnome-terminal) or terminals (Ctrl-Alt-F1, Ctrl-Alt-F2, ...) and issue the **who am i** in both. Then try to echo a word from one terminal to the other.

```
tty-terminal: echo Hello > /dev/tty1
```

```
pts-terminal: echo Hello > /dev/pts/1
```

14. Read the man page of **random** and explain the difference between **/dev/random** and /**dev/urandom**.

```
man 4 random
```

Part IV. shell expansion

Table of Contents

Chapter 12. commands and arguments

This chapter introduces you to **shell expansion** by taking a close look at **commands** and **arguments**. Knowing **shell expansion** is important because many **commands** on your Linux system are processed and most likely changed by the **shell** before they are executed.

The command line interface or **shell** used on most Linux systems is called **bash**, which stands for **Bourne again shell**. The **bash** shell incorporates features from **sh** (the original Bourne shell), **csh** (the C shell), and **ksh** (the Korn shell).

This chapter frequently uses the **echo** command to demonstrate shell features. The **echo** command is very simple: it echoes the input that it receives.

```
paul@laika:~$ echo Burtonville
Burtonville
paul@laika:~$ echo Smurfs are blue
Smurfs are blue
```

12.1. arguments

One of the primary features of a shell is to perform a **command line scan**. When you enter a command at the shell's command prompt and press the enter key, then the shell will start scanning that line, cutting it up in **arguments**. While scanning the line, the shell may make many changes to the **arguments** you typed.

This process is called **shell expansion**. When the shell has finished scanning and modifying that line, then it will be executed.

12.2. white space removal

Parts that are separated by one or more consecutive **white spaces** (or tabs) are considered separate **arguments**, any white space is removed. The first **argument** is the command to be executed, the other **arguments** are given to the command. The shell effectively cuts your command into one or more arguments.

This explains why the following four different command lines are the same after **shell expansion**.

```
[paul@RHELv4u3 ~]$ echo Hello World
Hello World
[paul@RHELv4u3 ~]$ echo Hello    World
Hello World
[paul@RHELv4u3 ~]$ echo   Hello    World
Hello World
[paul@RHELv4u3 ~]$    echo       Hello       World
Hello World
```

The **echo** command will display each argument it receives from the shell. The **echo** command will also add a new white space between the arguments it received.

12.3. single quotes

You can prevent the removal of white spaces by quoting the spaces. The contents of the quoted string are considered as one argument. In the screenshot below the **echo** receives only one **argument**.

```
[paul@RHEL4b ~]$ echo 'A line with     single    quotes'
A line with     single    quotes
[paul@RHEL4b ~]$
```

12.4. double quotes

You can also prevent the removal of white spaces by double quoting the spaces. Same as above, **echo** only receives one **argument**.

```
[paul@RHEL4b ~]$ echo "A line with     double    quotes"
A line with     double    quotes
[paul@RHEL4b ~]$
```

Later in this book, when discussing **variables** we will see important differences between single and double quotes.

12.5. echo and quotes

Quoted lines can include special escaped characters recognised by the **echo** command (when using **echo -e**). The screenshot below shows how to use \n for a newline and \t for a tab (usually eight white spaces).

```
[paul@RHEL4b ~]$ echo -e "A line with \na newline"
A line with
a newline
[paul@RHEL4b ~]$ echo -e 'A line with \na newline'
A line with
a newline
[paul@RHEL4b ~]$ echo -e "A line with \ta tab"
A line with     a tab
[paul@RHEL4b ~]$ echo -e 'A line with \ta tab'
A line with     a tab
[paul@RHEL4b ~]$
```

The echo command can generate more than white spaces, tabs and newlines. Look in the man page for a list of options.

12.6. commands

12.6.1. external or builtin commands ?

Not all commands are external to the shell, some are **builtin**. **External commands** are programs that have their own binary and reside somewhere in the file system. Many external commands are located in **/bin** or **/sbin**. **Builtin commands** are an integral part of the shell program itself.

12.6.2. type

To find out whether a command given to the shell will be executed as an **external command** or as a **builtin command**, use the **type** command.

```
paul@laika:~$ type cd
cd is a shell builtin
paul@laika:~$ type cat
cat is /bin/cat
```

As you can see, the **cd** command is **builtin** and the **cat** command is **external**.

You can also use this command to show you whether the command is **aliased** or not.

```
paul@laika:~$ type ls
ls is aliased to `ls --color=auto'
```

12.6.3. running external commands

Some commands have both builtin and external versions. When one of these commands is executed, the builtin version takes priority. To run the external version, you must enter the full path to the command.

```
paul@laika:~$ type -a echo
echo is a shell builtin
echo is /bin/echo
paul@laika:~$ /bin/echo Running the external echo command...
Running the external echo command...
```

12.6.4. which

The **which** command will search for binaries in the **$PATH** environment variable (variables will be explained later). In the screenshot below, it is determined that **cd** is **builtin**, and **ls, cp, rm, mv, mkdir, pwd,** and **which** are external commands.

```
[root@RHEL4b ~]# which cp ls cd mkdir pwd
/bin/cp
/bin/ls
/usr/bin/which: no cd in (/usr/kerberos/sbin:/usr/kerberos/bin:...
/bin/mkdir
/bin/pwd
```

12.7. aliases

12.7.1. create an alias

The shell allows you to create **aliases**. Aliases are often used to create an easier to remember name for an existing command or to easily supply parameters.

```
[paul@RHELv4u3 ~]$ cat count.txt
one
two
three
[paul@RHELv4u3 ~]$ alias dog=tac
[paul@RHELv4u3 ~]$ dog count.txt
three
two
one
```

12.7.2. abbreviate commands

An **alias** can also be useful to abbreviate an existing command.

```
paul@laika:~$ alias ll='ls -lh --color=auto'
paul@laika:~$ alias c='clear'
paul@laika:~$
```

12.7.3. default options

Aliases can be used to supply commands with default options. The example below shows how to set the **-i** option default when typing **rm**.

```
[paul@RHELv4u3 ~]$ rm -i winter.txt
rm: remove regular file `winter.txt'? no
[paul@RHELv4u3 ~]$ rm winter.txt
[paul@RHELv4u3 ~]$ ls winter.txt
ls: winter.txt: No such file or directory
[paul@RHELv4u3 ~]$ touch winter.txt
[paul@RHELv4u3 ~]$ alias rm='rm -i'
[paul@RHELv4u3 ~]$ rm winter.txt
rm: remove regular empty file `winter.txt'? no
[paul@RHELv4u3 ~]$
```

Some distributions enable default aliases to protect users from accidentally erasing files ('rm -i', 'mv -i', 'cp -i')

12.7.4. viewing aliases

You can provide one or more aliases as arguments to the **alias** command to get their definitions. Providing no arguments gives a complete list of current aliases.

```
paul@laika:~$ alias c ll
alias c='clear'
alias ll='ls -lh --color=auto'
```

12.7.5. unalias

You can undo an alias with the **unalias** command.

```
[paul@RHEL4b ~]$ which rm
/bin/rm
[paul@RHEL4b ~]$ alias rm='rm -i'
[paul@RHEL4b ~]$ which rm
alias rm='rm -i'
        /bin/rm
[paul@RHEL4b ~]$ unalias rm
[paul@RHEL4b ~]$ which rm
/bin/rm
[paul@RHEL4b ~]$
```

12.8. displaying shell expansion

You can display shell expansion with **set -x**, and stop displaying it with **set +x**. You might want to use this further on in this course, or when in doubt about exactly what the shell is doing with your command.

```
[paul@RHELv4u3 ~]$ set -x
++ echo -ne '\033]0;paul@RHELv4u3:~\007'
[paul@RHELv4u3 ~]$ echo $USER
+ echo paul
paul
++ echo -ne '\033]0;paul@RHELv4u3:~\007'
[paul@RHELv4u3 ~]$ echo \$USER
+ echo '$USER'
$USER
++ echo -ne '\033]0;paul@RHELv4u3:~\007'
[paul@RHELv4u3 ~]$ set +x
+ set +x
[paul@RHELv4u3 ~]$ echo $USER
paul
```

12.9. practice: commands and arguments

1. How many **arguments** are in this line (not counting the command itself).

```
touch '/etc/cron/cron.allow' 'file 42.txt' "file 33.txt"
```

2. Is **tac** a shell builtin command ?

3. Is there an existing alias for **rm** ?

4. Read the man page of **rm**, make sure you understand the **-i** option of rm. Create and remove a file to test the **-i** option.

5. Execute: **alias rm='rm -i'** . Test your alias with a test file. Does this work as expected ?

6. List all current aliases.

7a. Create an alias called 'city' that echoes your hometown.

7b. Use your alias to test that it works.

8. Execute **set -x** to display shell expansion for every command.

9. Test the functionality of **set -x** by executing your **city** and **rm** aliases.

10 Execute **set +x** to stop displaying shell expansion.

11. Remove your city alias.

12. What is the location of the **cat** and the **passwd** commands ?

13. Explain the difference between the following commands:

```
echo
/bin/echo
```

14. Explain the difference between the following commands:

```
echo Hello
echo -n Hello
```

15. Display **A B C** with two spaces between B and C.

(optional)16. Complete the following command (do not use spaces) to display exactly the following output:

```
4+4      =8
10+14    =24
```

17. Use **echo** to display the following exactly:

```
??\\
```

Find two solutions with single quotes, two with double quotes and one without quotes (and say thank you to René and Darioush from Google for this extra).

18. Use one **echo** command to display three words on three lines.

12.10. solution: commands and arguments

1. How many **arguments** are in this line (not counting the command itself).

```
touch '/etc/cron/cron.allow' 'file 42.txt' "file 33.txt"

answer: three
```

2. Is **tac** a shell builtin command ?

```
type tac
```

3. Is there an existing alias for **rm** ?

```
alias rm
```

4. Read the man page of **rm**, make sure you understand the **-i** option of rm. Create and remove a file to test the **-i** option.

```
man rm

touch testfile

rm -i testfile
```

5. Execute: **alias rm='rm -i'** . Test your alias with a test file. Does this work as expected ?

```
touch testfile

rm testfile (should ask for confirmation)
```

6. List all current aliases.

```
alias
```

7a. Create an alias called 'city' that echoes your hometown.

```
alias city='echo Antwerp'
```

7b. Use your alias to test that it works.

```
city (it should display Antwerp)
```

8. Execute **set -x** to display shell expansion for every command.

```
set -x
```

9. Test the functionality of **set -x** by executing your **city** and **rm** aliases.

```
shell should display the resolved aliases and then execute the command:
paul@deb503:~$ set -x
paul@deb503:~$ city
+ echo antwerp
antwerp
```

10 Execute **set +x** to stop displaying shell expansion.

```
set +x
```

11. Remove your city alias.

```
unalias city
```

12. What is the location of the **cat** and the **passwd** commands ?

```
which cat (probably /bin/cat)
```

```
which passwd (probably /usr/bin/passwd)
```

13. Explain the difference between the following commands:

```
echo
```

```
/bin/echo
```

The **echo** command will be interpreted by the shell as the **built-in echo** command. The **/bin/echo** command will make the shell execute the **echo binary** located in the **/bin** directory.

14. Explain the difference between the following commands:

```
echo Hello
```

```
echo -n Hello
```

The -n option of the **echo** command will prevent echo from echoing a trailing newline. **echo Hello** will echo six characters in total, **echo -n hello** only echoes five characters.

(The -n option might not work in the Korn shell.)

15. Display **A B C** with two spaces between B and C.

```
echo "A B  C"
```

16. Complete the following command (do not use spaces) to display exactly the following output:

```
4+4     =8
10+14   =24
```

The solution is to use tabs with \t.

```
echo -e "4+4\t=8" ; echo -e "10+14\t=24"
```

17. Use **echo** to display the following exactly:

```
??\\
echo '??\\'
echo -e '??\\\\'
echo "??\\\\"
echo -e "??\\\\\\"
echo ??\\\\
```

Find two solutions with single quotes, two with double quotes and one without quotes (and say thank you to René and Darioush from Google for this extra).

18. Use one **echo** command to display three words on three lines.

```
echo -e "one \ntwo \nthree"
```

Chapter 13. control operators

In this chapter we put more than one command on the command line using **control operators**. We also briefly discuss related parameters ($?) and similar special characters(&).

13.1. ; semicolon

You can put two or more commands on the same line separated by a semicolon ; . The shell will scan the line until it reaches the semicolon. All the arguments before this semicolon will be considered a separate command from all the arguments after the semicolon. Both series will be executed sequentially with the shell waiting for each command to finish before starting the next one.

```
[paul@RHELv4u3 ~]$ echo Hello
Hello
[paul@RHELv4u3 ~]$ echo World
World
[paul@RHELv4u3 ~]$ echo Hello ; echo World
Hello
World
[paul@RHELv4u3 ~]$
```

13.2. & ampersand

When a line ends with an ampersand &, the shell will not wait for the command to finish. You will get your shell prompt back, and the command is executed in background. You will get a message when this command has finished executing in background.

```
[paul@RHELv4u3 ~]$ sleep 20 &
[1] 7925
[paul@RHELv4u3 ~]$
...wait 20 seconds...
[paul@RHELv4u3 ~]$
[1]+  Done                    sleep 20
```

The technical explanation of what happens in this case is explained in the chapter about **processes**.

13.3. $? dollar question mark

The exit code of the previous command is stored in the shell variable $?. Actually $? is a shell parameter and not a variable, since you cannot assign a value to $?.

```
paul@debian5:~/test$ touch file1
paul@debian5:~/test$ echo $?
0
paul@debian5:~/test$ rm file1
paul@debian5:~/test$ echo $?
0
paul@debian5:~/test$ rm file1
rm: cannot remove `file1': No such file or directory
paul@debian5:~/test$ echo $?
1
paul@debian5:~/test$
```

13.4. && double ampersand

The shell will interpret **&&** as a **logical AND**. When using **&&** the second command is executed only if the first one succeeds (returns a zero exit status).

```
paul@barry:~$ echo first && echo second
first
second
paul@barry:~$ zecho first && echo second
-bash: zecho: command not found
```

Another example of the same **logical AND** principle. This example starts with a working **cd** followed by **ls**, then a non-working **cd** which is **not** followed by **ls**.

```
[paul@RHELv4u3 ~]$ cd gen && ls
file1   file3   File55   fileab   FileAB    fileabc
file2   File4   FileA    Fileab   fileab2
[paul@RHELv4u3 gen]$ cd gen && ls
-bash: cd: gen: No such file or directory
```

13.5. || double vertical bar

The || represents a **logical OR**. The second command is executed only when the first command fails (returns a non-zero exit status).

```
paul@barry:~$ echo first || echo second ; echo third
first
third
paul@barry:~$ zecho first || echo second ; echo third
-bash: zecho: command not found
second
third
paul@barry:~$
```

Another example of the same **logical OR** principle.

```
[paul@RHELv4u3 ~]$ cd gen || ls
[paul@RHELv4u3 gen]$ cd gen || ls
-bash: cd: gen: No such file or directory
file1   file3   File55   fileab   FileAB    fileabc
file2   File4   FileA    Fileab   fileab2
```

13.6. combining && and ||

You can use this logical AND and logical OR to write an **if-then-else** structure on the command line. This example uses **echo** to display whether the **rm** command was successful.

```
paul@laika:~/test$ rm file1 && echo It worked! || echo It failed!
It worked!
paul@laika:~/test$ rm file1 && echo It worked! || echo It failed!
rm: cannot remove `file1': No such file or directory
It failed!
paul@laika:~/test$
```

13.7. # pound sign

Everything written after a **pound sign** (#) is ignored by the shell. This is useful to write a **shell comment**, but has no influence on the command execution or shell expansion.

```
paul@debian4:~$ mkdir test      # we create a directory
paul@debian4:~$ cd test         #### we enter the directory
paul@debian4:~/test$ ls         # is it empty ?
paul@debian4:~/test$
```

13.8. \ escaping special characters

The backslash \ character enables the use of control characters, but without the shell interpreting it, this is called **escaping** characters.

```
[paul@RHELv4u3 ~]$ echo hello \; world
hello ; world
[paul@RHELv4u3 ~]$ echo hello\ \ \ world
hello    world
[paul@RHELv4u3 ~]$ echo escaping \\\ \#\ \&\ \"\ \'
escaping \ # & " '
[paul@RHELv4u3 ~]$ echo escaping \\\?\*\"\'
escaping \?*"'
```

13.8.1. end of line backslash

Lines ending in a backslash are continued on the next line. The shell does not interpret the newline character and will wait on shell expansion and execution of the command line until a newline without backslash is encountered.

```
[paul@RHEL4b ~]$ echo This command line \
> is split in three \
> parts
This command line is split in three parts
[paul@RHEL4b ~]$
```

13.9. practice: control operators

0. Each question can be answered by one command line!

1. When you type **passwd**, which file is executed ?

2. What kind of file is that ?

3. Execute the **pwd** command twice. (remember 0.)

4. Execute **ls** after **cd /etc**, but only if **cd /etc** did not error.

5. Execute **cd /etc** after **cd etc**, but only if **cd etc** fails.

6. Echo **it worked** when **touch test42** works, and echo **it failed** when the **touch** failed. All on one command line as a normal user (not root). Test this line in your home directory and in **/bin/** .

7. Execute **sleep 6**, what is this command doing ?

8. Execute **sleep 200** in background (do not wait for it to finish).

9. Write a command line that executes **rm file55**. Your command line should print 'success' if file55 is removed, and print 'failed' if there was a problem.

(optional)10. Use echo to display "Hello World with strange' characters \ * [} ~ \ \ ." (including all quotes)

13.10. solution: control operators

0. Each question can be answered by one command line!

1. When you type **passwd**, which file is executed ?

```
which passwd
```

2. What kind of file is that ?

```
file /usr/bin/passwd
```

3. Execute the **pwd** command twice. (remember 0.)

```
pwd ; pwd
```

4. Execute **ls** after **cd /etc**, but only if **cd /etc** did not error.

```
cd /etc && ls
```

5. Execute **cd /etc** after **cd etc**, but only if **cd etc** fails.

```
cd etc || cd /etc
```

6. Echo **it worked** when **touch test42** works, and echo **it failed** when the **touch** failed. All on one command line as a normal user (not root). Test this line in your home directory and in **/bin/** .

```
paul@deb503:~$ cd ; touch test42 && echo it worked || echo it failed
it worked
paul@deb503:~$ cd /bin; touch test42 && echo it worked || echo it failed
touch: cannot touch `test42': Permission denied
it failed
```

7. Execute **sleep 6**, what is this command doing ?

```
pausing for six seconds
```

8. Execute **sleep 200** in background (do not wait for it to finish).

```
sleep 200 &
```

9. Write a command line that executes **rm file55**. Your command line should print 'success' if file55 is removed, and print 'failed' if there was a problem.

```
rm file55 && echo success || echo failed
```

(optional)10. Use echo to display "Hello World with strange' characters \ * [} ~ \ \ ." (including all quotes)

```
echo \"Hello World with strange\' characters \\ \* \[ \} \~ \\\\ \. \"
```

or

```
echo \""Hello World with strange' characters \ * [ } ~ \\ . "\"
```

Chapter 14. shell variables

In this chapter we learn to manage environment **variables** in the shell. These **variables** are often needed by applications.

14.1. $ dollar sign

Another important character interpreted by the shell is the dollar sign **$**. The shell will look for an **environment variable** named like the string following the **dollar sign** and replace it with the value of the variable (or with nothing if the variable does not exist).

These are some examples using $HOSTNAME, $USER, $UID, $SHELL, and $HOME.

```
[paul@RHELv4u3 ~]$ echo This is the $SHELL shell
This is the /bin/bash shell
[paul@RHELv4u3 ~]$ echo This is $SHELL on computer $HOSTNAME
This is /bin/bash on computer RHELv4u3.localdomain
[paul@RHELv4u3 ~]$ echo The userid of $USER is $UID
The userid of paul is 500
[paul@RHELv4u3 ~]$ echo My homedir is $HOME
My homedir is /home/paul
```

14.2. case sensitive

This example shows that shell variables are case sensitive!

```
[paul@RHELv4u3 ~]$ echo Hello $USER
Hello paul
[paul@RHELv4u3 ~]$ echo Hello $user
Hello
```

14.3. creating variables

This example creates the variable **$MyVar** and sets its value. It then uses **echo** to verify the value.

```
[paul@RHELv4u3 gen]$ MyVar=555
[paul@RHELv4u3 gen]$ echo $MyVar
555
[paul@RHELv4u3 gen]$
```

14.4. quotes

Notice that double quotes still allow the parsing of variables, whereas single quotes prevent this.

```
[paul@RHELv4u3 ~]$ MyVar=555
[paul@RHELv4u3 ~]$ echo $MyVar
555
[paul@RHELv4u3 ~]$ echo "$MyVar"
555
[paul@RHELv4u3 ~]$ echo '$MyVar'
$MyVar
```

The bash shell will replace variables with their value in double quoted lines, but not in single quoted lines.

```
paul@laika:~$ city=Burtonville
paul@laika:~$ echo "We are in $city today."
We are in Burtonville today.
paul@laika:~$ echo 'We are in $city today.'
We are in $city today.
```

14.5. set

You can use the **set** command to display a list of environment variables. On Ubuntu and Debian systems, the **set** command will also list shell functions after the shell variables. Use **set | more** to see the variables then.

14.6. unset

Use the **unset** command to remove a variable from your shell environment.

```
[paul@RHEL4b ~]$ MyVar=8472
[paul@RHEL4b ~]$ echo $MyVar
8472
[paul@RHEL4b ~]$ unset MyVar
[paul@RHEL4b ~]$ echo $MyVar

[paul@RHEL4b ~]$
```

14.7. $PS1

The **$PS1** variable determines your shell prompt. You can use backslash escaped special characters like **\u** for the username or **\w** for the working directory. The **bash** manual has a complete reference.

In this example we change the value of **$PS1** a couple of times.

```
paul@deb503:~$ PS1=prompt
prompt
promptPS1='prompt '
prompt
prompt PS1='> '
>
> PS1='\u@\h$ '
paul@deb503$
paul@deb503$ PS1='\u@\h:\W$'
paul@deb503:~$
```

To avoid unrecoverable mistakes, you can set normal user prompts to green and the root prompt to red. Add the following to your **.bashrc** for a green user prompt:

```
# color prompt by paul
RED='\[\033[01;31m\]'
WHITE='\[\033[01;00m\]'
GREEN='\[\033[01;32m\]'
BLUE='\[\033[01;34m\]'
export PS1="${debian_chroot:+($debian_chroot)}$GREEN\u$WHITE@$BLUE\h$WHITE\w\$ "
```

14.8. $PATH

The **$PATH** variable is determines where the shell is looking for commands to execute (unless the command is builtin or aliased). This variable contains a list of directories, separated by colons.

```
[[paul@RHEL4b ~]$ echo $PATH
/usr/kerberos/bin:/usr/local/bin:/bin:/usr/bin:
```

The shell will not look in the current directory for commands to execute! (Looking for executables in the current directory provided an easy way to hack PC-DOS computers). If you want the shell to look in the current directory, then add a . at the end of your $PATH.

```
[paul@RHEL4b ~]$ PATH=$PATH:.
[paul@RHEL4b ~]$ echo $PATH
/usr/kerberos/bin:/usr/local/bin:/bin:/usr/bin:.
[paul@RHEL4b ~]$
```

Your path might be different when using su instead of **su -** because the latter will take on the environment of the target user. The root user typically has **/sbin** directories added to the $PATH variable.

```
[paul@RHEL3 ~]$ su
Password:
[root@RHEL3 paul]# echo $PATH
/usr/local/bin:/bin:/usr/bin:/usr/X11R6/bin
[root@RHEL3 paul]# exit
[paul@RHEL3 ~]$ su -
Password:
[root@RHEL3 ~]# echo $PATH
/usr/local/sbin:/usr/local/bin:/sbin:/bin:/usr/sbin:/usr/bin:
[root@RHEL3 ~]#
```

14.9. env

The **env** command without options will display a list of **exported variables**. The difference with **set** with options is that **set** lists all variables, including those not exported to child shells.

But **env** can also be used to start a clean shell (a shell without any inherited environment). The **env -i** command clears the environment for the subshell.

Notice in this screenshot that **bash** will set the **$SHELL** variable on startup.

```
[paul@RHEL4b ~]$ bash -c 'echo $SHELL $HOME $USER'
/bin/bash /home/paul paul
[paul@RHEL4b ~]$ env -i bash -c 'echo $SHELL $HOME $USER'
/bin/bash
[paul@RHEL4b ~]$
```

You can use the **env** command to set the **$LANG**, or any other, variable for just one instance of **bash** with one command. The example below uses this to show the influence of the **$LANG** variable on file globbing (see the chapter on file globbing).

```
[paul@RHEL4b test]$ env LANG=C bash -c 'ls File[a-z]'
Filea   Fileb
[paul@RHEL4b test]$ env LANG=en_US.UTF-8 bash -c 'ls File[a-z]'
Filea   FileA   Fileb   FileB
[paul@RHEL4b test]$
```

14.10. export

You can export shell variables to other shells with the **export** command. This will export the variable to child shells.

```
[paul@RHEL4b ~]$ var3=three
[paul@RHEL4b ~]$ var4=four
[paul@RHEL4b ~]$ export var4
[paul@RHEL4b ~]$ echo $var3 $var4
three four
[paul@RHEL4b ~]$ bash
[paul@RHEL4b ~]$ echo $var3 $var4
four
```

But it will not export to the parent shell (previous screenshot continued).

```
[paul@RHEL4b ~]$ export var5=five
[paul@RHEL4b ~]$ echo $var3 $var4 $var5
four five
[paul@RHEL4b ~]$ exit
exit
[paul@RHEL4b ~]$ echo $var3 $var4 $var5
three four
[paul@RHEL4b ~]$
```

14.11. delineate variables

Until now, we have seen that bash interprets a variable starting from a dollar sign, continuing until the first occurrence of a non-alphanumeric character that is not an underscore. In some situations, this can be a problem. This issue can be resolved with curly braces like in this example.

```
[paul@RHEL4b ~]$ prefix=Super
[paul@RHEL4b ~]$ echo Hello $prefixman and $prefixgirl
Hello  and
[paul@RHEL4b ~]$ echo Hello ${prefix}man and ${prefix}girl
Hello Superman and Supergirl
[paul@RHEL4b ~]$
```

14.12. unbound variables

The example below tries to display the value of the **$MyVar** variable, but it fails because the variable does not exist. By default the shell will display nothing when a variable is unbound (does not exist).

```
[paul@RHELv4u3 gen]$ echo $MyVar

[paul@RHELv4u3 gen]$
```

There is, however, the **nounset** shell option that you can use to generate an error when a variable does not exist.

```
paul@laika:~$ set -u
paul@laika:~$ echo $Myvar
bash: Myvar: unbound variable
paul@laika:~$ set +u
paul@laika:~$ echo $Myvar

paul@laika:~$
```

In the bash shell **set -u** is identical to **set -o nounset** and likewise **set +u** is identical to **set +o nounset**.

14.13. practice: shell variables

1. Use echo to display Hello followed by your username. (use a bash variable!)

2. Create a variable **answer** with a value of **42**.

3. Copy the value of $LANG to $MyLANG.

4. List all current shell variables.

5. List all exported shell variables.

6. Do the **env** and **set** commands display your variable ?

6. Destroy your **answer** variable.

7. Create two variables, and **export** one of them.

8. Display the exported variable in an interactive child shell.

9. Create a variable, give it the value 'Dumb', create another variable with value 'do'. Use **echo** and the two variables to echo Dumbledore.

10. Find the list of backslash escaped characters in the manual of bash. Add the time to your **PS1** prompt.

14.14. solution: shell variables

1. Use echo to display Hello followed by your username. (use a bash variable!)

```
echo Hello $USER
```

2. Create a variable **answer** with a value of **42**.

```
answer=42
```

3. Copy the value of $LANG to $MyLANG.

```
MyLANG=$LANG
```

4. List all current shell variables.

```
set
```

```
set|more on Ubuntu/Debian
```

5. List all exported shell variables.

```
env
export
declare -x
```

6. Do the **env** and **set** commands display your variable ?

```
env | more
set | more
```

6. Destroy your **answer** variable.

```
unset answer
```

7. Create two variables, and **export** one of them.

```
var1=1; export var2=2
```

8. Display the exported variable in an interactive child shell.

```
bash
echo $var2
```

9. Create a variable, give it the value 'Dumb', create another variable with value 'do'. Use **echo** and the two variables to echo Dumbledore.

```
varx=Dumb; vary=do
```

```
echo ${varx}le${vary}re
solution by Yves from Dexia : echo $varx'le'$vary're'
solution by Erwin from Telenet : echo "$varx"le"$vary"re
```

10. Find the list of backslash escaped characters in the manual of bash. Add the time to your **PS1** prompt.

```
PS1='\t \u@\h \W$ '
```

Chapter 15. shell embedding and options

This chapter takes a brief look at **child shells**, **embedded shells** and **shell options**.

15.1. shell embedding

Shells can be **embedded** on the command line, or in other words, the command line scan can spawn new processes containing a fork of the current shell. You can use variables to prove that new shells are created. In the screenshot below, the variable $var1 only exists in the (temporary) sub shell.

```
[paul@RHELv4u3 gen]$ echo $var1

[paul@RHELv4u3 gen]$ echo $(var1=5;echo $var1)
5
[paul@RHELv4u3 gen]$ echo $var1

[paul@RHELv4u3 gen]$
```

You can embed a shell in an **embedded shell**, this is called **nested embedding** of shells.

This screenshot shows an embedded shell inside an embedded shell.

```
paul@deb503:~$ A=shell
paul@deb503:~$ echo $C$B$A $(B=sub;echo $C$B$A; echo $(C=sub;echo $C$B$A))
shell subshell subsubshell
```

15.1.1. backticks

Single embedding can be useful to avoid changing your current directory. The screenshot below uses **backticks** instead of dollar-bracket to embed.

```
[paul@RHELv4u3 ~]$ echo `cd /etc; ls -d * | grep pass`
passwd passwd- passwd.OLD
[paul@RHELv4u3 ~]$
```

You can only use the $() notation to nest embedded shells, **backticks** cannot do this.

15.1.2. backticks or single quotes

Placing the embedding between **backticks** uses one character less than the dollar and parenthesis combo. Be careful however, backticks are often confused with single quotes. The technical difference between ' and ` is significant!

```
[paul@RHELv4u3 gen]$ echo `var1=5;echo $var1`
5
[paul@RHELv4u3 gen]$ echo 'var1=5;echo $var1'
var1=5;echo $var1
[paul@RHELv4u3 gen]$
```

15.2. shell options

Both **set** and **unset** are builtin shell commands. They can be used to set options of the bash shell itself. The next example will clarify this. By default, the shell will treat unset variables as a variable having no value. By setting the -u option, the shell will treat any reference to unset variables as an error. See the man page of bash for more information.

```
[paul@RHEL4b ~]$ echo $var123

[paul@RHEL4b ~]$ set -u
[paul@RHEL4b ~]$ echo $var123
-bash: var123: unbound variable
[paul@RHEL4b ~]$ set +u
[paul@RHEL4b ~]$ echo $var123

[paul@RHEL4b ~]$
```

To list all the set options for your shell, use **echo $-**. The **noclobber** (or **-C**) option will be explained later in this book (in the I/O redirection chapter).

```
[paul@RHEL4b ~]$ echo $-
himBH
[paul@RHEL4b ~]$ set -C ; set -u
[paul@RHEL4b ~]$ echo $-
himuBCH
[paul@RHEL4b ~]$ set +C ; set +u
[paul@RHEL4b ~]$ echo $-
himBH
[paul@RHEL4b ~]$
```

When typing **set** without options, you get a list of all variables without function when the shell is on **posix** mode. You can set bash in posix mode typing **set -o posix**.

15.3. practice: shell embedding

1. Find the list of shell options in the man page of **bash**. What is the difference between **set -u** and **set -o nounset**?

2. Activate **nounset** in your shell. Test that it shows an error message when using non-existing variables.

3. Deactivate nounset.

4. Execute **cd /var** and **ls** in an embedded shell.

The **echo** command is only needed to show the result of the **ls** command. Omitting will result in the shell trying to execute the first file as a command.

5. Create the variable embvar in an embedded shell and echo it. Does the variable exist in your current shell now ?

6. Explain what "set -x" does. Can this be useful ?

(optional)7. Given the following screenshot, add exactly four characters to that command line so that the total output is FirstMiddleLast.

```
[paul@RHEL4b ~]$ echo  First; echo  Middle; echo  Last
```

8. Display a **long listing** (ls -l) of the **passwd** command using the **which** command inside an embedded shell.

15.4. solution: shell embedding

1. Find the list of shell options in the man page of **bash**. What is the difference between **set -u** and **set -o nounset**?

read the manual of bash (man bash), search for nounset -- both mean the same thing.

2. Activate **nounset** in your shell. Test that it shows an error message when using non-existing variables.

```
set -u
OR
set -o nounset
```

Both these lines have the same effect.

3. Deactivate nounset.

```
set +u
OR
set +o nounset
```

4. Execute **cd /var** and **ls** in an embedded shell.

```
echo $(cd /var ; ls)
```

The **echo** command is only needed to show the result of the **ls** command. Omitting will result in the shell trying to execute the first file as a command.

5. Create the variable embvar in an embedded shell and echo it. Does the variable exist in your current shell now ?

```
echo $(embvar=emb;echo $embvar) ; echo $embvar #the last echo fails
```

```
$embvar does not exist in your current shell
```

6. Explain what "set -x" does. Can this be useful ?

```
It displays shell expansion for troubleshooting your command.
```

(optional)7. Given the following screenshot, add exactly four characters to that command line so that the total output is FirstMiddleLast.

```
[paul@RHEL4b ~]$ echo  First; echo  Middle; echo  Last
```

```
echo -n First; echo -n Middle; echo Last
```

8. Display a **long listing** (ls -l) of the **passwd** command using the **which** command inside an embedded shell.

```
ls -l $(which passwd)
```

Chapter 16. shell history

The shell makes it easy for us to repeat commands, this chapter explains how.

16.1. repeating the last command

To repeat the last command in bash, type **!!**. This is pronounced as **bang bang**.

```
paul@debian5:~/test42$ echo this will be repeated > file42.txt
paul@debian5:~/test42$ !!
echo this will be repeated > file42.txt
paul@debian5:~/test42$
```

16.2. repeating other commands

You can repeat other commands using one **bang** followed by one or more characters. The shell will repeat the last command that started with those characters.

```
paul@debian5:~/test42$ touch file42
paul@debian5:~/test42$ cat file42
paul@debian5:~/test42$ !to
touch file42
paul@debian5:~/test42$
```

16.3. history

To see older commands, use **history** to display the shell command history (or use **history n** to see the last n commands).

```
paul@debian5:~/test$ history 10
38   mkdir test
39   cd test
40   touch file1
41   echo hello > file2
42   echo It is very cold today > winter.txt
43   ls
44   ls -l
45   cp winter.txt summer.txt
46   ls -l
47   history 10
```

16.4. !n

When typing **!** followed by the number preceding the command you want repeated, then the shell will echo the command and execute it.

```
paul@debian5:~/test$ !43
ls
file1   file2   summer.txt   winter.txt
```

16.5. Ctrl-r

Another option is to use **ctrl-r** to search in the history. In the screenshot below i only typed **ctrl-r** followed by four characters **apti** and it finds the last command containing these four consecutive characters.

```
paul@debian5:~$
(reverse-i-search)`apti': sudo aptitude install screen
```

16.6. $HISTSIZE

The $HISTSIZE variable determines the number of commands that will be remembered in your current environment. Most distributions default this variable to 500 or 1000.

```
paul@debian5:~$ echo $HISTSIZE
500
```

You can change it to any value you like.

```
paul@debian5:~$ HISTSIZE=15000
paul@debian5:~$ echo $HISTSIZE
15000
```

16.7. $HISTFILE

The $HISTFILE variable points to the file that contains your history. The **bash** shell defaults this value to ~/**.bash_history**.

```
paul@debian5:~$ echo $HISTFILE
/home/paul/.bash_history
```

A session history is saved to this file when you **exit** the session!

*Closing a gnome-terminal with the mouse, or typing **reboot** as root will NOT save your terminal's history.*

16.8. $HISTFILESIZE

The number of commands kept in your history file can be set using $HISTFILESIZE.

```
paul@debian5:~$ echo $HISTFILESIZE
15000
```

16.9. prevent recording a command

You can prevent a command from being recorded in **history** using a space prefix.

```
paul@debian8:~/github$ echo abc
abc
paul@debian8:~/github$  echo def
def
paul@debian8:~/github$ echo ghi
ghi
paul@debian8:~/github$ history 3
 9501  echo abc
 9502  echo ghi
 9503  history 3
```

16.10. (optional)regular expressions

It is possible to use **regular expressions** when using the **bang** to repeat commands. The screenshot below switches 1 into 2.

```
paul@debian5:~/test$ cat file1
paul@debian5:~/test$ !c:s/1/2
cat file2
hello
paul@debian5:~/test$
```

16.11. (optional) Korn shell history

Repeating a command in the **Korn shell** is very similar. The Korn shell also has the **history** command, but uses the letter **r** to recall lines from history.

This screenshot shows the history command. Note the different meaning of the parameter.

```
$ history 17
17  clear
18  echo hoi
19  history 12
20  echo world
21  history 17
```

Repeating with **r** can be combined with the line numbers given by the history command, or with the first few letters of the command.

```
$ r e
echo world
world
$ cd /etc
$ r
cd /etc
$
```

16.12. practice: shell history

1. Issue the command **echo The answer to the meaning of life, the universe and everything is 42**.

2. Repeat the previous command using only two characters (there are two solutions!)

3. Display the last 5 commands you typed.

4. Issue the long **echo** from question 1 again, using the line numbers you received from the command in question 3.

5. How many commands can be kept in memory for your current shell session ?

6. Where are these commands stored when exiting the shell ?

7. How many commands can be written to the **history file** when exiting your current shell session ?

8. Make sure your current bash shell remembers the next 5000 commands you type.

9. Open more than one console (by press Ctrl-shift-t in gnome-terminal, or by opening an extra putty.exe in MS Windows) with the same user account. When is command history written to the history file ?

16.13. solution: shell history

1. Issue the command **echo The answer to the meaning of life, the universe and everything is 42**.

```
echo The answer to the meaning of life, the universe and everything is 42
```

2. Repeat the previous command using only two characters (there are two solutions!)

```
!!
OR
!e
```

3. Display the last 5 commands you typed.

```
paul@ubu1010:~$ history 5
  52  ls -l
  53  ls
  54  df -h | grep sda
  55  echo The answer to the meaning of life, the universe and everything is 42
  56  history 5
```

You will receive different line numbers.

4. Issue the long **echo** from question 1 again, using the line numbers you received from the command in question 3.

```
paul@ubu1010:~$ !55
echo The answer to the meaning of life, the universe and everything is 42
The answer to the meaning of life, the universe and everything is 42
```

5. How many commands can be kept in memory for your current shell session ?

```
echo $HISTSIZE
```

6. Where are these commands stored when exiting the shell ?

```
echo $HISTFILE
```

7. How many commands can be written to the **history file** when exiting your current shell session ?

```
echo $HISTFILESIZE
```

8. Make sure your current bash shell remembers the next 5000 commands you type.

```
HISTSIZE=5000
```

9. Open more than one console (by press Ctrl-shift-t in gnome-terminal, or by opening an extra putty.exe in MS Windows) with the same user account. When is command history written to the history file ?

```
when you type exit
```

Chapter 17. file globbing

The shell is also responsible for **file globbing** (or dynamic filename generation). This chapter will explain **file globbing**.

17.1. * asterisk

The asterisk * is interpreted by the shell as a sign to generate filenames, matching the asterisk to any combination of characters (even none). When no path is given, the shell will use filenames in the current directory. See the man page of **glob(7)** for more information. (This is part of LPI topic 1.103.3.)

```
[paul@RHELv4u3 gen]$ ls
file1  file2  file3  File4  File55  FileA  fileab  Fileab  FileAB  fileabc
[paul@RHELv4u3 gen]$ ls File*
File4  File55  FileA  Fileab  FileAB
[paul@RHELv4u3 gen]$ ls file*
file1  file2  file3  fileab  fileabc
[paul@RHELv4u3 gen]$ ls *ile55
File55
[paul@RHELv4u3 gen]$ ls F*ile55
File55
[paul@RHELv4u3 gen]$ ls F*55
File55
[paul@RHELv4u3 gen]$
```

17.2. ? question mark

Similar to the asterisk, the question mark **?** is interpreted by the shell as a sign to generate filenames, matching the question mark with exactly one character.

```
[paul@RHELv4u3 gen]$ ls
file1  file2  file3  File4  File55  FileA  fileab  Fileab  FileAB  fileabc
[paul@RHELv4u3 gen]$ ls File?
File4  FileA
[paul@RHELv4u3 gen]$ ls Fil?4
File4
[paul@RHELv4u3 gen]$ ls Fil??
File4  FileA
[paul@RHELv4u3 gen]$ ls File??
File55  Fileab  FileAB
[paul@RHELv4u3 gen]$
```

17.3. [] square brackets

The square bracket [is interpreted by the shell as a sign to generate filenames, matching any of the characters between [and the first subsequent]. The order in this list between the brackets is not important. Each pair of brackets is replaced by exactly one character.

```
[paul@RHELv4u3 gen]$ ls
file1 file2 file3 File4 File55 FileA fileab Fileab FileAB fileabc
[paul@RHELv4u3 gen]$ ls File[5A]
FileA
[paul@RHELv4u3 gen]$ ls File[A5]
FileA
[paul@RHELv4u3 gen]$ ls File[A5][5b]
File55
[paul@RHELv4u3 gen]$ ls File[a5][5b]
File55 Fileab
[paul@RHELv4u3 gen]$ ls File[a5][5b][abcdefghijklm]
ls: File[a5][5b][abcdefghijklm]: No such file or directory
[paul@RHELv4u3 gen]$ ls file[a5][5b][abcdefghijklm]
fileabc
[paul@RHELv4u3 gen]$
```

You can also exclude characters from a list between square brackets with the exclamation mark !. And you are allowed to make combinations of these **wild cards**.

```
[paul@RHELv4u3 gen]$ ls
file1 file2 file3 File4 File55 FileA fileab Fileab FileAB fileabc
[paul@RHELv4u3 gen]$ ls file[a5][!Z]
fileab
[paul@RHELv4u3 gen]$ ls file[!5]*
file1 file2 file3 fileab fileabc
[paul@RHELv4u3 gen]$ ls file[!5]?
fileab
[paul@RHELv4u3 gen]$
```

17.4. a-z and 0-9 ranges

The bash shell will also understand ranges of characters between brackets.

```
[paul@RHELv4u3 gen]$ ls
file1  file3  File55  fileab  FileAB   fileabc
file2  File4  FileA   Fileab  fileab2
[paul@RHELv4u3 gen]$ ls file[a-z]*
fileab  fileab2  fileabc
[paul@RHELv4u3 gen]$ ls file[0-9]
file1  file2  file3
[paul@RHELv4u3 gen]$ ls file[a-z][a-z][0-9]*
fileab2
[paul@RHELv4u3 gen]$
```

17.5. $LANG and square brackets

But, don't forget the influence of the **LANG** variable. Some languages include lower case letters in an upper case range (and vice versa).

```
paul@RHELv4u4:~/test$ ls [A-Z]ile?
file1  file2  file3  File4
paul@RHELv4u4:~/test$ ls [a-z]ile?
file1  file2  file3  File4
paul@RHELv4u4:~/test$ echo $LANG
en_US.UTF-8
paul@RHELv4u4:~/test$ LANG=C
paul@RHELv4u4:~/test$ echo $LANG
C
paul@RHELv4u4:~/test$ ls [a-z]ile?
file1  file2  file3
paul@RHELv4u4:~/test$ ls [A-Z]ile?
File4
paul@RHELv4u4:~/test$
```

If **$LC_ALL** is set, then this will also need to be reset to prevent file globbing.

17.6. preventing file globbing

The screenshot below should be no surprise. The **echo** * will echo a * when in an empty directory. And it will echo the names of all files when the directory is not empty.

```
paul@ubu1010:~$ mkdir test42
paul@ubu1010:~$ cd test42
paul@ubu1010:~/test42$ echo *
*
paul@ubu1010:~/test42$ touch file42 file33
paul@ubu1010:~/test42$ echo *
file33 file42
```

Globbing can be prevented using quotes or by escaping the special characters, as shown in this screenshot.

```
paul@ubu1010:~/test42$ echo *
file33 file42
paul@ubu1010:~/test42$ echo \*
*
paul@ubu1010:~/test42$ echo '*'
*
paul@ubu1010:~/test42$ echo "*"
*
```

17.7. practice: shell globbing

1. Create a test directory and enter it.

2. Create the following files :

```
file1
file10
file11
file2
File2
File3
file33
fileAB
filea
fileA
fileAAA
file(
file 2
```

(the last one has 6 characters including a space)

3. List (with ls) all files starting with file

4. List (with ls) all files starting with File

5. List (with ls) all files starting with file and ending in a number.

6. List (with ls) all files starting with file and ending with a letter

7. List (with ls) all files starting with File and having a digit as fifth character.

8. List (with ls) all files starting with File and having a digit as fifth character and nothing else.

9. List (with ls) all files starting with a letter and ending in a number.

10. List (with ls) all files that have exactly five characters.

11. List (with ls) all files that start with f or F and end with 3 or A.

12. List (with ls) all files that start with f have i or R as second character and end in a number.

13. List all files that do not start with the letter F.

14. Copy the value of $LANG to $MyLANG.

15. Show the influence of $LANG in listing A-Z or a-z ranges.

16. You receive information that one of your servers was cracked, the cracker probably replaced the **ls** command. You know that the **echo** command is safe to use. Can **echo** replace **ls** ? How can you list the files in the current directory with **echo** ?

17. Is there another command besides cd to change directories ?

17.8. solution: shell globbing

1. Create a test directory and enter it.

```
mkdir testdir; cd testdir
```

2. Create the following files :

```
file1
file10
file11
file2
File2
File3
file33
fileAB
filea
fileA
fileAAA
file(
file 2
```

(the last one has 6 characters including a space)

```
touch file1 file10 file11 file2 File2 File3
touch file33 fileAB filea fileA fileAAA
touch "file("
touch "file 2"
```

3. List (with ls) all files starting with file

```
ls file*
```

4. List (with ls) all files starting with File

```
ls File*
```

5. List (with ls) all files starting with file and ending in a number.

```
ls file*[0-9]
```

6. List (with ls) all files starting with file and ending with a letter

```
ls file*[a-z]
```

7. List (with ls) all files starting with File and having a digit as fifth character.

```
ls File[0-9]*
```

8. List (with ls) all files starting with File and having a digit as fifth character and nothing else.

```
ls File[0-9]
```

9. List (with ls) all files starting with a letter and ending in a number.

```
ls [a-z]*[0-9]
```

10. List (with ls) all files that have exactly five characters.

```
ls ?????
```

11. List (with ls) all files that start with f or F and end with 3 or A.

```
ls [fF]*[3A]
```

12. List (with ls) all files that start with f have i or R as second character and end in a number.

```
ls f[iR]*[0-9]
```

13. List all files that do not start with the letter F.

```
ls [!F]*
```

14. Copy the value of $LANG to $MyLANG.

```
MyLANG=$LANG
```

15. Show the influence of $LANG in listing A-Z or a-z ranges.

```
see example in book
```

16. You receive information that one of your servers was cracked, the cracker probably replaced the **ls** command. You know that the **echo** command is safe to use. Can **echo** replace **ls** ? How can you list the files in the current directory with **echo** ?

```
echo *
```

17. Is there another command besides cd to change directories ?

```
pushd popd
```

Part V. pipes and commands

Table of Contents

Chapter 18. I/O redirection

One of the powers of the Unix command line is the use of **input/output redirection** and **pipes**.

This chapter explains **redirection** of input, output and error streams.

18.1. stdin, stdout, and stderr

The bash shell has three basic streams; it takes input from **stdin** (stream **0**), it sends output to **stdout** (stream **1**) and it sends error messages to **stderr** (stream **2**) .

The drawing below has a graphical interpretation of these three streams.

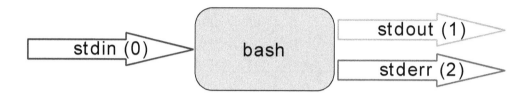

The keyboard often serves as **stdin**, whereas **stdout** and **stderr** both go to the display. This can be confusing to new Linux users because there is no obvious way to recognize **stdout** from **stderr**. Experienced users know that separating output from errors can be very useful.

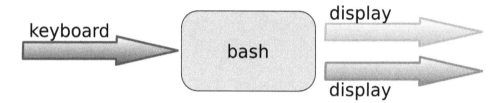

The next sections will explain how to redirect these streams.

18.2. output redirection

18.2.1. > stdout

stdout can be redirected with a **greater than** sign. While scanning the line, the shell will see the > sign and will clear the file.

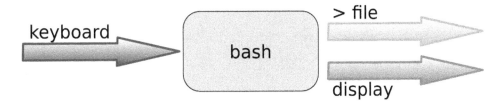

The > notation is in fact the abbreviation of **1>** (**stdout** being referred to as stream **1**).

```
[paul@RHELv4u3 ~]$ echo It is cold today!
It is cold today!
[paul@RHELv4u3 ~]$ echo It is cold today! > winter.txt
[paul@RHELv4u3 ~]$ cat winter.txt
It is cold today!
[paul@RHELv4u3 ~]$
```

Note that the bash shell effectively **removes** the redirection from the command line before argument 0 is executed. This means that in the case of this command:

```
echo hello > greetings.txt
```

the shell only counts two arguments (echo = argument 0, hello = argument 1). The redirection is removed before the argument counting takes place.

18.2.2. output file is erased

While scanning the line, the shell will see the > sign and **will clear the file**! Since this happens before resolving **argument 0**, this means that even when the command fails, the file will have been cleared!

```
[paul@RHELv4u3 ~]$ cat winter.txt
It is cold today!
[paul@RHELv4u3 ~]$ zcho It is cold today! > winter.txt
-bash: zcho: command not found
[paul@RHELv4u3 ~]$ cat winter.txt
[paul@RHELv4u3 ~]$
```

18.2.3. noclobber

Erasing a file while using > can be prevented by setting the **noclobber** option.

```
[paul@RHELv4u3 ~]$ cat winter.txt
It is cold today!
[paul@RHELv4u3 ~]$ set -o noclobber
[paul@RHELv4u3 ~]$ echo It is cold today! > winter.txt
-bash: winter.txt: cannot overwrite existing file
[paul@RHELv4u3 ~]$ set +o noclobber
[paul@RHELv4u3 ~]$
```

18.2.4. overruling noclobber

The **noclobber** can be overruled with >|.

```
[paul@RHELv4u3 ~]$ set -o noclobber
[paul@RHELv4u3 ~]$ echo It is cold today! > winter.txt
-bash: winter.txt: cannot overwrite existing file
[paul@RHELv4u3 ~]$ echo It is very cold today! >| winter.txt
[paul@RHELv4u3 ~]$ cat winter.txt
It is very cold today!
[paul@RHELv4u3 ~]$
```

18.2.5. >> append

Use >> to **append** output to a file.

```
[paul@RHELv4u3 ~]$ echo It is cold today! > winter.txt
[paul@RHELv4u3 ~]$ cat winter.txt
It is cold today!
[paul@RHELv4u3 ~]$ echo Where is the summer ? >> winter.txt
[paul@RHELv4u3 ~]$ cat winter.txt
It is cold today!
Where is the summer ?
[paul@RHELv4u3 ~]$
```

18.3. error redirection

18.3.1. 2> stderr

Redirecting **stderr** is done with **2>**. This can be very useful to prevent error messages from cluttering your screen.

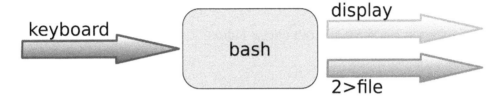

The screenshot below shows redirection of **stdout** to a file, and **stderr** to **/dev/null**. Writing **1>** is the same as **>**.

```
[paul@RHELv4u3 ~]$ find / > allfiles.txt 2> /dev/null
[paul@RHELv4u3 ~]$
```

18.3.2. 2>&1

To redirect both **stdout** and **stderr** to the same file, use **2>&1**.

```
[paul@RHELv4u3 ~]$ find / > allfiles_and_errors.txt 2>&1
[paul@RHELv4u3 ~]$
```

Note that the order of redirections is significant. For example, the command

```
ls > dirlist 2>&1
```

directs both standard output (file descriptor 1) and standard error (file descriptor 2) to the file dirlist, while the command

```
ls 2>&1 > dirlist
```

directs only the standard output to file dirlist, because the standard error made a copy of the standard output before the standard output was redirected to dirlist.

18.4. output redirection and pipes

By default you cannot grep inside **stderr** when using pipes on the command line, because only **stdout** is passed.

```
paul@debian7:~$ rm file42 file33 file1201 | grep file42
rm: cannot remove 'file42': No such file or directory
rm: cannot remove 'file33': No such file or directory
rm: cannot remove 'file1201': No such file or directory
```

With **2>&1** you can force **stderr** to go to **stdout**. This enables the next command in the pipe to act on both streams.

```
paul@debian7:~$ rm file42 file33 file1201 2>&1 | grep file42
rm: cannot remove 'file42': No such file or directory
```

You cannot use both **1>&2** and **2>&1** to switch **stdout** and **stderr**.

```
paul@debian7:~$ rm file42 file33 file1201 2>&1 1>&2 | grep file42
rm: cannot remove 'file42': No such file or directory
paul@debian7:~$ echo file42 2>&1 1>&2 | sed 's/file42/FILE42/'
FILE42
```

You need a third stream to switch stdout and stderr after a pipe symbol.

```
paul@debian7:~$ echo file42 3>&1 1>&2 2>&3 | sed 's/file42/FILE42/'
file42
paul@debian7:~$ rm file42 3>&1 1>&2 2>&3 | sed 's/file42/FILE42/'
rm: cannot remove 'FILE42': No such file or directory
```

18.5. joining stdout and stderr

The **&>** construction will put both **stdout** and **stderr** in one stream (to a file).

```
paul@debian7:~$ rm file42 &> out_and_err
paul@debian7:~$ cat out_and_err
rm: cannot remove 'file42': No such file or directory
paul@debian7:~$ echo file42 &> out_and_err
paul@debian7:~$ cat out_and_err
file42
paul@debian7:~$
```

18.6. input redirection

18.6.1. < stdin

Redirecting **stdin** is done with < (short for 0<).

```
[paul@RHEL4b ~]$ cat < text.txt
one
two
[paul@RHEL4b ~]$ tr 'onetw' 'ONEZZ' < text.txt
ONE
ZZO
[paul@RHEL4b ~]$
```

18.6.2. << here document

The **here document** (sometimes called here-is-document) is a way to append input until a certain sequence (usually EOF) is encountered. The **EOF** marker can be typed literally or can be called with Ctrl-D.

```
[paul@RHEL4b ~]$ cat <<EOF > text.txt
> one
> two
> EOF
[paul@RHEL4b ~]$ cat text.txt
one
two
[paul@RHEL4b ~]$ cat <<brol > text.txt
> brel
> brol
[paul@RHEL4b ~]$ cat text.txt
brel
[paul@RHEL4b ~]$
```

18.6.3. <<< here string

The **here string** can be used to directly pass strings to a command. The result is the same as using **echo string | command** (but you have one less process running).

```
paul@ubu1110~$ base64 <<< linux-training.be
bGludXgtdHJhaW5pbmcuYmUK
paul@ubu1110~$ base64 -d <<< bGludXgtdHJhaW5pbmcuYmUK
linux-training.be
```

See rfc 3548 for more information about **base64**.

18.7. confusing redirection

The shell will scan the whole line before applying redirection. The following command line is very readable and is correct.

```
cat winter.txt > snow.txt 2> errors.txt
```

But this one is also correct, but less readable.

```
2> errors.txt cat winter.txt > snow.txt
```

Even this will be understood perfectly by the shell.

```
< winter.txt > snow.txt 2> errors.txt cat
```

18.8. quick file clear

So what is the quickest way to clear a file ?

```
>foo
```

And what is the quickest way to clear a file when the **noclobber** option is set ?

```
>|bar
```

18.9. practice: input/output redirection

1. Activate the **noclobber** shell option.

2. Verify that **noclobber** is active by repeating an **ls** on /**etc**/ with redirected output to a file.

3. When listing all shell options, which character represents the **noclobber** option ?

4. Deactivate the **noclobber** option.

5. Make sure you have two shells open on the same computer. Create an empty **tailing.txt** file. Then type **tail -f tailing.txt**. Use the second shell to **append** a line of text to that file. Verify that the first shell displays this line.

6. Create a file that contains the names of five people. Use **cat** and output redirection to create the file and use a **here document** to end the input.

18.10. solution: input/output redirection

1. Activate the **noclobber** shell option.

```
set -o noclobber
set -C
```

2. Verify that **noclobber** is active by repeating an **ls** on **/etc/** with redirected output to a file.

```
ls /etc > etc.txt
ls /etc > etc.txt (should not work)
```

4. When listing all shell options, which character represents the **noclobber** option ?

```
echo $- (noclobber is visible as C)
```

5. Deactivate the **noclobber** option.

```
set +o noclobber
```

6. Make sure you have two shells open on the same computer. Create an empty **tailing.txt** file. Then type **tail -f tailing.txt**. Use the second shell to **append** a line of text to that file. Verify that the first shell displays this line.

```
paul@deb503:~$ > tailing.txt
paul@deb503:~$ tail -f tailing.txt
hello
world

in the other shell:
paul@deb503:~$ echo hello >> tailing.txt
paul@deb503:~$ echo world >> tailing.txt
```

7. Create a file that contains the names of five people. Use **cat** and output redirection to create the file and use a **here document** to end the input.

```
paul@deb503:~$ cat > tennis.txt << ace
> Justine Henin
> Venus Williams
> Serena Williams
> Martina Hingis
> Kim Clijsters
> ace
paul@deb503:~$ cat tennis.txt
Justine Henin
Venus Williams
Serena Williams
Martina Hingis
Kim Clijsters
paul@deb503:~$
```

Chapter 19. filters

Commands that are created to be used with a **pipe** are often called **filters**. These **filters** are very small programs that do one specific thing very efficiently. They can be used as **building blocks**.

This chapter will introduce you to the most common **filters**. The combination of simple commands and filters in a long **pipe** allows you to design elegant solutions.

19.1. cat

When between two **pipes**, the **cat** command does nothing (except putting **stdin** on **stdout**).

```
[paul@RHEL4b pipes]$ tac count.txt | cat | cat | cat | cat | cat
five
four
three
two
one
[paul@RHEL4b pipes]$
```

19.2. tee

Writing long **pipes** in Unix is fun, but sometimes you may want intermediate results. This is were **tee** comes in handy. The **tee** filter puts **stdin** on **stdout** and also into a file. So **tee** is almost the same as **cat**, except that it has two identical outputs.

```
[paul@RHEL4b pipes]$ tac count.txt | tee temp.txt | tac
one
two
three
four
five
[paul@RHEL4b pipes]$ cat temp.txt
five
four
three
two
one
[paul@RHEL4b pipes]$
```

19.3. grep

The **grep** filter is famous among Unix users. The most common use of **grep** is to filter lines of text containing (or not containing) a certain string.

```
[paul@RHEL4b pipes]$ cat tennis.txt
Amelie Mauresmo, Fra
Kim Clijsters, BEL
Justine Henin, Bel
Serena Williams, usa
Venus Williams, USA
[paul@RHEL4b pipes]$ cat tennis.txt | grep Williams
Serena Williams, usa
Venus Williams, USA
```

You can write this without the cat.

```
[paul@RHEL4b pipes]$ grep Williams tennis.txt
Serena Williams, usa
Venus Williams, USA
```

One of the most useful options of grep is **grep -i** which filters in a case insensitive way.

```
[paul@RHEL4b pipes]$ grep Bel tennis.txt
Justine Henin, Bel
[paul@RHEL4b pipes]$ grep -i Bel tennis.txt
```

```
Kim Clijsters, BEL
Justine Henin, Bel
[paul@RHEL4b pipes]$
```

Another very useful option is **grep -v** which outputs lines not matching the string.

```
[paul@RHEL4b pipes]$ grep -v Fra tennis.txt
Kim Clijsters, BEL
Justine Henin, Bel
Serena Williams, usa
Venus Williams, USA
[paul@RHEL4b pipes]$
```

And of course, both options can be combined to filter all lines not containing a case insensitive string.

```
[paul@RHEL4b pipes]$ grep -vi usa tennis.txt
Amelie Mauresmo, Fra
Kim Clijsters, BEL
Justine Henin, Bel
[paul@RHEL4b pipes]$
```

With **grep -A1** one line **after** the result is also displayed.

```
paul@debian5:~/pipes$ grep -A1 Henin tennis.txt
Justine Henin, Bel
Serena Williams, usa
```

With **grep -B1** one line **before** the result is also displayed.

```
paul@debian5:~/pipes$ grep -B1 Henin tennis.txt
Kim Clijsters, BEL
Justine Henin, Bel
```

With **grep -C1** (context) one line **before** and one **after** are also displayed. All three options (A,B, and C) can display any number of lines (using e.g. A2, B4 or C20).

```
paul@debian5:~/pipes$ grep -C1 Henin tennis.txt
Kim Clijsters, BEL
Justine Henin, Bel
Serena Williams, usa
```

19.4. cut

The **cut** filter can select columns from files, depending on a delimiter or a count of bytes. The screenshot below uses **cut** to filter for the username and userid in the **/etc/passwd** file. It uses the colon as a delimiter, and selects fields 1 and 3.

```
[[paul@RHEL4b pipes]$ cut -d: -f1,3 /etc/passwd | tail -4
Figo:510
Pfaff:511
Harry:516
Hermione:517
[paul@RHEL4b pipes]$
```

When using a space as the delimiter for **cut**, you have to quote the space.

```
[paul@RHEL4b pipes]$ cut -d" " -f1 tennis.txt
Amelie
Kim
Justine
Serena
Venus
[paul@RHEL4b pipes]$
```

This example uses **cut** to display the second to the seventh character of **/etc/passwd**.

```
[paul@RHEL4b pipes]$ cut -c2-7 /etc/passwd | tail -4
igo:x:
faff:x
arry:x
ermion
[paul@RHEL4b pipes]$
```

19.5. tr

You can translate characters with **tr**. The screenshot shows the translation of all occurrences of e to E.

```
[paul@RHEL4b pipes]$ cat tennis.txt | tr 'e' 'E'
AmEliE MaurEsmo, Fra
Kim ClijstErs, BEL
JustinE HEnin, BEl
SErEna Williams, usa
VEnus Williams, USA
```

Here we set all letters to uppercase by defining two ranges.

```
[paul@RHEL4b pipes]$ cat tennis.txt | tr 'a-z' 'A-Z'
AMELIE MAURESMO, FRA
KIM CLIJSTERS, BEL
JUSTINE HENIN, BEL
SERENA WILLIAMS, USA
VENUS WILLIAMS, USA
[paul@RHEL4b pipes]$
```

Here we translate all newlines to spaces.

```
[paul@RHEL4b pipes]$ cat count.txt
one
two
```

```
three
four
five
[paul@RHEL4b pipes]$ cat count.txt | tr '\n' ' '
one two three four five [paul@RHEL4b pipes]$
```

The **tr -s** filter can also be used to squeeze multiple occurrences of a character to one.

```
[paul@RHEL4b pipes]$ cat spaces.txt
one      two        three
     four   five  six
[paul@RHEL4b pipes]$ cat spaces.txt | tr -s ' '
one two three
 four five six
[paul@RHEL4b pipes]$
```

You can also use **tr** to 'encrypt' texts with **rot13**.

```
[paul@RHEL4b pipes]$ cat count.txt | tr 'a-z' 'nopqrstuvwxyzabcdefghijklm'
bar
gjb
guerr
sbhe
svir
[paul@RHEL4b pipes]$ cat count.txt | tr 'a-z' 'n-za-m'
bar
gjb
guerr
sbhe
svir
[paul@RHEL4b pipes]$
```

This last example uses **tr -d** to delete characters.

```
paul@debian5:~/pipes$ cat tennis.txt | tr -d e
Amli Maursmo, Fra
Kim Clijstrs, BEL
Justin Hnin, Bl
Srna Williams, usa
Vnus Williams, USA
```

19.6. wc

Counting words, lines and characters is easy with **wc**.

```
[paul@RHEL4b pipes]$ wc tennis.txt
  5  15 100 tennis.txt
[paul@RHEL4b pipes]$ wc -l tennis.txt
5 tennis.txt
[paul@RHEL4b pipes]$ wc -w tennis.txt
15 tennis.txt
[paul@RHEL4b pipes]$ wc -c tennis.txt
100 tennis.txt
[paul@RHEL4b pipes]$
```

19.7. sort

The **sort** filter will default to an alphabetical sort.

```
paul@debian5:~/pipes$ cat music.txt
Queen
Brel
Led Zeppelin
Abba
paul@debian5:~/pipes$ sort music.txt
Abba
Brel
Led Zeppelin
Queen
```

But the **sort** filter has many options to tweak its usage. This example shows sorting different columns (column 1 or column 2).

```
[paul@RHEL4b pipes]$ sort -k1 country.txt
Belgium, Brussels, 10
France, Paris, 60
Germany, Berlin, 100
Iran, Teheran, 70
Italy, Rome, 50
[paul@RHEL4b pipes]$ sort -k2 country.txt
Germany, Berlin, 100
Belgium, Brussels, 10
France, Paris, 60
Italy, Rome, 50
Iran, Teheran, 70
```

The screenshot below shows the difference between an alphabetical sort and a numerical sort (both on the third column).

```
[paul@RHEL4b pipes]$ sort -k3 country.txt
Belgium, Brussels, 10
Germany, Berlin, 100
Italy, Rome, 50
France, Paris, 60
Iran, Teheran, 70
[paul@RHEL4b pipes]$ sort -n -k3 country.txt
Belgium, Brussels, 10
Italy, Rome, 50
France, Paris, 60
Iran, Teheran, 70
Germany, Berlin, 100
```

19.8. uniq

With **uniq** you can remove duplicates from a **sorted list**.

```
paul@debian5:~/pipes$ cat music.txt
Queen
Brel
Queen
Abba
paul@debian5:~/pipes$ sort music.txt
Abba
Brel
Queen
Queen
paul@debian5:~/pipes$ sort music.txt |uniq
Abba
Brel
Queen
```

uniq can also count occurrences with the **-c** option.

```
paul@debian5:~/pipes$ sort music.txt |uniq -c
      1 Abba
      1 Brel
      2 Queen
```

19.9. comm

Comparing streams (or files) can be done with the **comm**. By default **comm** will output three columns. In this example, Abba, Cure and Queen are in both lists, Bowie and Sweet are only in the first file, Turner is only in the second.

```
paul@debian5:~/pipes$ cat > list1.txt
Abba
Bowie
Cure
Queen
Sweet
paul@debian5:~/pipes$ cat > list2.txt
Abba
Cure
Queen
Turner
paul@debian5:~/pipes$ comm list1.txt list2.txt
                Abba
Bowie
                Cure
                Queen
Sweet
        Turner
```

The output of **comm** can be easier to read when outputting only a single column. The digits point out which output columns should not be displayed.

```
paul@debian5:~/pipes$ comm -12 list1.txt list2.txt
Abba
Cure
Queen
paul@debian5:~/pipes$ comm -13 list1.txt list2.txt
Turner
paul@debian5:~/pipes$ comm -23 list1.txt list2.txt
Bowie
Sweet
```

19.10. od

European humans like to work with ascii characters, but computers store files in bytes. The example below creates a simple file, and then uses **od** to show the contents of the file in hexadecimal bytes

```
paul@laika:~/test$ cat > text.txt
abcdefg
1234567
paul@laika:~/test$ od -t x1 text.txt
0000000 61 62 63 64 65 66 67 0a 31 32 33 34 35 36 37 0a
0000020
```

The same file can also be displayed in octal bytes.

```
paul@laika:~/test$ od -b text.txt
0000000 141 142 143 144 145 146 147 012 061 062 063 064 065 066 067 012
0000020
```

And here is the file in ascii (or backslashed) characters.

```
paul@laika:~/test$ od -c text.txt
0000000   a   b   c   d   e   f   g  \n   1   2   3   4   5   6   7  \n
0000020
```

19.11. sed

The **stream ed**itor **sed** can perform editing functions in the stream, using **regular expressions**.

```
paul@debian5:~/pipes$ echo level5 | sed 's/5/42/'
level42
paul@debian5:~/pipes$ echo level5 | sed 's/level/jump/'
jump5
```

Add **g** for global replacements (all occurrences of the string per line).

```
paul@debian5:~/pipes$ echo level5 level7 | sed 's/level/jump/'
jump5 level7
paul@debian5:~/pipes$ echo level5 level7 | sed 's/level/jump/g'
jump5 jump7
```

With **d** you can remove lines from a stream containing a character.

```
paul@debian5:~/test42$ cat tennis.txt
Venus Williams, USA
Martina Hingis, SUI
Justine Henin, BE
Serena williams, USA
Kim Clijsters, BE
Yanina Wickmayer, BE
paul@debian5:~/test42$ cat tennis.txt | sed '/BE/d'
Venus Williams, USA
Martina Hingis, SUI
Serena williams, USA
```

19.12. pipe examples

19.12.1. who | wc

How many users are logged on to this system ?

```
[paul@RHEL4b pipes]$ who
root      tty1        Jul 25 10:50
paul      pts/0       Jul 25 09:29 (laika)
Harry     pts/1       Jul 25 12:26 (barry)
paul      pts/2       Jul 25 12:26 (pasha)
[paul@RHEL4b pipes]$ who | wc -l
4
```

19.12.2. who | cut | sort

Display a sorted list of logged on users.

```
[paul@RHEL4b pipes]$ who | cut -d' ' -f1 | sort
Harry
paul
paul
root
```

Display a sorted list of logged on users, but every user only once .

```
[paul@RHEL4b pipes]$ who | cut -d' ' -f1 | sort | uniq
Harry
paul
root
```

19.12.3. grep | cut

Display a list of all bash **user accounts** on this computer. Users accounts are explained in detail later.

```
paul@debian5:~$ grep bash /etc/passwd
root:x:0:0:root:/root:/bin/bash
paul:x:1000:1000:paul,,,:/home/paul:/bin/bash
serena:x:1001:1001::/home/serena:/bin/bash
paul@debian5:~$ grep bash /etc/passwd | cut -d: -f1
root
paul
serena
```

19.13. practice: filters

1. Put a sorted list of all bash users in bashusers.txt.

2. Put a sorted list of all logged on users in onlineusers.txt.

3. Make a list of all filenames in **/etc** that contain the string **conf** in their filename.

4. Make a sorted list of all files in **/etc** that contain the case insensitive string **conf** in their filename.

5. Look at the output of **/sbin/ifconfig**. Write a line that displays only ip address and the subnet mask.

6. Write a line that removes all non-letters from a stream.

7. Write a line that receives a text file, and outputs all words on a separate line.

8. Write a spell checker on the command line. (There may be a dictionary in **/usr/share/ dict/** .)

19.14. solution: filters

1. Put a sorted list of all bash users in bashusers.txt.

```
grep bash /etc/passwd | cut -d: -f1 | sort > bashusers.txt
```

2. Put a sorted list of all logged on users in onlineusers.txt.

```
who | cut -d' ' -f1 | sort > onlineusers.txt
```

3. Make a list of all filenames in **/etc** that contain the string **conf** in their filename.

```
ls /etc | grep conf
```

4. Make a sorted list of all files in **/etc** that contain the case insensitive string **conf** in their filename.

```
ls /etc | grep -i conf | sort
```

5. Look at the output of **/sbin/ifconfig**. Write a line that displays only ip address and the subnet mask.

```
/sbin/ifconfig | head -2 | grep 'inet ' | tr -s ' ' | cut -d' ' -f3,5
```

6. Write a line that removes all non-letters from a stream.

```
paul@deb503:~$ cat text
This is, yes really! , a text with ?&* too many str$ange# characters ;-)
paul@deb503:~$ cat text | tr -d ',!$?.*&^%#;()-'
This is yes really  a text with  too many strange characters
```

7. Write a line that receives a text file, and outputs all words on a separate line.

```
paul@deb503:~$ cat text2
it is very cold today without the sun

paul@deb503:~$ cat text2 | tr ' ' '\n'
it
is
very
cold
today
without
the
sun
```

8. Write a spell checker on the command line. (There may be a dictionary in **/usr/share/ dict/** .)

```
paul@rhel ~$ echo "The zun is shining today" > text

paul@rhel ~$ cat > DICT
is
shining
sun
the
```

```
today

paul@rhel ~$ cat text | tr 'A-Z ' 'a-z\n' | sort | uniq | comm -23 - DICT
zun
```

You could also add the solution from question number 6 to remove non-letters, and **tr -s '** ' to remove redundant spaces.

Chapter 20. basic Unix tools

This chapter introduces commands to **find** or **locate** files and to **compress** files, together with other common tools that were not discussed before. While the tools discussed here are technically not considered **filters**, they can be used in **pipes**.

20.1. find

The **find** command can be very useful at the start of a pipe to search for files. Here are some examples. You might want to add **2>/dev/null** to the command lines to avoid cluttering your screen with error messages.

Find all files in **/etc** and put the list in etcfiles.txt

```
find /etc > etcfiles.txt
```

Find all files of the entire system and put the list in allfiles.txt

```
find / > allfiles.txt
```

Find files that end in .conf in the current directory (and all subdirs).

```
find . -name "*.conf"
```

Find files of type file (not directory, pipe or etc.) that end in .conf.

```
find . -type f -name "*.conf"
```

Find files of type directory that end in .bak .

```
find /data -type d -name "*.bak"
```

Find files that are newer than file42.txt

```
find . -newer file42.txt
```

Find can also execute another command on every file found. This example will look for *.odf files and copy them to /backup/.

```
find /data -name "*.odf" -exec cp {} /backup/ \;
```

Find can also execute, after your confirmation, another command on every file found. This example will remove *.odf files if you approve of it for every file found.

```
find /data -name "*.odf" -ok rm {} \;
```

20.2. locate

The **locate** tool is very different from **find** in that it uses an index to locate files. This is a lot faster than traversing all the directories, but it also means that it is always outdated. If the index does not exist yet, then you have to create it (as root on Red Hat Enterprise Linux) with the **updatedb** command.

```
[paul@RHEL4b ~]$ locate Samba
warning: locate: could not open database: /var/lib/slocate/slocate.db:...
warning: You need to run the 'updatedb' command (as root) to create th...
Please have a look at /etc/updatedb.conf to enable the daily cron job.
[paul@RHEL4b ~]$ updatedb
fatal error: updatedb: You are not authorized to create a default sloc...
[paul@RHEL4b ~]$ su -
Password:
[root@RHEL4b ~]# updatedb
[root@RHEL4b ~]#
```

Most Linux distributions will schedule the **updatedb** to run once every day.

20.3. date

The **date** command can display the date, time, time zone and more.

```
paul@rhel55 ~$ date
Sat Apr 17 12:44:30 CEST 2010
```

A date string can be customised to display the format of your choice. Check the man page for more options.

```
paul@rhel55 ~$ date +'%A %d-%m-%Y'
Saturday 17-04-2010
```

Time on any Unix is calculated in number of seconds since 1969 (the first second being the first second of the first of January 1970). Use **date +%s** to display Unix time in seconds.

```
paul@rhel55 ~$ date +%s
1271501080
```

When will this seconds counter reach two thousand million ?

```
paul@rhel55 ~$ date -d '1970-01-01 + 2000000000 seconds'
Wed May 18 04:33:20 CEST 2033
```

20.4. cal

The **cal** command displays the current month, with the current day highlighted.

```
paul@rhel55 ~$ cal
      April 2010
Su Mo Tu We Th Fr Sa
             1  2  3
 4  5  6  7  8  9 10
11 12 13 14 15 16 17
18 19 20 21 22 23 24
25 26 27 28 29 30
```

You can select any month in the past or the future.

```
paul@rhel55 ~$ cal 2 1970
    February 1970
Su Mo Tu We Th Fr Sa
 1  2  3  4  5  6  7
 8  9 10 11 12 13 14
15 16 17 18 19 20 21
22 23 24 25 26 27 28
```

20.5. sleep

The **sleep** command is sometimes used in scripts to wait a number of seconds. This example shows a five second **sleep**.

```
paul@rhel55 ~$ sleep 5
paul@rhel55 ~$
```

20.6. time

The **time** command can display how long it takes to execute a command. The **date** command takes only a little time.

```
paul@rhel55 ~$ time date
Sat Apr 17 13:08:27 CEST 2010

real    0m0.014s
user    0m0.008s
sys     0m0.006s
```

The **sleep 5** command takes five **real** seconds to execute, but consumes little **cpu time**.

```
paul@rhel55 ~$ time sleep 5

real    0m5.018s
user    0m0.005s
sys     0m0.011s
```

This **bzip2** command compresses a file and uses a lot of **cpu time**.

```
paul@rhel55 ~$ time bzip2 text.txt

real    0m2.368s
user    0m0.847s
sys     0m0.539s
```

20.7. gzip - gunzip

Users never have enough disk space, so compression comes in handy. The **gzip** command can make files take up less space.

```
paul@rhel55 ~$ ls -lh text.txt
-rw-rw-r-- 1 paul paul 6.4M Apr 17 13:11 text.txt
paul@rhel55 ~$ gzip text.txt
paul@rhel55 ~$ ls -lh text.txt.gz
-rw-rw-r-- 1 paul paul 760K Apr 17 13:11 text.txt.gz
```

You can get the original back with **gunzip**.

```
paul@rhel55 ~$ gunzip text.txt.gz
paul@rhel55 ~$ ls -lh text.txt
-rw-rw-r-- 1 paul paul 6.4M Apr 17 13:11 text.txt
```

20.8. zcat - zmore

Text files that are compressed with **gzip** can be viewed with **zcat** and **zmore**.

```
paul@rhel55 ~$ head -4 text.txt
/
/opt
/opt/VBoxGuestAdditions-3.1.6
/opt/VBoxGuestAdditions-3.1.6/routines.sh
paul@rhel55 ~$ gzip text.txt
paul@rhel55 ~$ zcat text.txt.gz | head -4
/
/opt
/opt/VBoxGuestAdditions-3.1.6
/opt/VBoxGuestAdditions-3.1.6/routines.sh
```

20.9. bzip2 - bunzip2

Files can also be compressed with **bzip2** which takes a little more time than **gzip**, but compresses better.

```
paul@rhel55 ~$ bzip2 text.txt
paul@rhel55 ~$ ls -lh text.txt.bz2
-rw-rw-r-- 1 paul paul 569K Apr 17 13:11 text.txt.bz2
```

Files can be uncompressed again with **bunzip2**.

```
paul@rhel55 ~$ bunzip2 text.txt.bz2
paul@rhel55 ~$ ls -lh text.txt
-rw-rw-r-- 1 paul paul 6.4M Apr 17 13:11 text.txt
```

20.10. bzcat - bzmore

And in the same way **bzcat** and **bzmore** can display files compressed with **bzip2**.

```
paul@rhel55 ~$ bzip2 text.txt
paul@rhel55 ~$ bzcat text.txt.bz2 | head -4
/
/opt
/opt/VBoxGuestAdditions-3.1.6
/opt/VBoxGuestAdditions-3.1.6/routines.sh
```

20.11. practice: basic Unix tools

1. Explain the difference between these two commands. This question is very important. If you don't know the answer, then look back at the **shell** chapter.

```
find /data -name "*.txt"

find /data -name *.txt
```

2. Explain the difference between these two statements. Will they both work when there are 200 **.odf** files in **/data** ? How about when there are 2 million .odf files ?

```
find /data -name "*.odf" > data_odf.txt

find /data/*.odf > data_odf.txt
```

3. Write a find command that finds all files created after January 30th 2010.

4. Write a find command that finds all *.odf files created in September 2009.

5. Count the number of *.conf files in /etc and all its subdirs.

6. Here are two commands that do the same thing: copy *.odf files to /backup/ . What would be a reason to replace the first command with the second ? Again, this is an important question.

```
cp -r /data/*.odf /backup/

find /data -name "*.odf" -exec cp {} /backup/ \;
```

7. Create a file called **loctest.txt**. Can you find this file with **locate** ? Why not ? How do you make locate find this file ?

8. Use find and -exec to rename all .htm files to .html.

9. Issue the **date** command. Now display the date in YYYY/MM/DD format.

10. Issue the **cal** command. Display a calendar of 1582 and 1752. Notice anything special ?

20.12. solution: basic Unix tools

1. Explain the difference between these two commands. This question is very important. If you don't know the answer, then look back at the **shell** chapter.

```
find /data -name "*.txt"

find /data -name *.txt
```

When ***.txt** is quoted then the shell will not touch it. The **find** tool will look in the **/data** for all files ending in **.txt**.

When ***.txt** is not quoted then the shell might expand this (when one or more files that ends in **.txt** exist in the current directory). The **find** might show a different result, or can result in a syntax error.

2. Explain the difference between these two statements. Will they both work when there are 200 **.odf** files in **/data** ? How about when there are 2 million .odf files ?

```
find /data -name "*.odf" > data_odf.txt

find /data/*.odf > data_odf.txt
```

The first **find** will output all **.odf** filenames in **/data** and all subdirectories. The shell will redirect this to a file.

The second find will output all files named **.odf** in **/data** and will also output all files that exist in directories named ***.odf** (in **/data**).

With two million files the command line would be expanded beyond the maximum that the shell can accept. The last part of the command line would be lost.

3. Write a find command that finds all files created after January 30th 2010.

```
touch -t 201001302359 marker_date
find . -type f -newer marker_date

There is another solution :
find . -type f -newerat "20100130 23:59:59"
```

4. Write a find command that finds all *.odf files created in September 2009.

```
touch -t 200908312359 marker_start
touch -t 200910010000 marker_end
find . -type f -name "*.odf" -newer marker_start ! -newer marker_end
```

The exclamation mark **! -newer** can be read as **not newer**.

5. Count the number of *.conf files in /etc and all its subdirs.

```
find /etc -type f -name '*.conf' | wc -l
```

6. Here are two commands that do the same thing: copy *.odf files to /backup/ . What would be a reason to replace the first command with the second ? Again, this is an important question.

```
cp -r /data/*.odf /backup/
```

```
find /data -name "*.odf" -exec cp {} /backup/ \;
```

The first might fail when there are too many files to fit on one command line.

7. Create a file called **loctest.txt**. Can you find this file with **locate** ? Why not ? How do you make locate find this file ?

You cannot locate this with **locate** because it is not yet in the index.

```
updatedb
```

8. Use find and -exec to rename all .htm files to .html.

```
paul@rhel55 ~$ find . -name '*.htm'
./one.htm
./two.htm
paul@rhel55 ~$ find . -name '*.htm' -exec mv {} {}l \;
paul@rhel55 ~$ find . -name '*.htm*'
./one.html
./two.html
```

9. Issue the **date** command. Now display the date in YYYY/MM/DD format.

```
date +%Y/%m/%d
```

10. Issue the **cal** command. Display a calendar of 1582 and 1752. Notice anything special ?

```
cal 1582
```

The calendars are different depending on the country. Check http://linux-training.be/files/studentfiles/dates.txt

Chapter 21. regular expressions

Regular expressions are a very powerful tool in Linux. They can be used with a variety of programs like bash, vi, rename, grep, sed, and more.

This chapter introduces you to the basics of **regular expressions**.

21.1. regex versions

There are three different versions of regular expression syntax:

```
BRE: Basic Regular Expressions
ERE: Extended Regular Expressions
PRCE: Perl Regular Expressions
```

Depending on the tool being used, one or more of these syntaxes can be used.

For example the **grep** tool has the **-E** option to force a string to be read as ERE while **-G** forces BRE and **-P** forces PRCE.

Note that **grep** also has **-F** to force the string to be read literally.

The **sed** tool also has options to choose a regex syntax.

Read the manual of the tools you use!

21.2. grep

21.2.1. print lines matching a pattern

grep is a popular Linux tool to search for lines that match a certain pattern. Below are some examples of the simplest **regular expressions**.

This is the contents of the test file. This file contains three lines (or three **newline** characters).

```
paul@rhel65:~$ cat names
Tania
Laura
Valentina
```

When **grepping** for a single character, only the lines containing that character are returned.

```
paul@rhel65:~$ grep u names
Laura
paul@rhel65:~$ grep e names
Valentina
paul@rhel65:~$ grep i names
Tania
Valentina
```

The pattern matching in this example should be very straightforward; if the given character occurs on a line, then **grep** will return that line.

21.2.2. concatenating characters

Two concatenated characters will have to be concatenated in the same way to have a match.

This example demonstrates that **ia** will match Tan**ia** but not Valentina and **in** will match Valent**in**a but not Tania.

```
paul@rhel65:~$ grep a names
Tania
Laura
Valentina
paul@rhel65:~$ grep ia names
Tania
paul@rhel65:~$ grep in names
Valentina
paul@rhel65:~$
```

21.2.3. one or the other

PRCE and ERE both use the pipe symbol to signify OR. In this example we **grep** for lines containing the letter i or the letter a.

```
paul@debian7:~$ cat list
Tania
Laura
paul@debian7:~$ grep -E 'i|a' list
Tania
Laura
```

Note that we use the **-E** switch of grep to force interpretion of our string as an ERE.

We need to **escape** the pipe symbol in a BRE to get the same logical OR.

```
paul@debian7:~$ grep -G 'i|a' list
paul@debian7:~$ grep -G 'i\|a' list
Tania
Laura
```

21.2.4. one or more

The * signifies zero, one or more occurences of the previous and the + signifies one or more of the previous.

```
paul@debian7:~$ cat list2
ll
lol
lool
loool
paul@debian7:~$ grep -E 'o*' list2
ll
lol
lool
loool
paul@debian7:~$ grep -E 'o+' list2
lol
lool
loool
paul@debian7:~$
```

21.2.5. match the end of a string

For the following examples, we will use this file.

```
paul@debian7:~$ cat names
Tania
Laura
Valentina
Fleur
Floor
```

The two examples below show how to use the **dollar character** to match the end of a string.

```
paul@debian7:~$ grep a$ names
Tania
Laura
Valentina
paul@debian7:~$ grep r$ names
Fleur
Floor
```

21.2.6. match the start of a string

The **caret character (^)** will match a string at the start (or the beginning) of a line.

Given the same file as above, here are two examples.

```
paul@debian7:~$ grep ^Val names
Valentina
paul@debian7:~$ grep ^F names
Fleur
Floor
```

Both the dollar sign and the little hat are called **anchors** in a regex.

21.2.7. separating words

Regular expressions use a \b sequence to reference a word separator. Take for example this file:

```
paul@debian7:~$ cat text
The governer is governing.
The winter is over.
Can you get over there?
```

Simply grepping for **over** will give too many results.

```
paul@debian7:~$ grep over text
The governer is governing.
The winter is over.
Can you get over there?
```

Surrounding the searched word with spaces is not a good solution (because other characters can be word separators). This screenshot below show how to use **\b** to find only the searched word:

```
paul@debian7:~$ grep '\bover\b' text
The winter is over.
Can you get over there?
paul@debian7:~$
```

Note that **grep** also has a **-w** option to grep for words.

```
paul@debian7:~$ cat text
The governer is governing.
The winter is over.
Can you get over there?
paul@debian7:~$ grep -w over text
The winter is over.
Can you get over there?
paul@debian7:~$
```

21.2.8. grep features

Sometimes it is easier to combine a simple regex with **grep** options, than it is to write a more complex regex. These options where discussed before:

```
grep -i
grep -v
grep -w
grep -A5
grep -B5
grep -C5
```

21.2.9. preventing shell expansion of a regex

The dollar sign is a special character, both for the regex and also for the shell (remember variables and embedded shells). Therefore it is advised to always quote the regex, this prevents shell expansion.

```
paul@debian7:~$ grep 'r$' names
Fleur
Floor
```

21.3. rename

21.3.1. the rename command

On Debian Linux the **/usr/bin/rename** command is a link to **/usr/bin/prename** installed by the **perl** package.

```
paul@pi ~ $ dpkg -S $(readlink -f $(which rename))
perl: /usr/bin/prename
```

Red Hat derived systems do not install the same **rename** command, so this section does not describe **rename** on Red Hat (unless you copy the perl script manually).

There is often confusion on the internet about the rename command because solutions that work fine in Debian (and Ubuntu, xubuntu, Mint, ...) cannot be used in Red Hat (and CentOS, Fedora, ...).

21.3.2. perl

The **rename** command is actually a perl script that uses **perl regular expressions**. The complete manual for these can be found by typing **perldoc perlrequick** (after installing **perldoc**).

```
root@pi:~# aptitude install perl-doc
The following NEW packages will be installed:
  perl-doc
0 packages upgraded, 1 newly installed, 0 to remove and 0 not upgraded.
Need to get 8,170 kB of archives. After unpacking 13.2 MB will be used.
Get: 1 http://mirrordirector.raspbian.org/raspbian/ wheezy/main perl-do...
Fetched 8,170 kB in 19s (412 kB/s)
Selecting previously unselected package perl-doc.
(Reading database ... 67121 files and directories currently installed.)
Unpacking perl-doc (from .../perl-doc_5.14.2-21+rpi2_all.deb) ...
Adding 'diversion of /usr/bin/perldoc to /usr/bin/perldoc.stub by perl-doc'
Processing triggers for man-db ...
Setting up perl-doc (5.14.2-21+rpi2) ...

root@pi:~# perldoc perlrequick
```

21.3.3. well known syntax

The most common use of the **rename** is to search for filenames matching a certain **string** and replacing this string with an **other string**.

This is often presented as **s/string/other string/** as seen in this example:

```
paul@pi ~ $ ls
abc        allfiles.TXT  bllfiles.TXT  Scratch    tennis2.TXT
abc.conf   backup        cllfiles.TXT  temp.TXT   tennis.TXT
paul@pi ~ $ rename 's/TXT/text/' *
paul@pi ~ $ ls
abc        allfiles.text  bllfiles.text  Scratch   tennis2.text
abc.conf   backup         cllfiles.text  temp.text  tennis.text
```

And here is another example that uses **rename** with the well know syntax to change the extensions of the same files once more:

```
paul@pi ~ $ ls
abc        allfiles.text  bllfiles.text  Scratch   tennis2.text
abc.conf   backup         cllfiles.text  temp.text  tennis.text
paul@pi ~ $ rename 's/text/txt/' *.text
paul@pi ~ $ ls
abc        allfiles.txt  bllfiles.txt  Scratch   tennis2.txt
abc.conf   backup        cllfiles.txt  temp.txt  tennis.txt
paul@pi ~ $
```

These two examples appear to work because the strings we used only exist at the end of the filename. Remember that file extensions have no meaning in the bash shell.

The next example shows what can go wrong with this syntax.

```
paul@pi ~ $ touch atxt.txt
paul@pi ~ $ rename 's/txt/problem/' atxt.txt
paul@pi ~ $ ls
abc        allfiles.txt  backup        cllfiles.txt  temp.txt   tennis.txt
abc.conf   aproblem.txt  bllfiles.txt  Scratch       tennis2.txt
paul@pi ~ $
```

Only the first occurrence of the searched string is replaced.

21.3.4. a global replace

The syntax used in the previous example can be described as **s/regex/replacement/**. This is simple and straightforward, you enter a **regex** between the first two slashes and a **replacement string** between the last two.

This example expands this syntax only a little, by adding a **modifier**.

```
paul@pi ~ $ rename -n 's/TXT/txt/g' aTXT.TXT
aTXT.TXT renamed as atxt.txt
paul@pi ~ $
```

The syntax we use now can be described as **s/regex/replacement/g** where s signifies **switch** and g stands for **global**.

Note that this example used the **-n** switch to show what is being done (instead of actually renaming the file).

21.3.5. case insensitive replace

Another **modifier** that can be useful is **i**. this example shows how to replace a case insensitive string with another string.

```
paul@debian7:~/files$ ls
file1.text  file2.TEXT  file3.txt
paul@debian7:~/files$ rename 's/.text/.txt/i' *
paul@debian7:~/files$ ls
file1.txt  file2.txt  file3.txt
paul@debian7:~/files$
```

21.3.6. renaming extensions

Command line Linux has no knowledge of MS-DOS like extensions, but many end users and graphical application do use them.

Here is an example on how to use **rename** to only rename the file extension. It uses the dollar sign to mark the ending of the filename.

```
paul@pi ~ $ ls *.txt
allfiles.txt  bllfiles.txt  cllfiles.txt  really.txt.txt  temp.txt  tennis.txt
paul@pi ~ $ rename 's/.txt$/.TXT/' *.txt
paul@pi ~ $ ls *.TXT
allfiles.TXT  bllfiles.TXT  cllfiles.TXT  really.txt.TXT
temp.TXT      tennis.TXT
paul@pi ~ $
```

Note that the **dollar sign** in the regex means **at the end**. Without the dollar sign this command would fail on the really.txt.txt file.

21.4. sed

21.4.1. stream editor

The **stream editor** or short **sed** uses **regex** for stream editing.

In this example **sed** is used to replace a string.

```
echo Sunday | sed 's/Sun/Mon/'
Monday
```

The slashes can be replaced by a couple of other characters, which can be handy in some cases to improve readability.

```
echo Sunday | sed 's:Sun:Mon:'
Monday
echo Sunday | sed 's_Sun_Mon_'
Monday
echo Sunday | sed 's|Sun|Mon|'
Monday
```

21.4.2. interactive editor

While **sed** is meant to be used in a stream, it can also be used interactively on a file.

```
paul@debian7:~/files$ echo Sunday > today
paul@debian7:~/files$ cat today
Sunday
paul@debian7:~/files$ sed -i 's/Sun/Mon/' today
paul@debian7:~/files$ cat today
Monday
```

21.4.3. simple back referencing

The **ampersand** character can be used to reference the searched (and found) string.

In this example the **ampersand** is used to double the occurence of the found string.

```
echo Sunday | sed 's/Sun/&&/'
SunSunday
echo Sunday | sed 's/day/&&/'
Sundayday
```

21.4.4. back referencing

Parentheses (often called round brackets) are used to group sections of the regex so they can leter be referenced.

Consider this simple example:

```
paul@debian7:~$ echo Sunday | sed 's_\(Sun\)_\1ny_'
Sunnyday
paul@debian7:~$ echo Sunday | sed 's_\(Sun\)_\1ny \1_'
Sunny Sunday
```

21.4.5. a dot for any character

In a **regex** a simple dot can signify any character.

```
paul@debian7:~$ echo 2014-04-01 | sed 's/....-..-../YYYY-MM-DD/'
YYYY-MM-DD
paul@debian7:~$ echo abcd-ef-gh | sed 's/....-..-../YYYY-MM-DD/'
YYYY-MM-DD
```

21.4.6. multiple back referencing

When more than one pair of **parentheses** is used, each of them can be referenced separately by consecutive numbers.

```
paul@debian7:~$ echo 2014-04-01 | sed 's/\(....\)-\(..\)-\(..\)/\1+\2+\3/'
2014+04+01
paul@debian7:~$ echo 2014-04-01 | sed 's/\(....\)-\(..\)-\(..\)/\3:\2:\1/'
01:04:2014
```

This feature is called **grouping**.

21.4.7. white space

The **\s** can refer to white space such as a space or a tab.

This example looks for white spaces (\s) globally and replaces them with 1 space.

```
paul@debian7:~$ echo -e 'today\tis\twarm'
today    is        warm
paul@debian7:~$ echo -e 'today\tis\twarm' | sed 's_\s_ _g'
today is warm
```

21.4.8. optional occurrence

A question mark signifies that the previous is **optional**.

The example below searches for three consecutive letter o, but the third o is optional.

```
paul@debian7:~$ cat list2
ll
lol
lool
loool
paul@debian7:~$ grep -E 'ooo?' list2
lool
loool
paul@debian7:~$ cat list2 | sed 's/ooo\?/A/'
ll
lol
lAl
lAl
```

21.4.9. exactly n times

You can demand an exact number of times the oprevious has to occur.

This example wants exactly three o's.

```
paul@debian7:~$ cat list2
ll
lol
lool
loool
paul@debian7:~$ grep -E 'o{3}' list2
loool
paul@debian7:~$ cat list2 | sed 's/o\{3\}/A/'
ll
lol
lool
lAl
paul@debian7:~$
```

21.4.10. between n and m times

And here we demand exactly from minimum 2 to maximum 3 times.

```
paul@debian7:~$ cat list2
ll
lol
lool
loool
paul@debian7:~$ grep -E 'o{2,3}' list2
lool
loool
paul@debian7:~$ grep 'o\{2,3\}' list2
lool
loool
paul@debian7:~$ cat list2 | sed 's/o\{2,3\}/A/'
ll
lol
lAl
lAl
paul@debian7:~$
```

21.5. bash history

The **bash shell** can also interpret some regular expressions.

This example shows how to manipulate the exclamation mask history feature of the bash shell.

```
paul@debian7:~$ mkdir hist
paul@debian7:~$ cd hist/
paul@debian7:~/hist$ touch file1 file2 file3
paul@debian7:~/hist$ ls -l file1
-rw-r--r-- 1 paul paul 0 Apr 15 22:07 file1
paul@debian7:~/hist$ !l
ls -l file1
-rw-r--r-- 1 paul paul 0 Apr 15 22:07 file1
paul@debian7:~/hist$ !l:s/1/3
ls -l file3
-rw-r--r-- 1 paul paul 0 Apr 15 22:07 file3
paul@debian7:~/hist$
```

This also works with the history numbers in bash.

```
paul@debian7:~/hist$ history 6
 2089  mkdir hist
 2090  cd hist/
 2091  touch file1 file2 file3
 2092  ls -l file1
 2093  ls -l file3
 2094  history 6
paul@debian7:~/hist$ !2092
ls -l file1
-rw-r--r-- 1 paul paul 0 Apr 15 22:07 file1
paul@debian7:~/hist$ !2092:s/1/2
ls -l file2
-rw-r--r-- 1 paul paul 0 Apr 15 22:07 file2
paul@debian7:~/hist$
```

Part VI. vi

Table of Contents

Chapter 22. Introduction to vi

The **vi** editor is installed on almost every Unix. Linux will very often install **vim (vi improved)** which is similar. Every system administrator should know **vi(m)**, because it is an easy tool to solve problems.

The **vi** editor is not intuitive, but once you get to know it, **vi** becomes a very powerful application. Most Linux distributions will include the **vimtutor** which is a 45 minute lesson in **vi(m)**.

22.1. command mode and insert mode

The vi editor starts in **command mode**. In command mode, you can type commands. Some commands will bring you into **insert mode**. In insert mode, you can type text. The **escape key** will return you to command mode.

Table 22.1. getting to command mode

key	action
Esc	set vi(m) in command mode.

22.2. start typing (a A i I o O)

The difference between a A i I o and O is the location where you can start typing. a will append after the current character and A will append at the end of the line. i will insert before the current character and I will insert at the beginning of the line. o will put you in a new line after the current line and O will put you in a new line before the current line.

Table 22.2. switch to insert mode

command	action
a	start typing after the current character
A	start typing at the end of the current line
i	start typing before the current character
I	start typing at the start of the current line
o	start typing on a new line after the current line
O	start typing on a new line before the current line

22.3. replace and delete a character (r x X)

When in command mode (it doesn't hurt to hit the escape key more than once) you can use the x key to delete the current character. The big X key (or shift x) will delete the character left of the cursor. Also when in command mode, you can use the r key to replace one single character. The r key will bring you in insert mode for just one key press, and will return you immediately to command mode.

Table 22.3. replace and delete

command	action
x	delete the character below the cursor
X	delete the character before the cursor
r	replace the character below the cursor
p	paste after the cursor (here the last deleted character)
xp	switch two characters

22.4. undo and repeat (u .)

When in command mode, you can undo your mistakes with u. You can do your mistakes twice with . (in other words, the . will repeat your last command).

Table 22.4. undo and repeat

command	action
u	undo the last action
.	repeat the last action

22.5. cut, copy and paste a line (dd yy p P)

When in command mode, dd will cut the current line. yy will copy the current line. You can paste the last copied or cut line after (p) or before (P) the current line.

Table 22.5. cut, copy and paste a line

command	action
dd	cut the current line
yy	(yank yank) copy the current line
p	paste after the current line
P	paste before the current line

22.6. cut, copy and paste lines (3dd 2yy)

When in command mode, before typing dd or yy, you can type a number to repeat the command a number of times. Thus, 5dd will cut 5 lines and 4yy will copy (yank) 4 lines. That last one will be noted by vi in the bottom left corner as "4 line yanked".

Table 22.6. cut, copy and paste lines

command	action
3dd	cut three lines
4yy	copy four lines

22.7. start and end of a line (0 or ^ and $)

When in command mode, the 0 and the caret ^ will bring you to the start of the current line, whereas the $ will put the cursor at the end of the current line. You can add 0 and $ to the d command, d0 will delete every character between the current character and the start of the line. Likewise d$ will delete everything from the current character till the end of the line. Similarly y0 and y$ will yank till start and end of the current line.

Table 22.7. start and end of line

command	action
0	jump to start of current line
^	jump to start of current line
$	jump to end of current line
d0	delete until start of line
d$	delete until end of line

22.8. join two lines (J) and more

When in command mode, pressing **J** will append the next line to the current line. With **yyp** you duplicate a line and with **ddp** you switch two lines.

Table 22.8. join two lines

command	action
J	join two lines
yyp	duplicate a line
ddp	switch two lines

22.9. words (w b)

When in command mode, **w** will jump to the next word and **b** will move to the previous word. w and b can also be combined with d and y to copy and cut words (dw db yw yb).

Table 22.9. words

command	action
w	forward one word
b	back one word
3w	forward three words
dw	delete one word
yw	yank (copy) one word
5yb	yank five words back
7dw	delete seven words

22.10. save (or not) and exit (:w :q :q!)

Pressing the colon : will allow you to give instructions to vi (technically speaking, typing the colon will open the **ex** editor). **:w** will write (save) the file, **:q** will quit an unchanged file without saving, and **:q!** will quit vi discarding any changes. **:wq** will save and quit and is the same as typing **ZZ** in command mode.

Table 22.10. save and exit vi

command	action
:w	save (write)
:w fname	save as fname
:q	quit
:wq	save and quit
ZZ	save and quit
:q!	quit (discarding your changes)
:w!	save (and write to non-writable file!)

The last one is a bit special. With **:w! vi** will try to **chmod** the file to get write permission (this works when you are the owner) and will **chmod** it back when the write succeeds. This should always work when you are root (and the file system is writable).

22.11. Searching (/ ?)

When in command mode typing / will allow you to search in vi for strings (can be a regular expression). Typing /foo will do a forward search for the string foo and typing ?bar will do a backward search for bar.

Table 22.11. searching

command	action
/string	forward search for string

command	action
?string	backward search for string
n	go to next occurrence of search string
/^string	forward search string at beginning of line
/string$	forward search string at end of line
/br[aeio]l	search for bral brel bril and brol
/\<he\>	search for the word **he** (and not for **he**re or t**he**)

22.12. replace all (:1,$ s/foo/bar/g)

To replace all occurrences of the string foo with bar, first switch to ex mode with : . Then tell vi which lines to use, for example 1,$ will do the replace all from the first to the last line. You can write 1,5 to only process the first five lines. The s/foo/bar/g will replace all occurrences of foo with bar.

Table 22.12. replace

command	action
:4,8 s/foo/bar/g	replace foo with bar on lines 4 to 8
:1,$ s/foo/bar/g	replace foo with bar on all lines

22.13. reading files (:r :r !cmd)

When in command mode, :r foo will read the file named foo, :r !foo will execute the command foo. The result will be put at the current location. Thus :r !ls will put a listing of the current directory in your text file.

Table 22.13. read files and input

command	action
:r fname	(read) file fname and paste contents
:r !cmd	execute cmd and paste its output

22.14. text buffers

There are 36 buffers in vi to store text. You can use them with the " character.

Table 22.14. text buffers

command	action
"add	delete current line and put text in buffer a
"g7yy	copy seven lines into buffer g
"ap	paste from buffer a

22.15. multiple files

You can edit multiple files with vi. Here are some tips.

Table 22.15. multiple files

command	action
vi file1 file2 file3	start editing three files
:args	lists files and marks active file
:n	start editing the next file
:e	toggle with last edited file
:rew	rewind file pointer to first file

22.16. abbreviations

With **:ab** you can put abbreviations in vi. Use **:una** to undo the abbreviation.

Table 22.16. abbreviations

command	action
:ab str long string	abbreviate **str** to be 'long string'
:una str	un-abbreviate str

22.17. key mappings

Similarly to their abbreviations, you can use mappings with **:map** for command mode and **:map!** for insert mode.

This example shows how to set the F6 function key to toggle between **set number** and **set nonumber**. The <bar> separates the two commands, **set number!** toggles the state and **set number?** reports the current state.

```
:map <F6> :set number!<bar>set number?<CR>
```

22.18. setting options

Some options that you can set in vim.

```
:set number  ( also try :se nu )
:set nonumber
:syntax on
:syntax off
:set all  (list all options)
:set tabstop=8
:set tx   (CR/LF style endings)
:set notx
```

You can set these options (and much more) in ~/**.vimrc** for vim or in ~/**.exrc** for standard vi.

```
paul@barry:~$ cat ~/.vimrc
set number
set tabstop=8
set textwidth=78
map <F6> :set number!<bar>set number?<CR>
paul@barry:~$
```

22.19. practice: vi(m)

1. Start the vimtutor and do some or all of the exercises. You might need to run **aptitude install vim** on xubuntu.

2. What 3 key sequence in command mode will duplicate the current line.

3. What 3 key sequence in command mode will switch two lines' place (line five becomes line six and line six becomes line five).

4. What 2 key sequence in command mode will switch a character's place with the next one.

5. vi can understand macro's. A macro can be recorded with q followed by the name of the macro. So qa will record the macro named a. Pressing q again will end the recording. You can recall the macro with @ followed by the name of the macro. Try this example: i 1 'Escape Key' qa yyp 'Ctrl a' q 5@a (Ctrl a will increase the number with one).

6. Copy /etc/passwd to your ~/passwd. Open the last one in vi and press Ctrl v. Use the arrow keys to select a Visual Block, you can copy this with y or delete it with d. Try pasting it.

7. What does dwwP do when you are at the beginning of a word in a sentence ?

22.20. solution: vi(m)

1. Start the vimtutor and do some or all of the exercises. You might need to run **aptitude install vim** on xubuntu.

```
vimtutor
```

2. What 3 key sequence in command mode will duplicate the current line.

```
yyp
```

3. What 3 key sequence in command mode will switch two lines' place (line five becomes line six and line six becomes line five).

```
ddp
```

4. What 2 key sequence in command mode will switch a character's place with the next one.

```
xp
```

5. vi can understand macro's. A macro can be recorded with q followed by the name of the macro. So qa will record the macro named a. Pressing q again will end the recording. You can recall the macro with @ followed by the name of the macro. Try this example: i 1 'Escape Key' qa yyp 'Ctrl a' q 5@a (Ctrl a will increase the number with one).

6. Copy /etc/passwd to your ~/passwd. Open the last one in vi and press Ctrl v. Use the arrow keys to select a Visual Block, you can copy this with y or delete it with d. Try pasting it.

```
cp /etc/passwd ~
vi passwd
(press Ctrl-V)
```

7. What does **dwwP** do when you are at the beginning of a word in a sentence ?

dwwP can switch the current word with the next word.

Part VII. scripting

Table of Contents

Chapter 23. scripting introduction

Shells like **bash** and **Korn** have support for programming constructs that can be saved as **scripts**. These **scripts** in turn then become more **shell** commands. Many Linux commands are **scripts**. **User profile scripts** are run when a user logs on and **init scripts** are run when a **daemon** is stopped or started.

This means that system administrators also need basic knowledge of **scripting** to understand how their servers and their applications are started, updated, upgraded, patched, maintained, configured and removed, and also to understand how a user environment is built.

The goal of this chapter is to give you enough information to be able to read and understand scripts. Not to become a writer of complex scripts.

23.1. prerequisites

You should have read and understood **part III shell expansion** and **part IV pipes and commands** before starting this chapter.

23.2. hello world

Just like in every programming course, we start with a simple **hello_world** script. The following script will output **Hello World**.

```
echo Hello World
```

After creating this simple script in **vi** or with **echo**, you'll have to **chmod +x hello_world** to make it executable. And unless you add the scripts directory to your path, you'll have to type the path to the script for the shell to be able to find it.

```
[paul@RHEL4a ~]$ echo echo Hello World > hello_world
[paul@RHEL4a ~]$ chmod +x hello_world
[paul@RHEL4a ~]$ ./hello_world
Hello World
[paul@RHEL4a ~]$
```

23.3. she-bang

Let's expand our example a little further by putting **#!/bin/bash** on the first line of the script. The **#!** is called a **she-bang** (sometimes called **sha-bang**), where the **she-bang** is the first two characters of the script.

```
#!/bin/bash
echo Hello World
```

You can never be sure which shell a user is running. A script that works flawlessly in **bash** might not work in **ksh**, **csh**, or **dash**. To instruct a shell to run your script in a certain shell, you can start your script with a **she-bang** followed by the shell it is supposed to run in. This script will run in a bash shell.

```
#!/bin/bash
echo -n hello
echo A bash subshell `echo -n hello`
```

This script will run in a Korn shell (unless **/bin/ksh** is a hard link to **/bin/bash**). The **/etc/shells** file contains a list of shells on your system.

```
#!/bin/ksh
echo -n hello
echo a Korn subshell `echo -n hello`
```

23.4. comment

Let's expand our example a little further by adding comment lines.

```
#!/bin/bash
#
# Hello World Script
#
echo Hello World
```

23.5. variables

Here is a simple example of a variable inside a script.

```
#!/bin/bash
#
# simple variable in script
#
var1=4
echo var1 = $var1
```

Scripts can contain variables, but since scripts are run in their own shell, the variables do not survive the end of the script.

```
[paul@RHEL4a ~]$ echo $var1

[paul@RHEL4a ~]$ ./vars
var1 = 4
[paul@RHEL4a ~]$ echo $var1

[paul@RHEL4a ~]$
```

23.6. sourcing a script

Luckily, you can force a script to run in the same shell; this is called **sourcing** a script.

```
[paul@RHEL4a ~]$ source ./vars
var1 = 4
[paul@RHEL4a ~]$ echo $var1
4
[paul@RHEL4a ~]$
```

The above is identical to the below.

```
[paul@RHEL4a ~]$ . ./vars
var1 = 4
[paul@RHEL4a ~]$ echo $var1
4
[paul@RHEL4a ~]$
```

23.7. troubleshooting a script

Another way to run a script in a separate shell is by typing **bash** with the name of the script as a parameter.

```
paul@debian6~/test$ bash runme
42
```

Expanding this to **bash -x** allows you to see the commands that the shell is executing (after shell expansion).

```
paul@debian6~/test$ bash -x runme
+ var4=42
+ echo 42
42
paul@debian6~/test$ cat runme
# the runme script
var4=42
echo $var4
paul@debian6~/test$
```

Notice the absence of the commented (#) line, and the replacement of the variable before execution of **echo**.

23.8. prevent setuid root spoofing

Some user may try to perform **setuid** based script **root spoofing**. This is a rare but possible attack. To improve script security and to avoid interpreter spoofing, you need to add -- after the **#!/bin/bash**, which disables further option processing so the shell will not accept any options.

```
#!/bin/bash -
or
#!/bin/bash --
```

Any arguments after the -- are treated as filenames and arguments. An argument of - is equivalent to --.

23.9. practice: introduction to scripting

0. Give each script a different name, keep them for later!

1. Write a script that outputs the name of a city.

2. Make sure the script runs in the bash shell.

3. Make sure the script runs in the Korn shell.

4. Create a script that defines two variables, and outputs their value.

5. The previous script does not influence your current shell (the variables do not exist outside of the script). Now run the script so that it influences your current shell.

6. Is there a shorter way to **source** the script ?

7. Comment your scripts so that you know what they are doing.

23.10. solution: introduction to scripting

0. Give each script a different name, keep them for later!

1. Write a script that outputs the name of a city.

```
$ echo 'echo Antwerp' > first.bash
$ chmod +x first.bash
$ ./first.bash
Antwerp
```

2. Make sure the script runs in the bash shell.

```
$ cat first.bash
#!/bin/bash
echo Antwerp
```

3. Make sure the script runs in the Korn shell.

```
$ cat first.bash
#!/bin/ksh
echo Antwerp
```

Note that while first.bash will technically work as a Korn shell script, the name ending in .bash is confusing.

4. Create a script that defines two variables, and outputs their value.

```
$ cat second.bash
#!/bin/bash

var33=300
var42=400

echo $var33 $var42
```

5. The previous script does not influence your current shell (the variables do not exist outside of the script). Now run the script so that it influences your current shell.

```
source second.bash
```

6. Is there a shorter way to **source** the script ?

```
. ./second.bash
```

7. Comment your scripts so that you know what they are doing.

```
$ cat second.bash
#!/bin/bash
# script to test variables and sourcing

# define two variables
var33=300
var42=400

# output the value of these variables
echo $var33 $var42
```

Chapter 24. scripting loops

24.1. test [ ]

The **test** command can test whether something is true or false. Let's start by testing whether 10 is greater than 55.

```
[paul@RHEL4b ~]$ test 10 -gt 55 ; echo $?
1
[paul@RHEL4b ~]$
```

The test command returns 1 if the test fails. And as you see in the next screenshot, test returns 0 when a test succeeds.

```
[paul@RHEL4b ~]$ test 56 -gt 55 ; echo $?
0
[paul@RHEL4b ~]$
```

If you prefer true and false, then write the test like this.

```
[paul@RHEL4b ~]$ test 56 -gt 55 && echo true || echo false
true
[paul@RHEL4b ~]$ test 6 -gt 55 && echo true || echo false
false
```

The test command can also be written as square brackets, the screenshot below is identical to the one above.

```
[paul@RHEL4b ~]$ [ 56 -gt 55 ] && echo true || echo false
true
[paul@RHEL4b ~]$ [ 6 -gt 55 ] && echo true || echo false
false
```

Below are some example tests. Take a look at **man test** to see more options for tests.

```
[ -d foo ]            Does the directory foo exist ?
[ -e bar ]            Does the file bar exist ?
[ '/etc' = $PWD ]     Is the string /etc equal to the variable $PWD ?
[ $1 != 'secret' ]    Is the first parameter different from secret ?
[ 55 -lt $bar ]       Is 55 less than the value of $bar ?
[ $foo -ge 1000 ]     Is the value of $foo greater or equal to 1000 ?
[ "abc" < $bar ]      Does abc sort before the value of $bar ?
[ -f foo ]            Is foo a regular file ?
[ -r bar ]            Is bar a readable file ?
[ foo -nt bar ]       Is file foo newer than file bar ?
[ -o nounset ]        Is the shell option nounset set ?
```

Tests can be combined with logical AND and OR.

```
paul@RHEL4b:~$ [ 66 -gt 55 -a 66 -lt 500 ] && echo true || echo false
true
paul@RHEL4b:~$ [ 66 -gt 55 -a 660 -lt 500 ] && echo true || echo false
false
paul@RHEL4b:~$ [ 66 -gt 55 -o 660 -lt 500 ] && echo true || echo false
true
```

24.2. if then else

The **if then else** construction is about choice. If a certain condition is met, then execute something, else execute something else. The example below tests whether a file exists, and if the file exists then a proper message is echoed.

```
#!/bin/bash

if [ -f isit.txt ]
then echo isit.txt exists!
else echo isit.txt not found!
fi
```

If we name the above script 'choice', then it executes like this.

```
[paul@RHEL4a scripts]$ ./choice
isit.txt not found!
[paul@RHEL4a scripts]$ touch isit.txt
[paul@RHEL4a scripts]$ ./choice
isit.txt exists!
[paul@RHEL4a scripts]$
```

24.3. if then elif

You can nest a new **if** inside an **else** with **elif**. This is a simple example.

```
#!/bin/bash
count=42
if [ $count -eq 42 ]
then
  echo "42 is correct."
elif [ $count -gt 42 ]
then
  echo "Too much."
else
  echo "Not enough."
fi
```

24.4. for loop

The example below shows the syntax of a classical **for loop** in bash.

```
for i in 1 2 4
do
   echo $i
done
```

An example of a **for loop** combined with an embedded shell.

```
#!/bin/ksh
for counter in `seq 1 20`
do
   echo counting from 1 to 20, now at $counter
   sleep 1
done
```

The same example as above can be written without the embedded shell using the bash **{from..to}** shorthand.

```
#!/bin/bash
for counter in {1..20}
do
    echo counting from 1 to 20, now at $counter
    sleep 1
done
```

This **for loop** uses file globbing (from the shell expansion). Putting the instruction on the command line has identical functionality.

```
kahlan@solexp11$ ls
count.ksh  go.ksh
kahlan@solexp11$ for file in *.ksh ; do cp $file $file.backup ; done
kahlan@solexp11$ ls
count.ksh  count.ksh.backup  go.ksh  go.ksh.backup
```

24.5. while loop

Below a simple example of a **while loop**.

```
i=100;
while [ $i -ge 0 ] ;
do
    echo Counting down, from 100 to 0, now at $i;
    let i--;
done
```

Endless loops can be made with **while true** or **while :** , where the **colon** is the equivalent of **no operation** in the **Korn** and **bash** shells.

```
#!/bin/ksh
# endless loop
while :
do
 echo hello
 sleep 1
done
```

24.6. until loop

Below a simple example of an **until loop**.

```
let i=100;
until [ $i -le 0 ] ;
do
    echo Counting down, from 100 to 1, now at $i;
    let i--;
done
```

24.7. practice: scripting tests and loops

1. Write a script that uses a **for** loop to count from 3 to 7.

2. Write a script that uses a **for** loop to count from 1 to 17000.

3. Write a script that uses a **while** loop to count from 3 to 7.

4. Write a script that uses an **until** loop to count down from 8 to 4.

5. Write a script that counts the number of files ending in **.txt** in the current directory.

6. Wrap an **if** statement around the script so it is also correct when there are zero files ending in **.txt**.

24.8. solution: scripting tests and loops

1. Write a script that uses a **for** loop to count from 3 to 7.

```
#!/bin/bash

for i in 3 4 5 6 7
do
 echo Counting from 3 to 7, now at $i
done
```

2. Write a script that uses a **for** loop to count from 1 to 17000.

```
#!/bin/bash

for i in `seq 1 17000`
do
 echo Counting from 1 to 17000, now at $i
done
```

3. Write a script that uses a **while** loop to count from 3 to 7.

```
#!/bin/bash

i=3
while [ $i -le 7 ]
do
 echo Counting from 3 to 7, now at $i
 let i=i+1
done
```

4. Write a script that uses an **until** loop to count down from 8 to 4.

```
#!/bin/bash

i=8
until [ $i -lt 4 ]
do
 echo Counting down from 8 to 4, now at $i
 let i=i-1
done
```

5. Write a script that counts the number of files ending in **.txt** in the current directory.

```
#!/bin/bash

let i=0
for file in *.txt
do
 let i++
done
echo "There are $i files ending in .txt"
```

6. Wrap an **if** statement around the script so it is also correct when there are zero files ending in **.txt**.

```
#!/bin/bash

ls *.txt > /dev/null 2>&1
if [ $? -ne 0 ]
```

```
then echo "There are 0 files ending in .txt"
else
 let i=0
 for file in *.txt
 do
  let i++
 done
 echo "There are $i files ending in .txt"
fi
```

Chapter 25. scripting parameters

25.1. script parameters

A **bash** shell script can have parameters. The numbering you see in the script below continues if you have more parameters. You also have special parameters containing the number of parameters, a string of all of them, and also the process id, and the last return code. The man page of **bash** has a full list.

```
#!/bin/bash
echo The first argument is $1
echo The second argument is $2
echo The third argument is $3

echo \$ $$  PID of the script
echo \# $#  count arguments
echo \? $?  last return code
echo \* $*  all the arguments
```

Below is the output of the script above in action.

```
[paul@RHEL4a scripts]$ ./pars one two three
The first argument is one
The second argument is two
The third argument is three
$ 5610 PID of the script
# 3 count arguments
? 0 last return code
* one two three all the arguments
```

Once more the same script, but with only two parameters.

```
[paul@RHEL4a scripts]$ ./pars 1 2
The first argument is 1
The second argument is 2
The third argument is
$ 5612 PID of the script
# 2 count arguments
? 0 last return code
* 1 2 all the arguments
[paul@RHEL4a scripts]$
```

Here is another example, where we use **$0**. The **$0** parameter contains the name of the script.

```
paul@debian6~$ cat myname
echo this script is called $0
paul@debian6~$ ./myname
this script is called ./myname
paul@debian6~$ mv myname test42
paul@debian6~$ ./test42
this script is called ./test42
```

25.2. shift through parameters

The **shift** statement can parse all **parameters** one by one. This is a sample script.

```
kahlan@solexp11$ cat shift.ksh
#!/bin/ksh

if [ "$#" == "0" ]
 then
   echo You have to give at least one parameter.
   exit 1
fi

while (( $# ))
 do
  echo You gave me $1
  shift
 done
```

Below is some sample output of the script above.

```
kahlan@solexp11$ ./shift.ksh one
You gave me one
kahlan@solexp11$ ./shift.ksh one two three 1201 "33 42"
You gave me one
You gave me two
You gave me three
You gave me 1201
You gave me 33 42
kahlan@solexp11$ ./shift.ksh
You have to give at least one parameter.
```

25.3. runtime input

You can ask the user for input with the **read** command in a script.

```
#!/bin/bash
echo -n Enter a number:
read number
```

25.4. sourcing a config file

The **source** (as seen in the shell chapters) can be used to source a configuration file.

Below a sample configuration file for an application.

```
[paul@RHEL4a scripts]$ cat myApp.conf
# The config file of myApp

# Enter the path here
myAppPath=/var/myApp

# Enter the number of quines here
quines=5
```

And here an application that uses this file.

```
[paul@RHEL4a scripts]$ cat myApp.bash
#!/bin/bash
#
# Welcome to the myApp application
#

. ./myApp.conf

echo There are $quines quines
```

The running application can use the values inside the sourced configuration file.

```
[paul@RHEL4a scripts]$ ./myApp.bash
There are 5 quines
[paul@RHEL4a scripts]$
```

25.5. get script options with getopts

The **getopts** function allows you to parse options given to a command. The following script allows for any combination of the options a, f and z.

```
kahlan@solexp11$ cat options.ksh
#!/bin/ksh

while getopts ":afz" option;
do
 case $option in
  a)
   echo received -a
   ;;
  f)
   echo received -f
   ;;
  z)
   echo received -z
   ;;
  *)
   echo "invalid option -$OPTARG"
   ;;
 esac
done
```

This is sample output from the script above. First we use correct options, then we enter twice an invalid option.

```
kahlan@solexp11$ ./options.ksh
kahlan@solexp11$ ./options.ksh -af
received -a
received -f
kahlan@solexp11$ ./options.ksh -zfg
received -z
received -f
invalid option -g
kahlan@solexp11$ ./options.ksh -a -b -z
received -a
invalid option -b
received -z
```

You can also check for options that need an argument, as this example shows.

```
kahlan@solexp11$ cat argoptions.ksh
#!/bin/ksh

while getopts ":af:z" option;
do
 case $option in
  a)
    echo received -a
    ;;
  f)
    echo received -f with $OPTARG
    ;;
  z)
    echo received -z
    ;;
  :)
    echo "option -$OPTARG needs an argument"
    ;;
  *)
    echo "invalid option -$OPTARG"
    ;;
 esac
done
```

This is sample output from the script above.

```
kahlan@solexp11$ ./argoptions.ksh -a -f hello -z
received -a
received -f with hello
received -z
kahlan@solexp11$ ./argoptions.ksh -zaf 42
received -z
received -a
received -f with 42
kahlan@solexp11$ ./argoptions.ksh -zf
received -z
option -f needs an argument
```

25.6. get shell options with shopt

You can toggle the values of variables controlling optional shell behaviour with the **shopt** built-in shell command. The example below first verifies whether the cdspell option is set; it is not. The next shopt command sets the value, and the third shopt command verifies that the option really is set. You can now use minor spelling mistakes in the cd command. The man page of bash has a complete list of options.

```
paul@laika:~$ shopt -q cdspell ; echo $?
1
paul@laika:~$ shopt -s cdspell
paul@laika:~$ shopt -q cdspell ; echo $?
0
paul@laika:~$ cd /Etc
/etc
```

25.7. practice: parameters and options

1. Write a script that receives four parameters, and outputs them in reverse order.

2. Write a script that receives two parameters (two filenames) and outputs whether those files exist.

3. Write a script that asks for a filename. Verify existence of the file, then verify that you own the file, and whether it is writable. If not, then make it writable.

4. Make a configuration file for the previous script. Put a logging switch in the config file, logging means writing detailed output of everything the script does to a log file in /tmp.

25.8. solution: parameters and options

1. Write a script that receives four parameters, and outputs them in reverse order.

```
echo $4 $3 $2 $1
```

2. Write a script that receives two parameters (two filenames) and outputs whether those files exist.

```
#!/bin/bash

if [ -f $1 ]
then echo $1 exists!
else echo $1 not found!
fi

if [ -f $2 ]
then echo $2 exists!
else echo $2 not found!
fi
```

3. Write a script that asks for a filename. Verify existence of the file, then verify that you own the file, and whether it is writable. If not, then make it writable.

4. Make a configuration file for the previous script. Put a logging switch in the config file, logging means writing detailed output of everything the script does to a log file in /tmp.

Chapter 26. more scripting

26.1. eval

eval reads arguments as input to the shell (the resulting commands are executed). This allows using the value of a variable as a variable.

```
paul@deb503:~/test42$ answer=42
paul@deb503:~/test42$ word=answer
paul@deb503:~/test42$ eval x=\$$word ; echo $x
42
```

Both in **bash** and **Korn** the arguments can be quoted.

```
kahlan@solexp11$ answer=42
kahlan@solexp11$ word=answer
kahlan@solexp11$ eval "y=\$$word" ; echo $y
42
```

Sometimes the **eval** is needed to have correct parsing of arguments. Consider this example where the **date** command receives one parameter **1 week ago**.

```
paul@debian6~$ date --date="1 week ago"
Thu Mar  8 21:36:25 CET 2012
```

When we set this command in a variable, then executing that variable fails unless we use **eval**.

```
paul@debian6~$ lastweek='date --date="1 week ago"'
paul@debian6~$ $lastweek
date: extra operand `ago"'
Try `date --help' for more information.
paul@debian6~$ eval $lastweek
Thu Mar  8 21:36:39 CET 2012
```

26.2. (( ))

The **(( ))** allows for evaluation of numerical expressions.

```
paul@deb503:~/test42$ (( 42 > 33 )) && echo true || echo false
true
paul@deb503:~/test42$ (( 42 > 1201 )) && echo true || echo false
false
paul@deb503:~/test42$ var42=42
paul@deb503:~/test42$ (( 42 == var42 )) && echo true || echo false
true
paul@deb503:~/test42$ (( 42 == $var42 )) && echo true || echo false
true
paul@deb503:~/test42$ var42=33
paul@deb503:~/test42$ (( 42 == var42 )) && echo true || echo false
false
```

26.3. let

The **let** built-in shell function instructs the shell to perform an evaluation of arithmetic expressions. It will return 0 unless the last arithmetic expression evaluates to 0.

```
[paul@RHEL4b ~]$ let x="3 + 4" ; echo $x
7
[paul@RHEL4b ~]$ let x="10 + 100/10" ; echo $x
20
[paul@RHEL4b ~]$ let x="10-2+100/10" ; echo $x
18
[paul@RHEL4b ~]$ let x="10*2+100/10" ; echo $x
30
```

The **shell** can also convert between different bases.

```
[paul@RHEL4b ~]$ let x="0xFF" ; echo $x
255
[paul@RHEL4b ~]$ let x="0xC0" ; echo $x
192
[paul@RHEL4b ~]$ let x="0xA8" ; echo $x
168
[paul@RHEL4b ~]$ let x="8#70" ; echo $x
56
[paul@RHEL4b ~]$ let x="8#77" ; echo $x
63
[paul@RHEL4b ~]$ let x="16#c0" ; echo $x
192
```

There is a difference between assigning a variable directly, or using **let** to evaluate the arithmetic expressions (even if it is just assigning a value).

```
kahlan@solexp11$ dec=15 ; oct=017 ; hex=0x0f
kahlan@solexp11$ echo $dec $oct $hex
15 017 0x0f
kahlan@solexp11$ let dec=15 ; let oct=017 ; let hex=0x0f
kahlan@solexp11$ echo $dec $oct $hex
15 15 15
```

26.4. case

You can sometimes simplify nested if statements with a **case** construct.

```
[paul@RHEL4b ~]$ ./help
What animal did you see ? lion
You better start running fast!
[paul@RHEL4b ~]$ ./help
What animal did you see ? dog
Don't worry, give it a cookie.
[paul@RHEL4b ~]$ cat help
#!/bin/bash
#
# Wild Animals Helpdesk Advice
#
echo -n "What animal did you see ? "
read animal
case $animal in
        "lion" | "tiger")
                echo "You better start running fast!"
        ;;
        "cat")
                echo "Let that mouse go..."
        ;;
        "dog")
                echo "Don't worry, give it a cookie."
        ;;
        "chicken" | "goose" | "duck" )
                echo "Eggs for breakfast!"
        ;;
        "liger")
                echo "Approach and say 'Ah you big fluffy kitty...'."
        ;;
        "babelfish")
                echo "Did it fall out your ear ?"
        ;;
        *)
                echo "You discovered an unknown animal, name it!"
        ;;
esac
[paul@RHEL4b ~]$
```

26.5. shell functions

Shell **functions** can be used to group commands in a logical way.

```
kahlan@solexp11$ cat funcs.ksh
#!/bin/ksh

function greetings {
echo Hello World!
echo and hello to $USER to!
}

echo We will now call a function
greetings
echo The end
```

This is sample output from this script with a **function**.

```
kahlan@solexp11$ ./funcs.ksh
We will now call a function
Hello World!
and hello to kahlan to!
The end
```

A shell function can also receive parameters.

```
kahlan@solexp11$ cat addfunc.ksh
#!/bin/ksh

function plus {
let result="$1 + $2"
echo  $1 + $2 = $result
}

plus 3 10
plus 20 13
plus 20 22
```

This script produces the following output.

```
kahlan@solexp11$ ./addfunc.ksh
3 + 10 = 13
20 + 13 = 33
20 + 22 = 42
```

26.6. practice : more scripting

1. Write a script that asks for two numbers, and outputs the sum and product (as shown here).

```
Enter a number: 5
Enter another number: 2

Sum:      5 + 2 = 7
Product:  5 x 2 = 10
```

2. Improve the previous script to test that the numbers are between 1 and 100, exit with an error if necessary.

3. Improve the previous script to congratulate the user if the sum equals the product.

4. Write a script with a case insensitive case statement, using the shopt nocasematch option. The nocasematch option is reset to the value it had before the scripts started.

5. If time permits (or if you are waiting for other students to finish this practice), take a look at Linux system scripts in /etc/init.d and /etc/rc.d and try to understand them. Where does execution of a script start in /etc/init.d/samba ? There are also some hidden scripts in ~, we will discuss them later.

26.7. solution : more scripting

1. Write a script that asks for two numbers, and outputs the sum and product (as shown here).

```
Enter a number: 5
Enter another number: 2

Sum:      5 + 2 = 7
Product:  5 x 2 = 10
```

```
#!/bin/bash

echo -n "Enter a number : "
read n1

echo -n "Enter another number : "
read n2

let sum="$n1+$n2"
let pro="$n1*$n2"

echo -e "Sum\t: $n1 + $n2 = $sum"
echo -e "Product\t: $n1 * $n2 = $pro"
```

2. Improve the previous script to test that the numbers are between 1 and 100, exit with an error if necessary.

```
echo -n "Enter a number between 1 and 100 : "
read n1

if [ $n1 -lt 1 -o $n1 -gt 100 ]
then
        echo Wrong number...
        exit 1
fi
```

3. Improve the previous script to congratulate the user if the sum equals the product.

```
if [ $sum -eq $pro ]
then echo Congratulations $sum == $pro
fi
```

4. Write a script with a case insensitive case statement, using the shopt nocasematch option. The nocasematch option is reset to the value it had before the scripts started.

```
#!/bin/bash
#
# Wild Animals Case Insensitive Helpdesk Advice
#

if shopt -q nocasematch; then
  nocase=yes;
else
  nocase=no;
  shopt -s nocasematch;
fi

echo -n "What animal did you see ? "
read animal

case $animal in
```

```
    "lion" | "tiger")
      echo "You better start running fast!"
    ;;
    "cat")
      echo "Let that mouse go..."
    ;;
    "dog")
      echo "Don't worry, give it a cookie."
    ;;
    "chicken" | "goose" | "duck" )
      echo "Eggs for breakfast!"
    ;;
    "liger")
      echo "Approach and say 'Ah you big fluffy kitty.'"
    ;;
    "babelfish")
      echo "Did it fall out your ear ?"
    ;;
    *)
      echo "You discovered an unknown animal, name it!"
    ;;
esac

if [ nocase = yes ] ; then
        shopt -s nocasematch;
else
        shopt -u nocasematch;
fi
```

5. If time permits (or if you are waiting for other students to finish this practice), take a look at Linux system scripts in /etc/init.d and /etc/rc.d and try to understand them. Where does execution of a script start in /etc/init.d/samba ? There are also some hidden scripts in ~, we will discuss them later.

Part VIII. local user management

Table of Contents

Chapter 27. introduction to users

This little chapter will teach you how to identify your user account on a Unix computer using commands like **who am i**, **id**, and more.

In a second part you will learn how to become another user with the **su** command.

And you will learn how to run a program as another user with **sudo**.

27.1. whoami

The **whoami** command tells you your username.

```
[paul@centos7 ~]$ whoami
paul
[paul@centos7 ~]$
```

27.2. who

The **who** command will give you information about who is logged on the system.

```
[paul@centos7 ~]$ who
root     pts/0        2014-10-10 23:07 (10.104.33.101)
paul     pts/1        2014-10-10 23:30 (10.104.33.101)
laura    pts/2        2014-10-10 23:34 (10.104.33.96)
tania    pts/3        2014-10-10 23:39 (10.104.33.91)
[paul@centos7 ~]$
```

27.3. who am i

With **who am i** the **who** command will display only the line pointing to your current session.

```
[paul@centos7 ~]$ who am i
paul     pts/1        2014-10-10 23:30 (10.104.33.101)
[paul@centos7 ~]$
```

27.4. w

The **w** command shows you who is logged on and what they are doing.

```
[paul@centos7 ~]$ w
 23:34:07 up 31 min,  2 users,  load average: 0.00, 0.01, 0.02
USER     TTY        LOGIN@   IDLE   JCPU   PCPU WHAT
root     pts/0      23:07    15.00s  0.01s  0.01s top
paul     pts/1      23:30     7.00s  0.00s  0.00s w
[paul@centos7 ~]$
```

27.5. id

The **id** command will give you your user id, primary group id, and a list of the groups that you belong to.

```
paul@debian7:~$ id
uid=1000(paul) gid=1000(paul) groups=1000(paul)
```

On RHEL/CentOS you will also get **SELinux** context information with this command.

```
[root@centos7 ~]# id
uid=0(root) gid=0(root) groups=0(root) context=unconfined_u:unconfined_r\
:unconfined_t:s0-s0:c0.c1023
```

27.6. su to another user

The **su** command allows a user to run a shell as another user.

```
laura@debian7:~$ su tania
Password:
tania@debian7:/home/laura$
```

27.7. su to root

Yes you can also **su** to become **root**, when you know the **root password**.

```
laura@debian7:~$ su root
Password:
root@debian7:/home/laura#
```

27.8. su as root

You need to know the password of the user you want to substitute to, unless your are logged in as **root**. The **root** user can become any existing user without knowing that user's password.

```
root@debian7:~# id
uid=0(root) gid=0(root) groups=0(root)
root@debian7:~# su - valentina
valentina@debian7:~$
```

27.9. su - $username

By default, the **su** command maintains the same shell environment. To become another user and also get the target user's environment, issue the **su -** command followed by the target username.

```
root@debian7:~# su laura
laura@debian7:/root$ exit
exit
root@debian7:~# su - laura
laura@debian7:~$ pwd
/home/laura
```

27.10. su -

When no username is provided to **su** or **su -**, the command will assume **root** is the target.

```
tania@debian7:~$ su -
Password:
root@debian7:~#
```

27.11. run a program as another user

The sudo program allows a user to start a program with the credentials of another user. Before this works, the system administrator has to set up the **/etc/sudoers** file. This can be useful to delegate administrative tasks to another user (without giving the root password).

The screenshot below shows the usage of **sudo**. User **paul** received the right to run **useradd** with the credentials of **root**. This allows **paul** to create new users on the system without becoming **root** and without knowing the **root password**.

First the command fails for **paul**.

```
paul@debian7:~$ /usr/sbin/useradd -m valentina
useradd: Permission denied.
useradd: cannot lock /etc/passwd; try again later.
```

But with **sudo** it works.

```
paul@debian7:~$ sudo /usr/sbin/useradd -m valentina
[sudo] password for paul:
paul@debian7:~$
```

27.12. visudo

Check the man page of **visudo** before playing with the **/etc/sudoers** file. Editing the **sudoers** is out of scope for this fundamentals book.

```
paul@rhel65:~$ apropos visudo
visudo              (8)  - edit the sudoers file
paul@rhel65:~$
```

27.13. sudo su -

On some Linux systems like Ubuntu and Xubuntu, the **root** user does not have a password set. This means that it is not possible to login as **root** (extra security). To perform tasks as **root**, the first user is given all **sudo rights** via the **/etc/sudoers**. In fact all users that are members of the admin group can use sudo to run all commands as root.

```
root@laika:~# grep admin /etc/sudoers
# Members of the admin group may gain root privileges
%admin ALL=(ALL) ALL
```

The end result of this is that the user can type **sudo su -** and become root without having to enter the root password. The sudo command does require you to enter your own password. Thus the password prompt in the screenshot below is for sudo, not for su.

```
paul@laika:~$ sudo su -
Password:
root@laika:~#
```

27.14. sudo logging

Using **sudo** without authorization will result in a severe warning:

```
paul@rhel65:~$ sudo su -

We trust you have received the usual lecture from the local System
Administrator. It usually boils down to these three things:

    #1) Respect the privacy of others.
    #2) Think before you type.
    #3) With great power comes great responsibility.

[sudo] password for paul:
paul is not in the sudoers file.  This incident will be reported.
paul@rhel65:~$
```

The root user can see this in the **/var/log/secure** on Red Hat and in **/var/log/auth.log** on Debian).

```
root@rhel65:~# tail /var/log/secure | grep sudo | tr -s ' '
Apr 13 16:03:42 rhel65 sudo: paul : user NOT in sudoers ; TTY=pts/0 ; PWD=\
/home/paul ; USER=root ; COMMAND=/bin/su -
root@rhel65:~#
```

27.15. practice: introduction to users

1. Run a command that displays only your currently logged on user name.

2. Display a list of all logged on users.

3. Display a list of all logged on users including the command they are running at this very moment.

4. Display your user name and your unique user identification (userid).

5. Use **su** to switch to another user account (unless you are root, you will need the password of the other account). And get back to the previous account.

6. Now use **su -** to switch to another user and notice the difference.

Note that **su -** gets you into the home directory of **Tania**.

7. Try to create a new user account (when using your normal user account). this should fail. (Details on adding user accounts are explained in the next chapter.)

8. Now try the same, but with **sudo** before your command.

27.16. solution: introduction to users

1. Run a command that displays only your currently logged on user name.

```
laura@debian7:~$ whoami
laura
laura@debian7:~$ echo $USER
laura
```

2. Display a list of all logged on users.

```
laura@debian7:~$ who
laura      pts/0          2014-10-13 07:22 (10.104.33.101)
laura@debian7:~$
```

3. Display a list of all logged on users including the command they are running at this very moment.

```
laura@debian7:~$ w
 07:47:02 up 16 min,  2 users,  load average: 0.00, 0.00, 0.00
USER     TTY       FROM            LOGIN@   IDLE   JCPU   PCPU WHAT
root     pts/0     10.104.33.101   07:30    6.00s  0.04s  0.00s w
root     pts/1     10.104.33.101   07:46    6.00s  0.01s  0.00s sleep 42
laura@debian7:~$
```

4. Display your user name and your unique user identification (userid).

```
laura@debian7:~$ id
uid=1005(laura) gid=1007(laura) groups=1007(laura)
laura@debian7:~$
```

5. Use **su** to switch to another user account (unless you are root, you will need the password of the other account). And get back to the previous account.

```
laura@debian7:~$ su tania
Password:
tania@debian7:/home/laura$ id
uid=1006(tania) gid=1008(tania) groups=1008(tania)
tania@debian7:/home/laura$ exit
laura@debian7:~$
```

6. Now use **su -** to switch to another user and notice the difference.

```
laura@debian7:~$ su - tania
Password:
tania@debian7:~$ pwd
/home/tania
tania@debian7:~$ logout
laura@debian7:~$
```

Note that **su -** gets you into the home directory of **Tania**.

7. Try to create a new user account (when using your normal user account). this should fail. (Details on adding user accounts are explained in the next chapter.)

```
laura@debian7:~$ useradd valentina
-su: useradd: command not found
laura@debian7:~$ /usr/sbin/useradd valentina
useradd: Permission denied.
useradd: cannot lock /etc/passwd; try again later.
```

It is possible that **useradd** is located in **/sbin/useradd** on your computer.

8. Now try the same, but with **sudo** before your command.

```
laura@debian7:~$ sudo /usr/sbin/useradd valentina
[sudo] password for laura:
laura is not in the sudoers file.  This incident will be reported.
laura@debian7:~$
```

Notice that **laura** has no permission to use the **sudo** on this system.

Chapter 28. user management

This chapter will teach you how to use **useradd**, **usermod** and **userdel** to create, modify and remove user accounts.

You will need **root** access on a Linux computer to complete this chapter.

28.1. user management

User management on Linux can be done in three complementary ways. You can use the **graphical** tools provided by your distribution. These tools have a look and feel that depends on the distribution. If you are a novice Linux user on your home system, then use the graphical tool that is provided by your distribution. This will make sure that you do not run into problems.

Another option is to use **command line tools** like useradd, usermod, gpasswd, passwd and others. Server administrators are likely to use these tools, since they are familiar and very similar across many different distributions. This chapter will focus on these command line tools.

A third and rather extremist way is to **edit the local configuration files** directly using vi (or vipw/vigr). Do not attempt this as a novice on production systems!

28.2. /etc/passwd

The local user database on Linux (and on most Unixes) is **/etc/passwd**.

```
[root@RHEL5 ~]# tail /etc/passwd
inge:x:518:524:art dealer:/home/inge:/bin/ksh
ann:x:519:525:flute player:/home/ann:/bin/bash
frederik:x:520:526:rubius poet:/home/frederik:/bin/bash
steven:x:521:527:roman emperor:/home/steven:/bin/bash
pascale:x:522:528:artist:/home/pascale:/bin/ksh
geert:x:524:530:kernel developer:/home/geert:/bin/bash
wim:x:525:531:master damuti:/home/wim:/bin/bash
sandra:x:526:532:radish stresser:/home/sandra:/bin/bash
annelies:x:527:533:sword fighter:/home/annelies:/bin/bash
laura:x:528:534:art dealer:/home/laura:/bin/ksh
```

As you can see, this file contains seven columns separated by a colon. The columns contain the username, an x, the user id, the primary group id, a description, the name of the home directory, and the login shell.

More information can be found by typing **man 5 passwd**.

```
[root@RHEL5 ~]# man 5 passwd
```

28.3. root

The **root** user also called the **superuser** is the most powerful account on your Linux system. This user can do almost anything, including the creation of other users. The root user always has userid 0 (regardless of the name of the account).

```
[root@RHEL5 ~]# head -1 /etc/passwd
root:x:0:0:root:/root:/bin/bash
```

28.4. useradd

You can add users with the **useradd** command. The example below shows how to add a user named yanina (last parameter) and at the same time forcing the creation of the home directory (-m), setting the name of the home directory (-d), and setting a description (-c).

```
[root@RHEL5 ~]# useradd -m -d /home/yanina -c "yanina wickmayer" yanina
[root@RHEL5 ~]# tail -1 /etc/passwd
yanina:x:529:529:yanina wickmayer:/home/yanina:/bin/bash
```

The user named yanina received userid 529 and **primary group** id 529.

28.5. /etc/default/useradd

Both Red Hat Enterprise Linux and Debian/Ubuntu have a file called **/etc/default/useradd** that contains some default user options. Besides using cat to display this file, you can also use **useradd -D**.

```
[root@RHEL4 ~]# useradd -D
GROUP=100
HOME=/home
INACTIVE=-1
EXPIRE=
SHELL=/bin/bash
SKEL=/etc/skel
```

28.6. userdel

You can delete the user yanina with **userdel**. The -r option of userdel will also remove the home directory.

```
[root@RHEL5 ~]# userdel -r yanina
```

28.7. usermod

You can modify the properties of a user with the **usermod** command. This example uses **usermod** to change the description of the user harry.

```
[root@RHEL4 ~]# tail -1 /etc/passwd
harry:x:516:520:harry potter:/home/harry:/bin/bash
[root@RHEL4 ~]# usermod -c 'wizard' harry
[root@RHEL4 ~]# tail -1 /etc/passwd
harry:x:516:520:wizard:/home/harry:/bin/bash
```

28.8. creating home directories

The easiest way to create a home directory is to supply the **-m** option with **useradd** (it is likely set as a default option on Linux).

A less easy way is to create a home directory manually with **mkdir** which also requires setting the owner and the permissions on the directory with **chmod** and **chown** (both commands are discussed in detail in another chapter).

```
[root@RHEL5 ~]# mkdir /home/laura
[root@RHEL5 ~]# chown laura:laura /home/laura
[root@RHEL5 ~]# chmod 700 /home/laura
[root@RHEL5 ~]# ls -ld /home/laura/
drwx------ 2 laura laura 4096 Jun 24 15:17 /home/laura/
```

28.9. /etc/skel/

When using **useradd** the **-m** option, the **/etc/skel/** directory is copied to the newly created home directory. The **/etc/skel/** directory contains some (usually hidden) files that contain profile settings and default values for applications. In this way **/etc/skel/** serves as a default home directory and as a default user profile.

```
[root@RHEL5 ~]# ls -la /etc/skel/
total 48
drwxr-xr-x  2 root root  4096 Apr  1 00:11 .
drwxr-xr-x 97 root root 12288 Jun 24 15:36 ..
-rw-r--r--  1 root root    24 Jul 12  2006 .bash_logout
-rw-r--r--  1 root root   176 Jul 12  2006 .bash_profile
-rw-r--r--  1 root root   124 Jul 12  2006 .bashrc
```

28.10. deleting home directories

The -r option of **userdel** will make sure that the home directory is deleted together with the user account.

```
[root@RHEL5 ~]# ls -ld /home/wim/
drwx------ 2 wim wim 4096 Jun 24 15:19 /home/wim/
[root@RHEL5 ~]# userdel -r wim
[root@RHEL5 ~]# ls -ld /home/wim/
ls: /home/wim/: No such file or directory
```

28.11. login shell

The **/etc/passwd** file specifies the **login shell** for the user. In the screenshot below you can see that user annelies will log in with the **/bin/bash** shell, and user laura with the **/bin/ksh** shell.

```
[root@RHEL5 ~]# tail -2 /etc/passwd
annelies:x:527:533:sword fighter:/home/annelies:/bin/bash
laura:x:528:534:art dealer:/home/laura:/bin/ksh
```

You can use the usermod command to change the shell for a user.

```
[root@RHEL5 ~]# usermod -s /bin/bash laura
[root@RHEL5 ~]# tail -1 /etc/passwd
laura:x:528:534:art dealer:/home/laura:/bin/bash
```

28.12. chsh

Users can change their login shell with the **chsh** command. First, user harry obtains a list of available shells (he could also have done a **cat /etc/shells**) and then changes his login shell to the **Korn shell** (/bin/ksh). At the next login, harry will default into ksh instead of bash.

```
[laura@centos7 ~]$ chsh -l
/bin/sh
/bin/bash
/sbin/nologin
/usr/bin/sh
/usr/bin/bash
/usr/sbin/nologin
/bin/ksh
/bin/tcsh
/bin/csh
[laura@centos7 ~]$
```

Note that the **-l** option does not exist on Debian and that the above screenshot assumes that **ksh** and **csh** shells are installed.

The screenshot below shows how **laura** can change her default shell (active on next login).

```
[laura@centos7 ~]$ chsh -s /bin/ksh
Changing shell for laura.
Password:
Shell changed.
```

28.13. practice: user management

1. Create a user account named **serena**, including a home directory and a description (or comment) that reads **Serena Williams**. Do all this in one single command.

2. Create a user named **venus**, including home directory, bash shell, a description that reads **Venus Williams** all in one single command.

3. Verify that both users have correct entries in **/etc/passwd**, **/etc/shadow** and **/etc/group**.

4. Verify that their home directory was created.

5. Create a user named **einstime** with **/bin/date** as his default logon shell.

7. What happens when you log on with the **einstime** user ? Can you think of a useful real world example for changing a user's login shell to an application ?

8. Create a file named **welcome.txt** and make sure every new user will see this file in their home directory.

9. Verify this setup by creating (and deleting) a test user account.

10. Change the default login shell for the **serena** user to **/bin/bash**. Verify before and after you make this change.

28.14. solution: user management

1. Create a user account named **serena**, including a home directory and a description (or comment) that reads **Serena Williams**. Do all this in one single command.

```
root@debian7:~# useradd -m -c 'Serena Williams' serena
```

2. Create a user named **venus**, including home directory, bash shell, a description that reads **Venus Williams** all in one single command.

```
root@debian7:~# useradd -m -c "Venus Williams" -s /bin/bash venus
```

3. Verify that both users have correct entries in **/etc/passwd**, **/etc/shadow** and **/etc/group**.

```
root@debian7:~# tail -2 /etc/passwd
serena:x:1008:1010:Serena Williams:/home/serena:/bin/sh
venus:x:1009:1011:Venus Williams:/home/venus:/bin/bash
root@debian7:~# tail -2 /etc/shadow
serena:!:16358:0:99999:7:::
venus:!:16358:0:99999:7:::
root@debian7:~# tail -2 /etc/group
serena:x:1010:
venus:x:1011:
```

4. Verify that their home directory was created.

```
root@debian7:~# ls -lrt /home | tail -2
drwxr-xr-x 2 serena     serena     4096 Oct 15 10:50 serena
drwxr-xr-x 2 venus      venus      4096 Oct 15 10:59 venus
root@debian7:~#
```

5. Create a user named **einstime** with **/bin/date** as his default logon shell.

```
root@debian7:~# useradd -s /bin/date einstime
```

Or even better:

```
root@debian7:~# useradd -s $(which date) einstime
```

7. What happens when you log on with the **einstime** user ? Can you think of a useful real world example for changing a user's login shell to an application ?

```
root@debian7:~# su - einstime
Wed Oct 15 11:05:56 UTC 2014 # You get the output of the date command
root@debian7:~#
```

It can be useful when users need to access only one application on the server. Just logging in opens the application for them, and closing the application automatically logs them out.

8. Create a file named **welcome.txt** and make sure every new user will see this file in their home directory.

```
root@debian7:~# echo Hello > /etc/skel/welcome.txt
```

9. Verify this setup by creating (and deleting) a test user account.

```
root@debian7:~# useradd -m test
root@debian7:~# ls -l /home/test
total 4
-rw-r--r-- 1 test test 6 Oct 15 11:16 welcome.txt
root@debian7:~# userdel -r test
root@debian7:~#
```

10. Change the default login shell for the **serena** user to **/bin/bash**. Verify before and after you make this change.

```
root@debian7:~# grep serena /etc/passwd
serena:x:1008:1010:Serena Williams:/home/serena:/bin/sh
root@debian7:~# usermod -s /bin/bash serena
root@debian7:~# grep serena /etc/passwd
serena:x:1008:1010:Serena Williams:/home/serena:/bin/bash
root@debian7:~#
```

Chapter 29. user passwords

This chapter will tell you more about passwords for local users.

Three methods for setting passwords are explained; using the **passwd** command, using **openssel passwd**, and using the **crypt** function in a C program.

The chapter will also discuss password settings and disabling, suspending or locking accounts.

29.1. passwd

Passwords of users can be set with the **passwd** command. Users will have to provide their old password before twice entering the new one.

```
[tania@centos7 ~]$ passwd
Changing password for user tania.
Changing password for tania.
(current) UNIX password:
New password:
BAD PASSWORD: The password is shorter than 8 characters
New password:
BAD PASSWORD: The password is a palindrome
New password:
BAD PASSWORD: The password is too similar to the old one
passwd: Have exhausted maximum number of retries for service
```

As you can see, the passwd tool will do some basic verification to prevent users from using too simple passwords. The **root** user does not have to follow these rules (there will be a warning though). The **root** user also does not have to provide the old password before entering the new password twice.

```
root@debian7:~# passwd tania
Enter new UNIX password:
Retype new UNIX password:
passwd: password updated successfully
```

29.2. shadow file

User passwords are encrypted and kept in **/etc/shadow**. The /etc/shadow file is read only and can only be read by root. We will see in the file permissions section how it is possible for users to change their password. For now, you will have to know that users can change their password with the **/usr/bin/passwd** command.

```
[root@centos7 ~]# tail -4 /etc/shadow
paul:$6$ikp2Xta5BT.Tml.p$2TZjNnOYNNQKpwLJqoGJbVsZG5/Fti8ovBRd.VzRbiDSl7TEq\
IaSMH.TeBKnTS/SjlMruW8qffC0JNORW.BTW1:16338:0:99999:7:::
tania:$6$8Z/zovxj$9qvoqT8i9KIrmN.k4EQwAF5ryz5yzNwEvYjAa9L5XVXQu.z4DlpvMREH\
eQpQzvRnqFdKkVj17H5ST.c79HDZw0:16356:0:99999:7:::
laura:$6$glDuTY5e$/NYYWLxfHgZFWeoujaXSMcR.Mz.lGOxtcxFocFVJNb98nbTPhWFXfKWG\
SyYh1WCv6763Wq54.w24Yr3uAZBOm/:16356:0:99999:7:::
valentina:$6$jrZa6PVI$1uQgqR6En9mZB6mKJ3LXRB4CnFko6LRhbh.v4iqUk9MVreuillv7\
GxHOUDSKA0N55ZRNhGHa6T2ouFnVno/0o1:16356:0:99999:7:::
[root@centos7 ~]#
```

The **/etc/shadow** file contains nine colon separated columns. The nine fields contain (from left to right) the user name, the encrypted password (note that only inge and laura have an encrypted password), the day the password was last changed (day 1 is January 1, 1970), number of days the password must be left unchanged, password expiry day, warning number of days before password expiry, number of days after expiry before disabling the account, and the day the account was disabled (again, since 1970). The last field has no meaning yet.

All the passwords in the screenshot above are hashes of **hunter2**.

29.3. encryption with passwd

Passwords are stored in an encrypted format. This encryption is done by the **crypt** function. The easiest (and recommended) way to add a user with a password to the system is to add the user with the **useradd -m user** command, and then set the user's password with **passwd**.

```
[root@RHEL4 ~]# useradd -m xavier
[root@RHEL4 ~]# passwd xavier
Changing password for user xavier.
New UNIX password:
Retype new UNIX password:
passwd: all authentication tokens updated successfully.
[root@RHEL4 ~]#
```

29.4. encryption with openssl

Another way to create users with a password is to use the -p option of useradd, but that option requires an encrypted password. You can generate this encrypted password with the **openssl passwd** command.

The **openssl passwd** command will generate several distinct hashes for the same password, for this it uses a **salt**.

```
paul@rhel65:~$ openssl passwd hunter2
86jcUNlnGDFpY
paul@rhel65:~$ openssl passwd hunter2
Yj7mDO9OAnvq6
paul@rhel65:~$ openssl passwd hunter2
YqDcJeGoDbzKA
paul@rhel65:~$
```

This **salt** can be chosen and is visible as the first two characters of the hash.

```
paul@rhel65:~$ openssl passwd -salt 42 hunter2
42ZrbtP1Ze8G.
paul@rhel65:~$ openssl passwd -salt 42 hunter2
42ZrbtP1Ze8G.
paul@rhel65:~$ openssl passwd -salt 42 hunter2
42ZrbtP1Ze8G.
paul@rhel65:~$
```

This example shows how to create a user with password.

```
root@rhel65:~# useradd -m -p $(openssl passwd hunter2) mohamed
```

Note that this command puts the password in your command history!

29.5. encryption with crypt

A third option is to create your own C program using the crypt function, and compile this into a command.

```
paul@rhel65:~$ cat MyCrypt.c
#include <stdio.h>
#define __USE_XOPEN
#include <unistd.h>

int main(int argc, char** argv)
{
 if(argc==3)
   {
       printf("%s\n", crypt(argv[1],argv[2]));
   }
   else
   {
       printf("Usage: MyCrypt $password $salt\n" );
   }
   return 0;
}
```

This little program can be compiled with **gcc** like this.

```
paul@rhel65:~$ gcc MyCrypt.c -o MyCrypt -lcrypt
```

To use it, we need to give two parameters to MyCrypt. The first is the unencrypted password, the second is the salt. The salt is used to perturb the encryption algorithm in one of 4096 different ways. This variation prevents two users with the same password from having the same entry in **/etc/shadow**.

```
paul@rhel65:~$ ./MyCrypt hunter2 42
42ZrbtP1Ze8G.
paul@rhel65:~$ ./MyCrypt hunter2 33
33d6taYSiEUXI
```

Did you notice that the first two characters of the password are the **salt**?

The standard output of the crypt function is using the DES algorithm which is old and can be cracked in minutes. A better method is to use **md5** passwords which can be recognized by a salt starting with 1.

```
paul@rhel65:~$ ./MyCrypt hunter2 '$1$42'
$1$42$716Y3xT5282XmZrtDOF9f0
paul@rhel65:~$ ./MyCrypt hunter2 '$6$42'
$6$42$OqFFAVnI3gTSYG0yI9TZWX9cpyQzwIop7HwpG1LLEsNBiMr4w6OvLX1KDa./UpwXfrFk1i...
```

The **md5** salt can be up to eight characters long. The salt is displayed in **/etc/shadow** between the second and third $, so never use the password as the salt!

```
paul@rhel65:~$ ./MyCrypt hunter2 '$1$hunter2'
$1$hunter2$YVxrxDmidq7Xf8Gdt6qM2.
```

29.6. /etc/login.defs

The **/etc/login.defs** file contains some default settings for user passwords like password aging and length settings. (You will also find the numerical limits of user ids and group ids and whether or not a home directory should be created by default).

```
root@rhel65:~# grep ^PASS /etc/login.defs
PASS_MAX_DAYS   99999
PASS_MIN_DAYS   0
PASS_MIN_LEN    5
PASS_WARN_AGE   7
```

Debian also has this file.

```
root@debian7:~# grep PASS /etc/login.defs
#   PASS_MAX_DAYS   Maximum number of days a password may be used.
#   PASS_MIN_DAYS   Minimum number of days allowed between password changes.
#   PASS_WARN_AGE   Number of days warning given before a password expires.
PASS_MAX_DAYS   99999
PASS_MIN_DAYS   0
PASS_WARN_AGE   7
#PASS_CHANGE_TRIES
#PASS_ALWAYS_WARN
#PASS_MIN_LEN
#PASS_MAX_LEN
# NO_PASSWORD_CONSOLE
root@debian7:~#
```

29.7. chage

The **chage** command can be used to set an expiration date for a user account (-E), set a minimum (-m) and maximum (-M) password age, a password expiration date, and set the number of warning days before the password expiration date. Much of this functionality is also available from the **passwd** command. The **-l** option of chage will list these settings for a user.

```
root@rhel65:~# chage -l paul
Last password change                                    : Mar 27, 2014
Password expires                                        : never
Password inactive                                       : never
Account expires                                         : never
Minimum number of days between password change          : 0
Maximum number of days between password change          : 99999
Number of days of warning before password expires       : 7
root@rhel65:~#
```

29.8. disabling a password

Passwords in **/etc/shadow** cannot begin with an exclamation mark. When the second field in **/etc/passwd** starts with an exclamation mark, then the password can not be used.

Using this feature is often called **locking**, **disabling**, or **suspending** a user account. Besides **vi** (or vipw) you can also accomplish this with **usermod**.

The first command in the next screenshot will show the hashed password of **laura** in **/etc/shadow**. The next command disables the password of **laura**, making it impossible for Laura to authenticate using this password.

```
root@debian7:~# grep laura /etc/shadow | cut -c1-70
laura:$6$JYj4JZqp$stwwWACp3OtE1R2aZuE87j.nbW.puDkNUYVk7mCHfCVMa3CoDUJV
root@debian7:~# usermod -L laura
```

As you can see below, the password hash is simply preceded with an exclamation mark.

```
root@debian7:~# grep laura /etc/shadow | cut -c1-70
laura:!$6$JYj4JZqp$stwwWACp3OtE1R2aZuE87j.nbW.puDkNUYVk7mCHfCVMa3CoDUJ
root@debian7:~#
```

The root user (and users with **sudo** rights on **su**) still will be able to **su** into the **laura** account (because the password is not needed here). Also note that **laura** will still be able to login if she has set up passwordless ssh!

```
root@debian7:~# su - laura
laura@debian7:~$
```

You can unlock the account again with **usermod -U**.

```
root@debian7:~# usermod -U laura
root@debian7:~# grep laura /etc/shadow | cut -c1-70
laura:$6$JYj4JZqp$stwwWACp3OtE1R2aZuE87j.nbW.puDkNUYVk7mCHfCVMa3CoDUJV
```

Watch out for tiny differences in the command line options of **passwd**, **usermod**, and **useradd** on different Linux distributions. Verify the local files when using features like **"disabling, suspending, or locking"** on user accounts and their passwords.

29.9. editing local files

If you still want to manually edit the **/etc/passwd** or **/etc/shadow**, after knowing these commands for password management, then use **vipw** instead of vi(m) directly. The **vipw** tool will do proper locking of the file.

```
[root@RHEL5 ~]# vipw /etc/passwd
vipw: the password file is busy (/etc/ptmp present)
```

29.10. practice: user passwords

1. Set the password for **serena** to **hunter2**.

2. Also set a password for **venus** and then lock the **venus** user account with **usermod**. Verify the locking in **/etc/shadow** before and after you lock it.

3. Use **passwd -d** to disable the **serena** password. Verify the **serena** line in **/etc/shadow** before and after disabling.

4. What is the difference between locking a user account and disabling a user account's password like we just did with **usermod -L** and **passwd -d**?

5. Try changing the password of serena to serena as serena.

6. Make sure **serena** has to change her password in 10 days.

7. Make sure every new user needs to change their password every 10 days.

8. Take a backup as root of **/etc/shadow**. Use **vi** to copy an encrypted **hunter2** hash from **venus** to **serena**. Can **serena** now log on with **hunter2** as a password ?

9. Why use **vipw** instead of **vi** ? What could be the problem when using **vi** or **vim** ?

10. Use **chsh** to list all shells (only works on RHEL/CentOS/Fedora), and compare to **cat /etc/shells**.

11. Which **useradd** option allows you to name a home directory ?

12. How can you see whether the password of user **serena** is locked or unlocked ? Give a solution with **grep** and a solution with **passwd**.

29.11. solution: user passwords

1. Set the password for **serena** to **hunter2**.

```
root@debian7:~# passwd serena
Enter new UNIX password:
Retype new UNIX password:
passwd: password updated successfully
```

2. Also set a password for **venus** and then lock the **venus** user account with **usermod**. Verify the locking in **/etc/shadow** before and after you lock it.

```
root@debian7:~# passwd venus
Enter new UNIX password:
Retype new UNIX password:
passwd: password updated successfully
root@debian7:~# grep venus /etc/shadow | cut -c1-70
venus:$6$gswzXICW$uSnKFV1kFKZmTPaMVS4AvNA/KO27OxN0v5LHdV9ed0gTyXrjUeM/
root@debian7:~# usermod -L venus
root@debian7:~# grep venus /etc/shadow | cut -c1-70
venus:!$6$gswzXICW$uSnKFV1kFKZmTPaMVS4AvNA/KO27OxN0v5LHdV9ed0gTyXrjUeM
```

Note that **usermod -L** precedes the password hash with an exclamation mark (!).

3. Use **passwd -d** to disable the **serena** password. Verify the **serena** line in **/etc/shadow** before and after disabling.

```
root@debian7:~# grep serena /etc/shadow | cut -c1-70
serena:$6$Es/omrPE$F2Ypu8kpLrfKdW0v/UIwA5jrYyBD2nwZ/dt.i/IypRgiPZSdB/B
root@debian7:~# passwd -d serena
passwd: password expiry information changed.
root@debian7:~# grep serena /etc/shadow
serena::16358:0:99999:7:::
root@debian7:~#
```

4. What is the difference between locking a user account and disabling a user account's password like we just did with **usermod -L** and **passwd -d**?

Locking will prevent the user from logging on to the system with his password by putting a ! in front of the password in **/etc/shadow**.

Disabling with **passwd** will erase the password from **/etc/shadow**.

5. Try changing the password of serena to serena as serena.

```
log on as serena, then execute: passwd serena... it should fail!
```

6. Make sure **serena** has to change her password in 10 days.

```
chage -M 10 serena
```

7. Make sure every new user needs to change their password every 10 days.

```
vi /etc/login.defs (and change PASS_MAX_DAYS to 10)
```

8. Take a backup as root of **/etc/shadow**. Use **vi** to copy an encrypted **hunter2** hash from **venus** to **serena**. Can **serena** now log on with **hunter2** as a password ?

```
Yes.
```

9. Why use **vipw** instead of **vi** ? What could be the problem when using **vi** or **vim** ?

```
vipw will give a warning when someone else is already using that file (with vipw).
```

10. Use **chsh** to list all shells (only works on RHEL/CentOS/Fedora), and compare to **cat /etc/shells**.

```
chsh -l
cat /etc/shells
```

11. Which **useradd** option allows you to name a home directory ?

```
-d
```

12. How can you see whether the password of user **serena** is locked or unlocked ? Give a solution with **grep** and a solution with **passwd**.

```
grep serena /etc/shadow
```

```
passwd -S serena
```

Chapter 30. user profiles

Logged on users have a number of preset (and customized) aliases, variables, and functions, but where do they come from ? The **shell** uses a number of startup files that are executed (or rather **sourced**) whenever the shell is invoked. What follows is an overview of startup scripts.

30.1. system profile

Both the **bash** and the **ksh** shell will verify the existence of **/etc/profile** and **source** it if it exists.

When reading this script, you will notice (both on Debian and on Red Hat Enterprise Linux) that it builds the PATH environment variable (among others). The script might also change the PS1 variable, set the HOSTNAME and execute even more scripts like **/etc/inputrc**

This screenshot uses grep to show PATH manipulation in **/etc/profile** on Debian.

```
root@debian7:~# grep PATH /etc/profile
  PATH="/usr/local/sbin:/usr/local/bin:/usr/sbin:/usr/bin:/sbin:/bin"
  PATH="/usr/local/bin:/usr/bin:/bin:/usr/local/games:/usr/games"
export PATH
root@debian7:~#
```

This screenshot uses grep to show PATH manipulation in **/etc/profile** on RHEL7/CentOS7.

```
[root@centos7 ~]# grep PATH /etc/profile
    case ":${PATH}:" in
                PATH=$PATH:$1
                PATH=$1:$PATH
export PATH USER LOGNAME MAIL HOSTNAME HISTSIZE HISTCONTROL
[root@centos7 ~]#
```

The **root user** can use this script to set aliases, functions, and variables for every user on the system.

30.2. ~/.bash_profile

When this file exists in the home directory, then **bash** will source it. On Debian Linux 5/6/7 this file does not exist by default.

RHEL7/CentOS7 uses a small ~/.**bash_profile** where it checks for the existence of ~/.**bashrc** and then sources it. It also adds $HOME/bin to the $PATH variable.

```
[root@rhel7 ~]# cat /home/paul/.bash_profile
# .bash_profile

# Get the aliases and functions
if [ -f ~/.bashrc ]; then
        . ~/.bashrc
fi

# User specific environment and startup programs

PATH=$PATH:$HOME/.local/bin:$HOME/bin

export PATH
[root@rhel7 ~]#
```

30.3. ~/.bash_login

When **.bash_profile** does not exist, then **bash** will check for ~/**.bash_login** and source it.

Neither Debian nor Red Hat have this file by default.

30.4. ~/.profile

When neither ~/**.bash_profile** and ~/**.bash_login** exist, then bash will verify the existence of ~/**.profile** and execute it. This file does not exist by default on Red Hat.

On Debian this script can execute ~/**.bashrc** and will add $HOME/bin to the $PATH variable.

```
root@debian7:~# tail -11 /home/paul/.profile
if [ -n "$BASH_VERSION" ]; then
    # include .bashrc if it exists
    if [ -f "$HOME/.bashrc" ]; then
        . "$HOME/.bashrc"
    fi
fi

# set PATH so it includes user's private bin if it exists
if [ -d "$HOME/bin" ] ; then
    PATH="$HOME/bin:$PATH"
fi
```

RHEL/CentOS does not have this file by default.

30.5. ~/.bashrc

The ~/**.bashrc** script is often sourced by other scripts. Let us take a look at what it does by default.

Red Hat uses a very simple ~/**.bashrc**, checking for **/etc/bashrc** and sourcing it. It also leaves room for custom aliases and functions.

```
[root@rhel7 ~]# cat /home/paul/.bashrc
# .bashrc

# Source global definitions
if [ -f /etc/bashrc ]; then
        . /etc/bashrc
fi

# Uncomment the following line if you don't like systemctl's auto-paging feature:
# export SYSTEMD_PAGER=

# User specific aliases and functions
```

On Debian this script is quite a bit longer and configures $PS1, some history variables and a number af active and inactive aliases.

```
root@debian7:~# wc -l /home/paul/.bashrc
110 /home/paul/.bashrc
```

30.6. ~/.bash_logout

When exiting **bash**, it can execute ~/**.bash_logout**.

Debian use this opportunity to clear the console screen.

```
serena@deb503:~$ cat .bash_logout
# ~/.bash_logout: executed by bash(1) when login shell exits.

# when leaving the console clear the screen to increase privacy

if [ "$SHLVL" = 1 ]; then
    [ -x /usr/bin/clear_console ] && /usr/bin/clear_console -q
fi
```

Red Hat Enterprise Linux 5 will simple call the **/usr/bin/clear** command in this script.

```
[serena@rhel53 ~]$ cat .bash_logout
# ~/.bash_logout

/usr/bin/clear
```

Red Hat Enterprise Linux 6 and 7 create this file, but leave it empty (except for a comment).

```
paul@rhel65:~$ cat .bash_logout
# ~/.bash_logout
```

30.7. Debian overview

Below is a table overview of when Debian is running any of these bash startup scripts.

Table 30.1. Debian User Environment

script	su	su -	ssh	gdm
~./bashrc	no	yes	yes	yes
~/.profile	no	yes	yes	yes
/etc/profile	no	yes	yes	yes
/etc/bash.bashrc	yes	no	no	yes

30.8. RHEL5 overview

Below is a table overview of when Red Hat Enterprise Linux 5 is running any of these bash startup scripts.

Table 30.2. Red Hat User Environment

script	su	su -	ssh	gdm
~./bashrc	yes	yes	yes	yes
~/.bash_profile	no	yes	yes	yes
/etc/profile	no	yes	yes	yes
/etc/bashrc	yes	yes	yes	yes

30.9. practice: user profiles

1. Make a list of all the profile files on your system.

2. Read the contents of each of these, often they **source** extra scripts.

3. Put a unique variable, alias and function in each of those files.

4. Try several different ways to obtain a shell (su, su -, ssh, tmux, gnome-terminal, Ctrl-alt-F1, ...) and verify which of your custom variables, aliases and function are present in your environment.

5. Do you also know the order in which they are executed?

6. When an application depends on a setting in $HOME/.profile, does it matter whether $HOME/.bash_profile exists or not ?

30.10. solution: user profiles

1. Make a list of all the profile files on your system.

```
ls -a ~ ; ls -l /etc/pro* /etc/bash*
```

2. Read the contents of each of these, often they **source** extra scripts.

3. Put a unique variable, alias and function in each of those files.

4. Try several different ways to obtain a shell (su, su -, ssh, tmux, gnome-terminal, Ctrl-alt-F1, ...) and verify which of your custom variables, aliases and function are present in your environment.

5. Do you also know the order in which they are executed?

```
same name aliases, functions and variables will overwrite each other
```

6. When an application depends on a setting in $HOME/.profile, does it matter whether $HOME/.bash_profile exists or not ?

```
Yes it does matter. (man bash /INVOCATION)
```

Chapter 31. groups

Users can be listed in **groups**. Groups allow you to set permissions on the group level instead of having to set permissions for every individual user.

Every Unix or Linux distribution will have a graphical tool to manage groups. Novice users are advised to use this graphical tool. More experienced users can use command line tools to manage users, but be careful: Some distributions do not allow the mixed use of GUI and CLI tools to manage groups (YaST in Novell Suse). Senior administrators can edit the relevant files directly with **vi** or **vigr**.

31.1. groupadd

Groups can be created with the **groupadd** command. The example below shows the creation of five (empty) groups.

```
root@laika:~# groupadd tennis
root@laika:~# groupadd football
root@laika:~# groupadd snooker
root@laika:~# groupadd formula1
root@laika:~# groupadd salsa
```

31.2. group file

Users can be a member of several groups. Group membership is defined by the **/etc/group** file.

```
root@laika:~# tail -5 /etc/group
tennis:x:1006:
football:x:1007:
snooker:x:1008:
formula1:x:1009:
salsa:x:1010:
root@laika:~#
```

The first field is the group's name. The second field is the group's (encrypted) password (can be empty). The third field is the group identification or **GID**. The fourth field is the list of members, these groups have no members.

31.3. groups

A user can type the **groups** command to see a list of groups where the user belongs to.

```
[harry@RHEL4b ~]$ groups
harry sports
[harry@RHEL4b ~]$
```

31.4. usermod

Group membership can be modified with the useradd or **usermod** command.

```
root@laika:~# usermod -a -G tennis inge
root@laika:~# usermod -a -G tennis katrien
root@laika:~# usermod -a -G salsa katrien
root@laika:~# usermod -a -G snooker sandra
root@laika:~# usermod -a -G formula1 annelies
root@laika:~# tail -5 /etc/group
tennis:x:1006:inge,katrien
football:x:1007:
snooker:x:1008:sandra
formula1:x:1009:annelies
salsa:x:1010:katrien
root@laika:~#
```

Be careful when using **usermod** to add users to groups. By default, the **usermod** command will **remove** the user from every group of which he is a member if the group is not listed in the command! Using the **-a** (append) switch prevents this behaviour.

31.5. groupmod

You can change the group name with the **groupmod** command.

```
root@laika:~# groupmod -n darts snooker
root@laika:~# tail -5 /etc/group
tennis:x:1006:inge,katrien
football:x:1007:
formula1:x:1009:annelies
salsa:x:1010:katrien
darts:x:1008:sandra
```

31.6. groupdel

You can permanently remove a group with the **groupdel** command.

```
root@laika:~# groupdel tennis
root@laika:~#
```

31.7. gpasswd

You can delegate control of group membership to another user with the **gpasswd** command. In the example below we delegate permissions to add and remove group members to serena for the sports group. Then we **su** to serena and add harry to the sports group.

```
[root@RHEL4b ~]# gpasswd -A serena sports
[root@RHEL4b ~]# su - serena
[serena@RHEL4b ~]$ id harry
uid=516(harry) gid=520(harry) groups=520(harry)
[serena@RHEL4b ~]$ gpasswd -a harry sports
Adding user harry to group sports
[serena@RHEL4b ~]$ id harry
uid=516(harry) gid=520(harry) groups=520(harry),522(sports)
[serena@RHEL4b ~]$ tail -1 /etc/group
sports:x:522:serena,venus,harry
[serena@RHEL4b ~]$
```

Group administrators do not have to be a member of the group. They can remove themselves from a group, but this does not influence their ability to add or remove members.

```
[serena@RHEL4b ~]$ gpasswd -d serena sports
Removing user serena from group sports
[serena@RHEL4b ~]$ exit
```

Information about group administrators is kept in the **/etc/gshadow** file.

```
[root@RHEL4b ~]# tail -1 /etc/gshadow
sports:!:serena:venus,harry
[root@RHEL4b ~]#
```

To remove all group administrators from a group, use the **gpasswd** command to set an empty administrators list.

```
[root@RHEL4b ~]# gpasswd -A "" sports
```

31.8. newgrp

You can start a **child shell** with a new temporary **primary group** using the **newgrp** command.

```
root@rhel65:~# mkdir prigroup
root@rhel65:~# cd prigroup/
root@rhel65:~/prigroup# touch standard.txt
root@rhel65:~/prigroup# ls -l
total 0
-rw-r--r--. 1 root root 0 Apr 13 17:49 standard.txt
root@rhel65:~/prigroup# echo $SHLVL
1
root@rhel65:~/prigroup# newgrp tennis
root@rhel65:~/prigroup# echo $SHLVL
2
root@rhel65:~/prigroup# touch newgrp.txt
root@rhel65:~/prigroup# ls -l
total 0
-rw-r--r--. 1 root tennis 0 Apr 13 17:49 newgrp.txt
-rw-r--r--. 1 root root   0 Apr 13 17:49 standard.txt
root@rhel65:~/prigroup# exit
exit
root@rhel65:~/prigroup#
```

31.9. vigr

Similar to vipw, the **vigr** command can be used to manually edit the **/etc/group** file, since it will do proper locking of the file. Only experienced senior administrators should use **vi** or **vigr** to manage groups.

31.10. practice: groups

1. Create the groups tennis, football and sports.

2. In one command, make venus a member of tennis and sports.

3. Rename the football group to foot.

4. Use vi to add serena to the tennis group.

5. Use the id command to verify that serena is a member of tennis.

6. Make someone responsible for managing group membership of foot and sports. Test that it works.

31.11. solution: groups

1. Create the groups tennis, football and sports.

`groupadd tennis ; groupadd football ; groupadd sports`

2. In one command, make venus a member of tennis and sports.

`usermod -a -G tennis,sports venus`

3. Rename the football group to foot.

`groupmod -n foot football`

4. Use vi to add serena to the tennis group.

`vi /etc/group`

5. Use the id command to verify that serena is a member of tennis.

`id (and after logoff logon serena should be member)`

6. Make someone responsible for managing group membership of foot and sports. Test that it works.

`gpasswd -A (to make manager)`

`gpasswd -a (to add member)`

Part IX. file security

Table of Contents

Chapter 32. standard file permissions

This chapter contains details about basic file security through **file ownership** and **file permissions**.

32.1. file ownership

32.1.1. user owner and group owner

The **users** and **groups** of a system can be locally managed in **/etc/passwd** and **/etc/group**, or they can be in a NIS, LDAP, or Samba domain. These users and groups can **own** files. Actually, every file has a **user owner** and a **group owner**, as can be seen in the following screenshot.

```
paul@rhel65:~/owners$ ls -lh
total 636K
-rw-r--r--. 1 paul snooker 1.1K Apr  8 18:47 data.odt
-rw-r--r--. 1 paul paul    626K Apr  8 18:46 file1
-rw-r--r--. 1 root tennis   185 Apr  8 18:46 file2
-rw-rw-r--. 1 root root       0 Apr  8 18:47 stuff.txt
paul@rhel65:~/owners$
```

User paul owns three files; file1 has paul as **user owner** and has the group paul as **group owner**, data.odt is **group owned** by the group snooker, file2 by the group tennis.

The last file is called stuff.txt and is owned by the root user and the root group.

32.1.2. listing user accounts

You can use the following command to list all local user accounts.

```
paul@debian7~$ cut -d: -f1 /etc/passwd | column
root          ntp          sam          bert         naomi
daemon        mysql        tom          rino         matthias2
bin           paul         wouter       antonio      bram
sys           maarten      robrecht     simon        fabrice
sync          kevin        bilal        sven         chimene
games         yuri         dimitri      wouter2      messagebus
man           william      ahmed        tarik        roger
lp            yves         dylan        jan          frank
mail          kris         robin        ian          toon
news          hamid        matthias     ivan         rinus
uucp          vladimir     ben          azeddine     eddy
proxy         abiy         mike         eric         bram2
www-data      david        kevin2       kamel        keith
backup        chahid       kenzo        ischa        jesse
list          stef         aaron        bart         frederick
irc           joeri        lorenzo      omer         hans
gnats         glenn        jens         kurt         dries
nobody        yannick      ruben        steve        steve2
libuuid       christof     jelle        constantin   tomas
Debian-exim   george       stefaan      sam2         johan
statd         joost        marc         bjorn        tom2
sshd          arno         thomas       ronald
```

32.1.3. chgrp

You can change the group owner of a file using the **chgrp** command.

```
root@rhel65:/home/paul/owners# ls -l file2
-rw-r--r--. 1 root tennis 185 Apr  8 18:46 file2
root@rhel65:/home/paul/owners# chgrp snooker file2
root@rhel65:/home/paul/owners# ls -l file2
-rw-r--r--. 1 root snooker 185 Apr  8 18:46 file2
root@rhel65:/home/paul/owners#
```

32.1.4. chown

The user owner of a file can be changed with **chown** command.

```
root@laika:/home/paul# ls -l FileForPaul
-rw-r--r-- 1 root paul 0 2008-08-06 14:11 FileForPaul
root@laika:/home/paul# chown paul FileForPaul
root@laika:/home/paul# ls -l FileForPaul
-rw-r--r-- 1 paul paul 0 2008-08-06 14:11 FileForPaul
```

You can also use **chown** to change both the user owner and the group owner.

```
root@laika:/home/paul# ls -l FileForPaul
-rw-r--r-- 1 paul paul 0 2008-08-06 14:11 FileForPaul
root@laika:/home/paul# chown root:project42 FileForPaul
root@laika:/home/paul# ls -l FileForPaul
-rw-r--r-- 1 root project42 0 2008-08-06 14:11 FileForPaul
```

32.2. list of special files

When you use **ls -l**, for each file you can see ten characters before the user and group owner. The first character tells us the type of file. Regular files get a **-**, directories get a **d**, symbolic links are shown with an **l**, pipes get a **p**, character devices a **c**, block devices a **b**, and sockets an **s**.

Table 32.1. Unix special files

first character	file type
-	normal file
d	directory
l	symbolic link
p	named pipe
b	block device
c	character device
s	socket

Below a screenshot of a character device (the console) and a block device (the hard disk).

```
paul@debian6lt~$ ls -ld /dev/console /dev/sda
crw-------  1 root root  5, 1 Mar 15 12:45 /dev/console
brw-rw----  1 root disk  8, 0 Mar 15 12:45 /dev/sda
```

And here you can see a directory, a regular file and a symbolic link.

```
paul@debian6lt~$ ls -ld /etc /etc/hosts /etc/motd
drwxr-xr-x 128 root root 12288 Mar 15 18:34 /etc
-rw-r--r--   1 root root   372 Dec 10 17:36 /etc/hosts
lrwxrwxrwx   1 root root    13 Dec  5 10:36 /etc/motd -> /var/run/motd
```

32.3. permissions

32.3.1. rwx

The nine characters following the file type denote the permissions in three triplets. A permission can be **r** for read access, **w** for write access, and **x** for execute. You need the **r** permission to list (ls) the contents of a directory. You need the **x** permission to enter (cd) a directory. You need the **w** permission to create files in or remove files from a directory.

Table 32.2. standard Unix file permissions

permission	on a file	on a directory
r (read)	read file contents (cat)	read directory contents (ls)
w (write)	change file contents (vi)	create files in (touch)
x (execute)	execute the file	enter the directory (cd)

32.3.2. three sets of rwx

We already know that the output of **ls -l** starts with ten characters for each file. This screenshot shows a regular file (because the first character is a -).

```
paul@RHELv4u4:~/test$ ls -l proc42.bash
-rwxr-xr--  1 paul proj 984 Feb  6 12:01 proc42.bash
```

Below is a table describing the function of all ten characters.

Table 32.3. Unix file permissions position

position	characters	function
1	-	this is a regular file
2-4	rwx	permissions for the **user owner**
5-7	r-x	permissions for the **group owner**
8-10	r--	permissions for **others**

When you are the **user owner** of a file, then the **user owner permissions** apply to you. The rest of the permissions have no influence on your access to the file.

When you belong to the **group** that is the **group owner** of a file, then the **group owner permissions** apply to you. The rest of the permissions have no influence on your access to the file.

When you are not the **user owner** of a file and you do not belong to the **group owner**, then the **others permissions** apply to you. The rest of the permissions have no influence on your access to the file.

32.3.3. permission examples

Some example combinations on files and directories are seen in this screenshot. The name of the file explains the permissions.

```
paul@laika:~/perms$ ls -lh
total 12K
drwxr-xr-x 2 paul paul 4.0K 2007-02-07 22:26 AllEnter_UserCreateDelete
-rwxrwxrwx 1 paul paul    0 2007-02-07 22:21 EveryoneFullControl.txt
-r--r----- 1 paul paul    0 2007-02-07 22:21 OnlyOwnersRead.txt
-rwxrwx--- 1 paul paul    0 2007-02-07 22:21 OwnersAll_RestNothing.txt
dr-xr-x--- 2 paul paul 4.0K 2007-02-07 22:25 UserAndGroupEnter
dr-x------ 2 paul paul 4.0K 2007-02-07 22:25 OnlyUserEnter
paul@laika:~/perms$
```

To summarise, the first **rwx** triplet represents the permissions for the **user owner**. The second triplet corresponds to the **group owner**; it specifies permissions for all members of that group. The third triplet defines permissions for all **other** users that are not the user owner and are not a member of the group owner.

32.3.4. setting permissions (chmod)

Permissions can be changed with **chmod**. The first example gives the user owner execute permissions.

```
paul@laika:~/perms$ ls -l permissions.txt
-rw-r--r-- 1 paul paul 0 2007-02-07 22:34 permissions.txt
paul@laika:~/perms$ chmod u+x permissions.txt
paul@laika:~/perms$ ls -l permissions.txt
-rwxr--r-- 1 paul paul 0 2007-02-07 22:34 permissions.txt
```

This example removes the group owners read permission.

```
paul@laika:~/perms$ chmod g-r permissions.txt
paul@laika:~/perms$ ls -l permissions.txt
-rwx---r-- 1 paul paul 0 2007-02-07 22:34 permissions.txt
```

This example removes the others read permission.

```
paul@laika:~/perms$ chmod o-r permissions.txt
paul@laika:~/perms$ ls -l permissions.txt
-rwx------ 1 paul paul 0 2007-02-07 22:34 permissions.txt
```

This example gives all of them the write permission.

```
paul@laika:~/perms$ chmod a+w permissions.txt
paul@laika:~/perms$ ls -l permissions.txt
-rwx-w--w- 1 paul paul 0 2007-02-07 22:34 permissions.txt
```

You don't even have to type the a.

```
paul@laika:~/perms$ chmod +x permissions.txt
paul@laika:~/perms$ ls -l permissions.txt
-rwx-wx-wx 1 paul paul 0 2007-02-07 22:34 permissions.txt
```

You can also set explicit permissions.

```
paul@laika:~/perms$ chmod u=rw permissions.txt
paul@laika:~/perms$ ls -l permissions.txt
-rw--wx-wx 1 paul paul 0 2007-02-07 22:34 permissions.txt
```

Feel free to make any kind of combination.

```
paul@laika:~/perms$ chmod u=rw,g=rw,o=r permissions.txt
paul@laika:~/perms$ ls -l permissions.txt
-rw-rw-r-- 1 paul paul 0 2007-02-07 22:34 permissions.txt
```

Even fishy combinations are accepted by chmod.

```
paul@laika:~/perms$ chmod u=rwx,ug+rw,o=r permissions.txt
paul@laika:~/perms$ ls -l permissions.txt
-rwxrw-r-- 1 paul paul 0 2007-02-07 22:34 permissions.txt
```

32.3.5. setting octal permissions

Most Unix administrators will use the **old school** octal system to talk about and set permissions. Look at the triplet bitwise, equating r to 4, w to 2, and x to 1.

Table 32.4. Octal permissions

binary	octal	permission
000	0	---
001	1	--x
010	2	-w-
011	3	-wx
100	4	r--
101	5	r-x
110	6	rw-
111	7	rwx

This makes **777** equal to rwxrwxrwx and by the same logic, 654 mean rw-r-xr-- . The **chmod** command will accept these numbers.

```
paul@laika:~/perms$ chmod 777 permissions.txt
paul@laika:~/perms$ ls -l permissions.txt
-rwxrwxrwx 1 paul paul 0 2007-02-07 22:34 permissions.txt
paul@laika:~/perms$ chmod 664 permissions.txt
paul@laika:~/perms$ ls -l permissions.txt
-rw-rw-r-- 1 paul paul 0 2007-02-07 22:34 permissions.txt
paul@laika:~/perms$ chmod 750 permissions.txt
paul@laika:~/perms$ ls -l permissions.txt
-rwxr-x--- 1 paul paul 0 2007-02-07 22:34 permissions.txt
```

32.3.6. umask

When creating a file or directory, a set of default permissions are applied. These default permissions are determined by the **umask**. The **umask** specifies permissions that you do not want set on by default. You can display the **umask** with the **umask** command.

```
[Harry@RHEL4b ~]$ umask
0002
[Harry@RHEL4b ~]$ touch test
[Harry@RHEL4b ~]$ ls -l test
-rw-rw-r--  1 Harry Harry 0 Jul 24 06:03 test
[Harry@RHEL4b ~]$
```

As you can also see, the file is also not executable by default. This is a general security feature among Unixes; newly created files are never executable by default. You have to explicitly do a **chmod +x** to make a file executable. This also means that the 1 bit in the **umask** has no meaning--a **umask** of 0022 is the same as 0033.

32.3.7. mkdir -m

When creating directories with **mkdir** you can use the **-m** option to set the **mode**. This screenshot explains.

```
paul@debian5~$ mkdir -m 700 MyDir
paul@debian5~$ mkdir -m 777 Public
paul@debian5~$ ls -dl MyDir/ Public/
drwx------ 2 paul paul 4096 2011-10-16 19:16 MyDir/
drwxrwxrwx 2 paul paul 4096 2011-10-16 19:16 Public/
```

32.3.8. cp -p

To preserve permissions and time stamps from source files, use **cp -p**.

```
paul@laika:~/perms$ cp file* cp
paul@laika:~/perms$ cp -p file* cpp
paul@laika:~/perms$ ll *
-rwx------ 1 paul paul    0 2008-08-25 13:26 file33
-rwxr-x--- 1 paul paul    0 2008-08-25 13:26 file42

cp:
total 0
-rwx------ 1 paul paul 0 2008-08-25 13:34 file33
-rwxr-x--- 1 paul paul 0 2008-08-25 13:34 file42

cpp:
total 0
-rwx------ 1 paul paul 0 2008-08-25 13:26 file33
-rwxr-x--- 1 paul paul 0 2008-08-25 13:26 file42
```

32.4. practice: standard file permissions

1. As normal user, create a directory ~/permissions. Create a file owned by yourself in there.

2. Copy a file owned by root from /etc/ to your permissions dir, who owns this file now ?

3. As root, create a file in the users ~/permissions directory.

4. As normal user, look at who owns this file created by root.

5. Change the ownership of all files in ~/permissions to yourself.

6. Make sure you have all rights to these files, and others can only read.

7. With chmod, is 770 the same as rwxrwx--- ?

8. With chmod, is 664 the same as r-xr-xr-- ?

9. With chmod, is 400 the same as r-------- ?

10. With chmod, is 734 the same as rwxr-xr-- ?

11a. Display the umask in octal and in symbolic form.

11b. Set the umask to 077, but use the symbolic format to set it. Verify that this works.

12. Create a file as root, give only read to others. Can a normal user read this file ? Test writing to this file with vi.

13a. Create a file as normal user, give only read to others. Can another normal user read this file ? Test writing to this file with vi.

13b. Can root read this file ? Can root write to this file with vi ?

14. Create a directory that belongs to a group, where every member of that group can read and write to files, and create files. Make sure that people can only delete their own files.

32.5. solution: standard file permissions

1. As normal user, create a directory ~/permissions. Create a file owned by yourself in there.

```
mkdir ~/permissions ; touch ~/permissions/myfile.txt
```

2. Copy a file owned by root from /etc/ to your permissions dir, who owns this file now ?

```
cp /etc/hosts ~/permissions/
```

The copy is owned by you.

3. As root, create a file in the users ~/permissions directory.

```
(become root)# touch /home/username/permissions/rootfile
```

4. As normal user, look at who owns this file created by root.

```
ls -l ~/permissions
```

The file created by root is owned by root.

5. Change the ownership of all files in ~/permissions to yourself.

```
chown user ~/permissions/*
```

You cannot become owner of the file that belongs to root.

6. Make sure you have all rights to these files, and others can only read.

```
chmod 644 (on files)
```

```
chmod 755 (on directories)
```

7. With chmod, is 770 the same as rwxrwx--- ?

yes

8. With chmod, is 664 the same as r-xr-xr-- ?

No

9. With chmod, is 400 the same as r-------- ?

yes

10. With chmod, is 734 the same as rwxr-xr-- ?

no

11a. Display the umask in octal and in symbolic form.

```
umask ; umask -S
```

11b. Set the umask to 077, but use the symbolic format to set it. Verify that this works.

```
umask -S u=rwx,go=
```

---

12. Create a file as root, give only read to others. Can a normal user read this file ? Test writing to this file with vi.

```
(become root)

# echo hello > /home/username/root.txt

# chmod 744 /home/username/root.txt

(become user)

vi ~/root.txt
```

13a. Create a file as normal user, give only read to others. Can another normal user read this file ? Test writing to this file with vi.

```
echo hello > file ; chmod 744 file
```

Yes, others can read this file

13b. Can root read this file ? Can root write to this file with vi ?

Yes, root can read and write to this file. Permissions do not apply to root.

14. Create a directory that belongs to a group, where every member of that group can read and write to files, and create files. Make sure that people can only delete their own files.

```
mkdir /home/project42 ; groupadd project42

chgrp project42 /home/project42 ; chmod 775 /home/project42
```

You can not yet do the last part of this exercise...

Chapter 33. advanced file permissions

33.1. sticky bit on directory

You can set the **sticky bit** on a directory to prevent users from removing files that they do not own as a user owner. The sticky bit is displayed at the same location as the x permission for others. The sticky bit is represented by a **t** (meaning x is also there) or a **T** (when there is no x for others).

```
root@RHELv4u4:~# mkdir /project55
root@RHELv4u4:~# ls -ld /project55
drwxr-xr-x  2 root root 4096 Feb  7 17:38 /project55
root@RHELv4u4:~# chmod +t /project55/
root@RHELv4u4:~# ls -ld /project55
drwxr-xr-t  2 root root 4096 Feb  7 17:38 /project55
root@RHELv4u4:~#
```

The **sticky bit** can also be set with octal permissions, it is binary 1 in the first of four triplets.

```
root@RHELv4u4:~# chmod 1775 /project55/
root@RHELv4u4:~# ls -ld /project55
drwxrwxr-t  2 root root 4096 Feb  7 17:38 /project55
root@RHELv4u4:~#
```

You will typically find the **sticky bit** on the **/tmp** directory.

```
root@barry:~# ls -ld /tmp
drwxrwxrwt 6 root root 4096 2009-06-04 19:02 /tmp
```

33.2. setgid bit on directory

setgid can be used on directories to make sure that all files inside the directory are owned by the group owner of the directory. The **setgid** bit is displayed at the same location as the x permission for group owner. The **setgid** bit is represented by an **s** (meaning x is also there) or a **S** (when there is no x for the group owner). As this example shows, even though **root** does not belong to the group proj55, the files created by root in /project55 will belong to proj55 since the **setgid** is set.

```
root@RHELv4u4:~# groupadd proj55
root@RHELv4u4:~# chown root:proj55 /project55/
root@RHELv4u4:~# chmod 2775 /project55/
root@RHELv4u4:~# touch /project55/fromroot.txt
root@RHELv4u4:~# ls -ld /project55/
drwxrwsr-x  2 root proj55 4096 Feb  7 17:45 /project55/
root@RHELv4u4:~# ls -l /project55/
total 4
-rw-r--r--  1 root proj55 0 Feb  7 17:45 fromroot.txt
root@RHELv4u4:~#
```

You can use the **find** command to find all **setgid** directories.

```
paul@laika:~$ find / -type d -perm -2000 2> /dev/null
/var/log/mysql
/var/log/news
/var/local
...
```

33.3. setgid and setuid on regular files

These two permissions cause an executable file to be executed with the permissions of the **file owner** instead of the **executing owner**. This means that if any user executes a program that belongs to the **root user**, and the **setuid** bit is set on that program, then the program runs as **root**. This can be dangerous, but sometimes this is good for security.

Take the example of passwords; they are stored in **/etc/shadow** which is only readable by **root**. (The **root** user never needs permissions anyway.)

```
root@RHELv4u4:~# ls -l /etc/shadow
-r--------  1 root root 1260 Jan 21 07:49 /etc/shadow
```

Changing your password requires an update of this file, so how can normal non-root users do this? Let's take a look at the permissions on the **/usr/bin/passwd**.

```
root@RHELv4u4:~# ls -l /usr/bin/passwd
-r-s--x--x  1 root root 21200 Jun 17  2005 /usr/bin/passwd
```

When running the **passwd** program, you are executing it with **root** credentials.

You can use the **find** command to find all **setuid** programs.

```
paul@laika:~$ find /usr/bin -type f -perm -04000
/usr/bin/arping
/usr/bin/kgrantpty
/usr/bin/newgrp
/usr/bin/chfn
/usr/bin/sudo
/usr/bin/fping6
/usr/bin/passwd
/usr/bin/gpasswd
...
```

In most cases, setting the **setuid** bit on executables is sufficient. Setting the **setgid** bit will result in these programs to run with the credentials of their group owner.

33.4. setuid on sudo

The **sudo** binary has the **setuid** bit set, so any user can run it with the effective userid of root.

```
paul@rhel65:~$ ls -l $(which sudo)
---s--x--x. 1 root root 123832 Oct  7  2013 /usr/bin/sudo
paul@rhel65:~$
```

33.5. practice: sticky, setuid and setgid bits

1a. Set up a directory, owned by the group sports.

1b. Members of the sports group should be able to create files in this directory.

1c. All files created in this directory should be group-owned by the sports group.

1d. Users should be able to delete only their own user-owned files.

1e. Test that this works!

2. Verify the permissions on **/usr/bin/passwd**. Remove the **setuid**, then try changing your password as a normal user. Reset the permissions back and try again.

3. If time permits (or if you are waiting for other students to finish this practice), read about file attributes in the man page of chattr and lsattr. Try setting the i attribute on a file and test that it works.

33.6. solution: sticky, setuid and setgid bits

1a. Set up a directory, owned by the group sports.

```
groupadd sports

mkdir /home/sports

chown root:sports /home/sports
```

1b. Members of the sports group should be able to create files in this directory.

```
chmod 770 /home/sports
```

1c. All files created in this directory should be group-owned by the sports group.

```
chmod 2770 /home/sports
```

1d. Users should be able to delete only their own user-owned files.

```
chmod +t /home/sports
```

1e. Test that this works!

Log in with different users (group members and others and root), create files and watch the permissions. Try changing and deleting files...

2. Verify the permissions on **/usr/bin/passwd**. Remove the **setuid**, then try changing your password as a normal user. Reset the permissions back and try again.

```
root@deb503:~# ls -l /usr/bin/passwd
-rwsr-xr-x 1 root root 31704 2009-11-14 15:41 /usr/bin/passwd
root@deb503:~# chmod 755 /usr/bin/passwd
root@deb503:~# ls -l /usr/bin/passwd
-rwxr-xr-x 1 root root 31704 2009-11-14 15:41 /usr/bin/passwd
```

A normal user cannot change password now.

```
root@deb503:~# chmod 4755 /usr/bin/passwd
root@deb503:~# ls -l /usr/bin/passwd
-rwsr-xr-x 1 root root 31704 2009-11-14 15:41 /usr/bin/passwd
```

3. If time permits (or if you are waiting for other students to finish this practice), read about file attributes in the man page of chattr and lsattr. Try setting the i attribute on a file and test that it works.

```
paul@laika:~$ sudo su -
[sudo] password for paul:
root@laika:~# mkdir attr
root@laika:~# cd attr/
root@laika:~/attr# touch file42
root@laika:~/attr# lsattr
------------------ ./file42
root@laika:~/attr# chattr +i file42
```

```
root@laika:~/attr# lsattr
----i------------- ./file42
root@laika:~/attr# rm -rf file42
rm: cannot remove `file42': Operation not permitted
root@laika:~/attr# chattr -i file42
root@laika:~/attr# rm -rf file42
root@laika:~/attr#
```

Chapter 34. access control lists

Standard Unix permissions might not be enough for some organisations. This chapter introduces **access control lists** or **acl's** to further protect files and directories.

34.1. acl in /etc/fstab

File systems that support **access control lists**, or **acls**, have to be mounted with the **acl** option listed in **/etc/fstab**. In the example below, you can see that the root file system has **acl** support, whereas /home/data does not.

```
root@laika:~# tail -4 /etc/fstab
/dev/sda1          /               ext3    acl,relatime    0  1
/dev/sdb2          /home/data      auto    noacl,defaults  0  0
pasha:/home/r      /home/pasha     nfs     defaults        0  0
wolf:/srv/data     /home/wolf      nfs     defaults        0  0
```

34.2. getfacl

Reading **acls** can be done with **/usr/bin/getfacl**. This screenshot shows how to read the **acl** of **file33** with **getfacl**.

```
paul@laika:~/test$ getfacl file33
# file: file33
# owner: paul
# group: paul
user::rw-
group::r--
mask::rwx
other::r--
```

34.3. setfacl

Writing or changing **acls** can be done with **/usr/bin/setfacl**. These screenshots show how to change the **acl** of **file33** with **setfacl**.

First we add **user sandra** with octal permission **7** to the **acl**.

```
paul@laika:~/test$ setfacl -m u:sandra:7 file33
```

Then we add the **group tennis** with octal permission **6** to the **acl** of the same file.

```
paul@laika:~/test$ setfacl -m g:tennis:6 file33
```

The result is visible with **getfacl**.

```
paul@laika:~/test$ getfacl file33
# file: file33
# owner: paul
# group: paul
user::rw-
user:sandra:rwx
group::r--
group:tennis:rw-
mask::rwx
other::r--
```

34.4. remove an acl entry

The **-x** option of the **setfacl** command will remove an **acl** entry from the targeted file.

```
paul@laika:~/test$ setfacl -m u:sandra:7 file33
paul@laika:~/test$ getfacl file33 | grep sandra
user:sandra:rwx
paul@laika:~/test$ setfacl -x sandra file33
paul@laika:~/test$ getfacl file33 | grep sandra
```

Note that omitting the **u** or **g** when defining the **acl** for an account will default it to a user account.

34.5. remove the complete acl

The **-b** option of the **setfacl** command will remove the **acl** from the targeted file.

```
paul@laika:~/test$ setfacl -b file33
paul@laika:~/test$ getfacl file33
# file: file33
# owner: paul
# group: paul
user::rw-
group::r--
other::r--
```

34.6. the acl mask

The **acl mask** defines the maximum effective permissions for any entry in the **acl**. This **mask** is calculated every time you execute the **setfacl** or **chmod** commands.

You can prevent the calculation by using the **--no-mask** switch.

```
paul@laika:~/test$ setfacl --no-mask -m u:sandra:7 file33
paul@laika:~/test$ getfacl file33
# file: file33
# owner: paul
# group: paul
user::rw-
user:sandra:rwx    #effective:rw-
group::r--
mask::rw-
other::r--
```

34.7. eiciel

Desktop users might want to use **eiciel** to manage **acls** with a graphical tool.

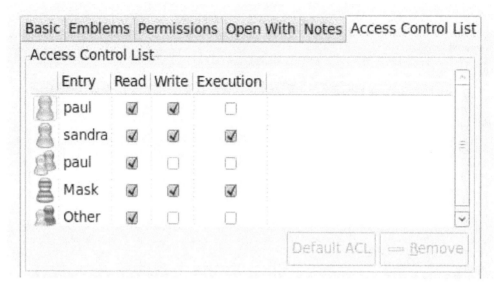

You will need to install **eiciel** and **nautilus-actions** to have an extra tab in **nautilus** to manage **acls**.

```
paul@laika:~$ sudo aptitude install eiciel nautilus-actions
```

Chapter 35. file links

An average computer using Linux has a file system with many **hard links** and **symbolic links**.

To understand links in a file system, you first have to understand what an **inode** is.

35.1. inodes

35.1.1. inode contents

An **inode** is a data structure that contains metadata about a file. When the file system stores a new file on the hard disk, it stores not only the contents (data) of the file, but also extra properties like the name of the file, the creation date, its permissions, the owner of the file, and more. All this information (except the name of the file and the contents of the file) is stored in the **inode** of the file.

The **ls -l** command will display some of the inode contents, as seen in this screenshot.

```
root@rhel53 ~# ls -ld /home/project42/
drwxr-xr-x 4 root pro42 4.0K Mar 27 14:29 /home/project42/
```

35.1.2. inode table

The **inode table** contains all of the **inodes** and is created when you create the file system (with **mkfs**). You can use the **df -i** command to see how many **inodes** are used and free on mounted file systems.

```
root@rhel53 ~# df -i
Filesystem              Inodes   IUsed   IFree IUse% Mounted on
/dev/mapper/VolGroup00-LogVol00
                       4947968  115326 4832642    3% /
/dev/hda1                26104      45   26059    1% /boot
tmpfs                    64417       1   64416    1% /dev/shm
/dev/sda1               262144    2207  259937    1% /home/project42
/dev/sdb1                74400    5519   68881    8% /home/project33
/dev/sdb5                    0       0       0    -  /home/sales
/dev/sdb6               100744      11  100733    1% /home/research
```

In the **df -i** screenshot above you can see the **inode** usage for several mounted **file systems**. You don't see numbers for **/dev/sdb5** because it is a **fat** file system.

35.1.3. inode number

Each **inode** has a unique number (the inode number). You can see the **inode** numbers with the **ls -li** command.

```
paul@RHELv4u4:~/test$ touch file1
paul@RHELv4u4:~/test$ touch file2
paul@RHELv4u4:~/test$ touch file3
paul@RHELv4u4:~/test$ ls -li
total 12
817266 -rw-rw-r--  1 paul paul 0 Feb  5 15:38 file1
817267 -rw-rw-r--  1 paul paul 0 Feb  5 15:38 file2
817268 -rw-rw-r--  1 paul paul 0 Feb  5 15:38 file3
paul@RHELv4u4:~/test$
```

These three files were created one after the other and got three different **inodes** (the first column). All the information you see with this **ls** command resides in the **inode**, except for the filename (which is contained in the directory).

35.1.4. inode and file contents

Let's put some data in one of the files.

```
paul@RHELv4u4:~/test$ ls -li
total 16
817266 -rw-rw-r-- 1 paul paul  0 Feb  5 15:38 file1
817270 -rw-rw-r-- 1 paul paul 92 Feb  5 15:42 file2
817268 -rw-rw-r-- 1 paul paul  0 Feb  5 15:38 file3
paul@RHELv4u4:~/test$ cat file2
It is winter now and it is very cold.
We do not like the cold, we prefer hot summer nights.
paul@RHELv4u4:~/test$
```

The data that is displayed by the **cat** command is not in the **inode**, but somewhere else on the disk. The **inode** contains a pointer to that data.

35.2. about directories

35.2.1. a directory is a table

A **directory** is a special kind of file that contains a table which maps filenames to inodes. Listing our current directory with **ls -ali** will display the contents of the directory file.

```
paul@RHELv4u4:~/test$ ls -ali
total 32
817262 drwxrwxr-x  2 paul paul 4096 Feb  5 15:42 .
800768 drwx------ 16 paul paul 4096 Feb  5 15:42 ..
817266 -rw-rw-r--  1 paul paul    0 Feb  5 15:38 file1
817270 -rw-rw-r--  1 paul paul   92 Feb  5 15:42 file2
817268 -rw-rw-r--  1 paul paul    0 Feb  5 15:38 file3
paul@RHELv4u4:~/test$
```

35.2.2. . and ..

You can see five names, and the mapping to their five inodes. The dot **.** is a mapping to itself, and the dotdot **..** is a mapping to the parent directory. The three other names are mappings to different inodes.

35.3. hard links

35.3.1. creating hard links

When we create a **hard link** to a file with **ln**, an extra entry is added in the directory. A new file name is mapped to an existing inode.

```
paul@RHELv4u4:~/test$ ln file2 hardlink_to_file2
paul@RHELv4u4:~/test$ ls -li
total 24
817266 -rw-rw-r--  1 paul paul  0 Feb  5 15:38 file1
817270 -rw-rw-r--  2 paul paul 92 Feb  5 15:42 file2
817268 -rw-rw-r--  1 paul paul  0 Feb  5 15:38 file3
817270 -rw-rw-r--  2 paul paul 92 Feb  5 15:42 hardlink_to_file2
paul@RHELv4u4:~/test$
```

Both files have the same inode, so they will always have the same permissions and the same owner. Both files will have the same content. Actually, both files are equal now, meaning you can safely remove the original file, the hardlinked file will remain. The inode contains a counter, counting the number of hard links to itself. When the counter drops to zero, then the inode is emptied.

35.3.2. finding hard links

You can use the **find** command to look for files with a certain inode. The screenshot below shows how to search for all filenames that point to **inode** 817270. Remember that an **inode** number is unique to its partition.

```
paul@RHELv4u4:~/test$ find / -inum 817270 2> /dev/null
/home/paul/test/file2
/home/paul/test/hardlink_to_file2
```

35.4. symbolic links

Symbolic links (sometimes called **soft links**) do not link to inodes, but create a name to name mapping. Symbolic links are created with **ln -s**. As you can see below, the **symbolic link** gets an inode of its own.

```
paul@RHELv4u4:~/test$ ln -s file2 symlink_to_file2
paul@RHELv4u4:~/test$ ls -li
total 32
817273 -rw-rw-r--  1 paul paul  13 Feb  5 17:06 file1
817270 -rw-rw-r--  2 paul paul 106 Feb  5 17:04 file2
817268 -rw-rw-r--  1 paul paul   0 Feb  5 15:38 file3
817270 -rw-rw-r--  2 paul paul 106 Feb  5 17:04 hardlink_to_file2
817267 lrwxrwxrwx  1 paul paul   5 Feb  5 16:55 symlink_to_file2 -> file2
paul@RHELv4u4:~/test$
```

Permissions on a symbolic link have no meaning, since the permissions of the target apply. Hard links are limited to their own partition (because they point to an inode), symbolic links can link anywhere (other file systems, even networked).

35.5. removing links

Links can be removed with **rm**.

```
paul@laika:~$ touch data.txt
paul@laika:~$ ln -s data.txt sl_data.txt
paul@laika:~$ ln data.txt hl_data.txt
paul@laika:~$ rm sl_data.txt
paul@laika:~$ rm hl_data.txt
```

35.6. practice : links

1. Create two files named winter.txt and summer.txt, put some text in them.

2. Create a hard link to winter.txt named hlwinter.txt.

3. Display the inode numbers of these three files, the hard links should have the same inode.

4. Use the find command to list the two hardlinked files

5. Everything about a file is in the inode, except two things : name them!

6. Create a symbolic link to summer.txt called slsummer.txt.

7. Find all files with inode number 2. What does this information tell you ?

8. Look at the directories /etc/init.d/ /etc/rc2.d/ /etc/rc3.d/ ... do you see the links ?

9. Look in /lib with ls -l...

10. Use **find** to look in your home directory for regular files that do not(!) have one hard link.

35.7. solution : links

1. Create two files named winter.txt and summer.txt, put some text in them.

```
echo cold > winter.txt ; echo hot > summer.txt
```

2. Create a hard link to winter.txt named hlwinter.txt.

```
ln winter.txt hlwinter.txt
```

3. Display the inode numbers of these three files, the hard links should have the same inode.

```
ls -li winter.txt summer.txt hlwinter.txt
```

4. Use the find command to list the two hardlinked files

```
find . -inum xyz #replace xyz with the inode number
```

5. Everything about a file is in the inode, except two things : name them!

The name of the file is in a directory, and the contents is somewhere on the disk.

6. Create a symbolic link to summer.txt called slsummer.txt.

```
ln -s summer.txt slsummer.txt
```

7. Find all files with inode number 2. What does this information tell you ?

It tells you there is more than one inode table (one for every formatted partition + virtual file systems)

8. Look at the directories /etc/init.d/ /etc/rc.d/ /etc/rc3.d/ ... do you see the links ?

```
ls -l /etc/init.d
```
```
ls -l /etc/rc2.d
```
```
ls -l /etc/rc3.d
```

9. Look in /lib with ls -l...

```
ls -l /lib
```

10. Use **find** to look in your home directory for regular files that do not(!) have one hard link.

```
find ~ ! -links 1 -type f
```

Part X. Appendices

Table of Contents

Appendix A. keyboard settings

A.1. about keyboard layout

Many people (like US-Americans) prefer the default US-qwerty keyboard layout. So when you are not from the USA and want a local keyboard layout on your system, then the best practice is to select this keyboard at installation time. Then the keyboard layout will always be correct. Also, whenever you use ssh to remotely manage a Linux system, your local keyboard layout will be used, independent of the server keyboard configuration. So you will not find much information on changing keyboard layout on the fly on linux, because not many people need it. Below are some tips to help you.

A.2. X Keyboard Layout

This is the relevant portion in /etc/X11/xorg.conf, first for Belgian azerty, then for US-qwerty.

```
[paul@RHEL5 ~]$ grep -i xkb /etc/X11/xorg.conf
        Option      "XkbModel" "pc105"
        Option      "XkbLayout" "be"


[paul@RHEL5 ~]$ grep -i xkb /etc/X11/xorg.conf
        Option      "XkbModel" "pc105"
        Option      "XkbLayout" "us"
```

When in Gnome or KDE or any other graphical environment, look in the graphical menu in preferences, there will be a keyboard section to choose your layout. Use the graphical menu instead of editing xorg.conf.

A.3. shell keyboard layout

When in bash, take a look in the /etc/sysconfig/keyboard file. Below a sample US-qwerty configuration, followed by a Belgian azerty configuration.

```
[paul@RHEL5 ~]$ cat /etc/sysconfig/keyboard
KEYBOARDTYPE="pc"
KEYTABLE="us"


[paul@RHEL5 ~]$ cat /etc/sysconfig/keyboard
KEYBOARDTYPE="pc"
KEYTABLE="be-latin1"
```

The keymaps themselves can be found in /usr/share/keymaps or /lib/kbd/keymaps.

```
[paul@RHEL5 ~]$ ls -l /lib/kbd/keymaps/
total 52
drwxr-xr-x 2 root root 4096 Apr  1 00:14 amiga
```

```
drwxr-xr-x 2 root root 4096 Apr  1 00:14 atari
drwxr-xr-x 8 root root 4096 Apr  1 00:14 i386
drwxr-xr-x 2 root root 4096 Apr  1 00:14 include
drwxr-xr-x 4 root root 4096 Apr  1 00:14 mac
lrwxrwxrwx 1 root root    3 Apr  1 00:14 ppc -> mac
drwxr-xr-x 2 root root 4096 Apr  1 00:14 sun
```

Appendix B. hardware

B.1. buses

B.1.1. about buses

Hardware components communicate with the **Central Processing Unit** or **cpu** over a **bus**. The most common buses today are **usb**, **pci**, **agp**, **pci-express** and **pcmcia** aka **pc-card**. These are all **Plag and Play** buses.

Older **x86** computers often had **isa** buses, which can be configured using **jumpers** or **dip switches**.

B.1.2. /proc/bus

To list the buses recognised by the Linux kernel on your computer, look at the contents of the **/proc/bus/** directory (screenshot from Ubuntu 7.04 and RHEL4u4 below).

```
root@laika:~# ls /proc/bus/
input  pccard  pci  usb


[root@RHEL4b ~]# ls /proc/bus/
input  pci  usb
```

Can you guess which of these two screenshots was taken on a laptop ?

B.1.3. /usr/sbin/lsusb

To list all the usb devices connected to your system, you could read the contents of **/proc/bus/usb/devices** (if it exists) or you could use the more readable output of **lsusb**, which is executed here on a SPARC system with Ubuntu.

```
root@shaka:~# lsusb
Bus 001 Device 002: ID 0430:0100 Sun Microsystems, Inc. 3-button Mouse
Bus 001 Device 003: ID 0430:0005 Sun Microsystems, Inc. Type 6 Keyboard
Bus 001 Device 001: ID 04b0:0136 Nikon Corp. Coolpix 7900 (storage)
root@shaka:~#
```

B.1.4. /var/lib/usbutils/usb.ids

The **/var/lib/usbutils/usb.ids** file contains a gzipped list of all known usb devices.

```
paul@barry:~$ zmore /var/lib/usbutils/usb.ids | head
------> /var/lib/usbutils/usb.ids <------
#
# List of USB ID's
#
# Maintained by Vojtech Pavlik <vojtech@suse.cz>
```

```
# If you have any new entries, send them to the maintainer.
# The latest version can be obtained from
#   http://www.linux-usb.org/usb.ids
#
# $Id: usb.ids,v 1.225 2006/07/13 04:18:02 dbrownell Exp $
```

B.1.5. /usr/sbin/lspci

To get a list of all pci devices connected, you could take a look at **/proc/bus/pci** or run **lspci** (partial output below).

```
paul@laika:~$ lspci
...
00:06.0 FireWire (IEEE 1394): Texas Instruments TSB43AB22/A IEEE-139...
00:08.0 Ethernet controller: Realtek Semiconductor Co., Ltd. RTL-816...
00:09.0 Multimedia controller: Philips Semiconductors SAA7133/SAA713...
00:0a.0 Network controller: RaLink RT2500 802.11g Cardbus/mini-PCI
00:0f.0 RAID bus controller: VIA Technologies, Inc. VIA VT6420 SATA ...
00:0f.1 IDE interface: VIA Technologies, Inc. VT82C586A/B/VT82C686/A...
00:10.0 USB Controller: VIA Technologies, Inc. VT82xxxxx UHCI USB 1....
00:10.1 USB Controller: VIA Technologies, Inc. VT82xxxxx UHCI USB 1....
...
```

B.2. interrupts

B.2.1. about interrupts

An **interrupt request** or **IRQ** is a request from a device to the CPU. A device raises an interrupt when it requires the attention of the CPU (could be because the device has data ready to be read by the CPU).

Since the introduction of pci, irq's can be shared among devices.

Interrupt 0 is always reserved for the timer, interrupt 1 for the keyboard. IRQ 2 is used as a channel for IRQ's 8 to 15, and thus is the same as IRQ 9.

B.2.2. /proc/interrupts

You can see a listing of interrupts on your system in **/proc/interrupts**.

```
paul@laika:~$ cat /proc/interrupts
        CPU0      CPU1
  0:  1320048      555   IO-APIC-edge      timer
  1:    10224        7   IO-APIC-edge      i8042
  7:        0        0   IO-APIC-edge      parport0
  8:        2        1   IO-APIC-edge      rtc
 10:     3062       21   IO-APIC-fasteoi   acpi
 12:      131        2   IO-APIC-edge      i8042
 15:    47073        0   IO-APIC-edge      ide1
 18:        0        1   IO-APIC-fasteoi   yenta
 19:    31056        1   IO-APIC-fasteoi   libata, ohci1394
 20:    19042        1   IO-APIC-fasteoi   eth0
 21:    44052        1   IO-APIC-fasteoi   uhci_hcd:usb1, uhci_hcd:usb2,...
 22:   188352        1   IO-APIC-fasteoi   ra0
```

```
23:    632444    1   IO-APIC-fasteoi   nvidia
24:      1585    1   IO-APIC-fasteoi   VIA82XX-MODEM, VIA8237
```

B.2.3. dmesg

You can also use **dmesg** to find irq's allocated at boot time.

```
paul@laika:~$ dmesg | grep "irq 1[45]"
[ 28.930069] ata3: PATA max UDMA/133 cmd 0x1f0 ctl 0x3f6 bmdma 0x2090 irq 14
[ 28.930071] ata4: PATA max UDMA/133 cmd 0x170 ctl 0x376 bmdma 0x2098 irq 15
```

B.3. io ports

B.3.1. about io ports

Communication in the other direction, from CPU to device, happens through **IO ports**. The CPU writes data or control codes to the IO port of the device. But this is not only a one way communication, the CPU can also use a device's IO port to read status information about the device. Unlike interrupts, ports cannot be shared!

B.3.2. /proc/ioports

You can see a listing of your system's IO ports via **/proc/ioports**.

```
[root@RHEL4b ~]# cat /proc/ioports
0000-001f : dma1
0020-0021 : pic1
0040-0043 : timer0
0050-0053 : timer1
0060-006f : keyboard
0070-0077 : rtc
0080-008f : dma page reg
00a0-00a1 : pic2
00c0-00df : dma2
00f0-00ff : fpu
0170-0177 : ide1
02f8-02ff : serial
...
```

B.4. dma

B.4.1. about dma

A device that needs a lot of data, interrupts and ports can pose a heavy load on the cpu. With **dma** or **Direct Memory Access** a device can gain (temporary) access to a specific range of the **ram** memory.

B.4.2. /proc/dma

Looking at **/proc/dma** might not give you the information that you want, since it only contains currently assigned **dma** channels for **isa** devices.

```
root@laika:~# cat /proc/dma
1: parport0
4: cascade
```

pci devices that are using dma are not listed in **/proc/dma**, in this case **dmesg** can be useful. The screenshot below shows that during boot the parallel port received dma channel 1, and the Infrared port received dma channel 3.

```
root@laika:~# dmesg | egrep -C 1 'dma 1|dma 3'
[   20.576000] parport: PnPBIOS parport detected.
[   20.580000] parport0: PC-style at 0x378 (0x778), irq 7, dma 1...
[   20.764000] irda_init()
--
[   21.204000] pnp: Device 00:0b activated.
[   21.204000] nsc_ircc_pnp_probe() : From PnP, found firbase 0x2F8...
[   21.204000] nsc-ircc, chip->init
```

Appendix C. License

0. PREAMBLE

The purpose of this License is to make a manual, textbook, or other
functional and useful document "free" in the sense of freedom: to
assure everyone the effective freedom to copy and redistribute it,
with or without modifying it, either commercially or noncommercially.
Secondarily, this License preserves for the author and publisher a way
to get credit for their work, while not being considered responsible
for modifications made by others.

This License is a kind of "copyleft", which means that derivative
works of the document must themselves be free in the same sense. It
complements the GNU General Public License, which is a copyleft
license designed for free software.

We have designed this License in order to use it for manuals for free
software, because free software needs free documentation: a free
program should come with manuals providing the same freedoms that the
software does. But this License is not limited to software manuals; it
can be used for any textual work, regardless of subject matter or
whether it is published as a printed book. We recommend this License
principally for works whose purpose is instruction or reference.

1. APPLICABILITY AND DEFINITIONS

This License applies to any manual or other work, in any medium, that
contains a notice placed by the copyright holder saying it can be
distributed under the terms of this License. Such a notice grants a
world-wide, royalty-free license, unlimited in duration, to use that
work under the conditions stated herein. The "Document", below, refers
to any such manual or work. Any member of the public is a licensee,
and is addressed as "you". You accept the license if you copy, modify
or distribute the work in a way requiring permission under copyright
law.

A "Modified Version" of the Document means any work containing the
Document or a portion of it, either copied verbatim, or with
modifications and/or translated into another language.

A "Secondary Section" is a named appendix or a front-matter section of
the Document that deals exclusively with the relationship of the
publishers or authors of the Document to the Document's overall
subject (or to related matters) and contains nothing that could fall
directly within that overall subject. (Thus, if the Document is in
part a textbook of mathematics, a Secondary Section may not explain
any mathematics.) The relationship could be a matter of historical
connection with the subject or with related matters, or of legal,
commercial, philosophical, ethical or political position regarding
them.

The "Invariant Sections" are certain Secondary Sections whose titles are designated, as being those of Invariant Sections, in the notice that says that the Document is released under this License. If a section does not fit the above definition of Secondary then it is not allowed to be designated as Invariant. The Document may contain zero Invariant Sections. If the Document does not identify any Invariant Sections then there are none.

The "Cover Texts" are certain short passages of text that are listed, as Front-Cover Texts or Back-Cover Texts, in the notice that says that the Document is released under this License. A Front-Cover Text may be at most 5 words, and a Back-Cover Text may be at most 25 words.

A "Transparent" copy of the Document means a machine-readable copy, represented in a format whose specification is available to the general public, that is suitable for revising the document straightforwardly with generic text editors or (for images composed of pixels) generic paint programs or (for drawings) some widely available drawing editor, and that is suitable for input to text formatters or for automatic translation to a variety of formats suitable for input to text formatters. A copy made in an otherwise Transparent file format whose markup, or absence of markup, has been arranged to thwart or discourage subsequent modification by readers is not Transparent. An image format is not Transparent if used for any substantial amount of text. A copy that is not "Transparent" is called "Opaque".

Examples of suitable formats for Transparent copies include plain ASCII without markup, Texinfo input format, LaTeX input format, SGML or XML using a publicly available DTD, and standard-conforming simple HTML, PostScript or PDF designed for human modification. Examples of transparent image formats include PNG, XCF and JPG. Opaque formats include proprietary formats that can be read and edited only by proprietary word processors, SGML or XML for which the DTD and/or processing tools are not generally available, and the machine-generated HTML, PostScript or PDF produced by some word processors for output purposes only.

The "Title Page" means, for a printed book, the title page itself, plus such following pages as are needed to hold, legibly, the material this License requires to appear in the title page. For works in formats which do not have any title page as such, "Title Page" means the text near the most prominent appearance of the work's title, preceding the beginning of the body of the text.

The "publisher" means any person or entity that distributes copies of the Document to the public.

A section "Entitled XYZ" means a named subunit of the Document whose title either is precisely XYZ or contains XYZ in parentheses following text that translates XYZ in another language. (Here XYZ stands for a specific section name mentioned below, such as "Acknowledgements", "Dedications", "Endorsements", or "History".) To "Preserve the Title" of such a section when you modify the Document means that it remains a section "Entitled XYZ" according to this definition.

The Document may include Warranty Disclaimers next to the notice which states that this License applies to the Document. These Warranty Disclaimers are considered to be included by reference in this License, but only as regards disclaiming warranties: any other implication that these Warranty Disclaimers may have is void and has no effect on the meaning of this License.

2. VERBATIM COPYING

You may copy and distribute the Document in any medium, either commercially or noncommercially, provided that this License, the copyright notices, and the license notice saying this License applies to the Document are reproduced in all copies, and that you add no other conditions whatsoever to those of this License. You may not use technical measures to obstruct or control the reading or further copying of the copies you make or distribute. However, you may accept compensation in exchange for copies. If you distribute a large enough number of copies you must also follow the conditions in section 3.

You may also lend copies, under the same conditions stated above, and you may publicly display copies.

3. COPYING IN QUANTITY

If you publish printed copies (or copies in media that commonly have printed covers) of the Document, numbering more than 100, and the Document's license notice requires Cover Texts, you must enclose the copies in covers that carry, clearly and legibly, all these Cover Texts: Front-Cover Texts on the front cover, and Back-Cover Texts on the back cover. Both covers must also clearly and legibly identify you as the publisher of these copies. The front cover must present the full title with all words of the title equally prominent and visible. You may add other material on the covers in addition. Copying with changes limited to the covers, as long as they preserve the title of the Document and satisfy these conditions, can be treated as verbatim copying in other respects.

If the required texts for either cover are too voluminous to fit legibly, you should put the first ones listed (as many as fit reasonably) on the actual cover, and continue the rest onto adjacent pages.

If you publish or distribute Opaque copies of the Document numbering more than 100, you must either include a machine-readable Transparent copy along with each Opaque copy, or state in or with each Opaque copy a computer-network location from which the general network-using public has access to download using public-standard network protocols a complete Transparent copy of the Document, free of added material. If you use the latter option, you must take reasonably prudent steps, when you begin distribution of Opaque copies in quantity, to ensure that this Transparent copy will remain thus accessible at the stated location until at least one year after the last time you distribute an Opaque copy (directly or through your agents or retailers) of that edition to the public.

It is requested, but not required, that you contact the authors of the Document well before redistributing any large number of copies, to give them a chance to provide you with an updated version of the Document.

4. MODIFICATIONS

You may copy and distribute a Modified Version of the Document under the conditions of sections 2 and 3 above, provided that you release the Modified Version under precisely this License, with the Modified Version filling the role of the Document, thus licensing distribution and modification of the Modified Version to whoever possesses a copy of it. In addition, you must do these things in the Modified Version:

  * A. Use in the Title Page (and on the covers, if any) a title distinct from that of the Document, and from those of previous versions (which should, if there were any, be listed in the History section of the Document). You may use the same title as a previous version if the original publisher of that version gives permission.

    * B. List on the Title Page, as authors, one or more persons or entities responsible for authorship of the modifications in the Modified Version, together with at least five of the principal authors of the Document (all of its principal authors, if it has fewer than five), unless they release you from this requirement.

    * C. State on the Title page the name of the publisher of the Modified Version, as the publisher.

    * D. Preserve all the copyright notices of the Document.

    * E. Add an appropriate copyright notice for your modifications adjacent to the other copyright notices.

    * F. Include, immediately after the copyright notices, a license notice giving the public permission to use the Modified Version under the terms of this License, in the form shown in the Addendum below.

    * G. Preserve in that license notice the full lists of Invariant Sections and required Cover Texts given in the Document's license notice.

    * H. Include an unaltered copy of this License.

    * I. Preserve the section Entitled "History", Preserve its Title, and add to it an item stating at least the title, year, new authors, and publisher of the Modified Version as given on the Title Page. If there is no section Entitled "History" in the Document, create one stating the title, year, authors, and publisher of the Document as given on its Title Page, then add an item describing the Modified Version as stated in the previous sentence.

    * J. Preserve the network location, if any, given in the Document for public access to a Transparent copy of the Document, and likewise the network locations given in the Document for previous versions it was based on. These may be placed in the "History" section. You may omit a network location for a work that was published at least four years before the Document itself, or if the original publisher of the version it refers to gives permission.

    * K. For any section Entitled "Acknowledgements" or "Dedications", Preserve the Title of the section, and preserve in the section all the substance and tone of each of the contributor acknowledgements and/or dedications given therein.

    * L. Preserve all the Invariant Sections of the Document, unaltered in their text and in their titles. Section numbers or the equivalent are not considered part of the section titles.

    * M. Delete any section Entitled "Endorsements". Such a section may not be included in the Modified Version.

    * N. Do not retitle any existing section to be Entitled "Endorsements" or to conflict in title with any Invariant Section.

    * O. Preserve any Warranty Disclaimers.

If the Modified Version includes new front-matter sections or appendices that qualify as Secondary Sections and contain no material copied from the Document, you may at your option designate some or all of these sections as invariant. To do this, add their titles to the list of Invariant Sections in the Modified Version's license notice. These titles must be distinct from any other section titles.

You may add a section Entitled "Endorsements", provided it contains nothing but endorsements of your Modified Version by various parties—for example, statements of peer review or that the text has been approved by an organization as the authoritative definition of a standard.

You may add a passage of up to five words as a Front-Cover Text, and a passage of up to 25 words as a Back-Cover Text, to the end of the list of Cover Texts in the Modified Version. Only one passage of Front-Cover Text and one of Back-Cover Text may be added by (or through arrangements made by) any one entity. If the Document already includes a cover text for the same cover, previously added by you or by arrangement made by the same entity you are acting on behalf of, you may not add another; but you may replace the old one, on explicit permission from the previous publisher that added the old one.

The author(s) and publisher(s) of the Document do not by this License give permission to use their names for publicity for or to assert or imply endorsement of any Modified Version.

5. COMBINING DOCUMENTS

You may combine the Document with other documents released under this License, under the terms defined in section 4 above for modified versions, provided that you include in the combination all of the Invariant Sections of all of the original documents, unmodified, and list them all as Invariant Sections of your combined work in its license notice, and that you preserve all their Warranty Disclaimers.

The combined work need only contain one copy of this License, and multiple identical Invariant Sections may be replaced with a single copy. If there are multiple Invariant Sections with the same name but different contents, make the title of each such section unique by adding at the end of it, in parentheses, the name of the original author or publisher of that section if known, or else a unique number. Make the same adjustment to the section titles in the list of Invariant Sections in the license notice of the combined work.

In the combination, you must combine any sections Entitled "History" in the various original documents, forming one section Entitled "History"; likewise combine any sections Entitled "Acknowledgements", and any sections Entitled "Dedications". You must delete all sections Entitled "Endorsements".

6. COLLECTIONS OF DOCUMENTS

You may make a collection consisting of the Document and other documents released under this License, and replace the individual copies of this License in the various documents with a single copy that is included in the collection, provided that you follow the rules of this License for verbatim copying of each of the documents in all other respects.

You may extract a single document from such a collection, and distribute it individually under this License, provided you insert a copy of this License into the extracted document, and follow this License in all other respects regarding verbatim copying of that document.

7. AGGREGATION WITH INDEPENDENT WORKS

A compilation of the Document or its derivatives with other separate and independent documents or works, in or on a volume of a storage or distribution medium, is called an "aggregate" if the copyright resulting from the compilation is not used to limit the legal rights of the compilation's users beyond what the individual works permit. When the Document is included in an aggregate, this License does not apply to the other works in the aggregate which are not themselves derivative works of the Document.

If the Cover Text requirement of section 3 is applicable to these copies of the Document, then if the Document is less than one half of the entire aggregate, the Document's Cover Texts may be placed on covers that bracket the Document within the aggregate, or the electronic equivalent of covers if the Document is in electronic form. Otherwise they must appear on printed covers that bracket the whole aggregate.

8. TRANSLATION

Translation is considered a kind of modification, so you may
distribute translations of the Document under the terms of section 4.
Replacing Invariant Sections with translations requires special
permission from their copyright holders, but you may include
translations of some or all Invariant Sections in addition to the
original versions of these Invariant Sections. You may include a
translation of this License, and all the license notices in the
Document, and any Warranty Disclaimers, provided that you also include
the original English version of this License and the original versions
of those notices and disclaimers. In case of a disagreement between
the translation and the original version of this License or a notice
or disclaimer, the original version will prevail.

If a section in the Document is Entitled "Acknowledgements",
"Dedications", or "History", the requirement (section 4) to Preserve
its Title (section 1) will typically require changing the actual
title.

9. TERMINATION

You may not copy, modify, sublicense, or distribute the Document
except as expressly provided under this License. Any attempt otherwise
to copy, modify, sublicense, or distribute it is void, and will
automatically terminate your rights under this License.

However, if you cease all violation of this License, then your license
from a particular copyright holder is reinstated (a) provisionally,
unless and until the copyright holder explicitly and finally
terminates your license, and (b) permanently, if the copyright holder
fails to notify you of the violation by some reasonable means prior to
60 days after the cessation.

Moreover, your license from a particular copyright holder is
reinstated permanently if the copyright holder notifies you of the
violation by some reasonable means, this is the first time you have
received notice of violation of this License (for any work) from that
copyright holder, and you cure the violation prior to 30 days after
your receipt of the notice.

Termination of your rights under this section does not terminate the
licenses of parties who have received copies or rights from you under
this License. If your rights have been terminated and not permanently
reinstated, receipt of a copy of some or all of the same material does
not give you any rights to use it.

10. FUTURE REVISIONS OF THIS LICENSE

The Free Software Foundation may publish new, revised versions of the
GNU Free Documentation License from time to time. Such new versions
will be similar in spirit to the present version, but may differ in
detail to address new problems or concerns. See
http://www.gnu.org/copyleft/.

Each version of the License is given a distinguishing version number.
If the Document specifies that a particular numbered version of this
License "or any later version" applies to it, you have the option of
following the terms and conditions either of that specified version or
of any later version that has been published (not as a draft) by the
Free Software Foundation. If the Document does not specify a version
number of this License, you may choose any version ever published (not
as a draft) by the Free Software Foundation. If the Document specifies

that a proxy can decide which future versions of this License can be used, that proxy's public statement of acceptance of a version permanently authorizes you to choose that version for the Document.

11. RELICENSING

"Massive Multiauthor Collaboration Site" (or "MMC Site") means any World Wide Web server that publishes copyrightable works and also provides prominent facilities for anybody to edit those works. A public wiki that anybody can edit is an example of such a server. A "Massive Multiauthor Collaboration" (or "MMC") contained in the site means any set of copyrightable works thus published on the MMC site.

"CC-BY-SA" means the Creative Commons Attribution-Share Alike 3.0 license published by Creative Commons Corporation, a not-for-profit corporation with a principal place of business in San Francisco, California, as well as future copyleft versions of that license published by that same organization.

"Incorporate" means to publish or republish a Document, in whole or in part, as part of another Document.

An MMC is "eligible for relicensing" if it is licensed under this License, and if all works that were first published under this License somewhere other than this MMC, and subsequently incorporated in whole or in part into the MMC, (1) had no cover texts or invariant sections, and (2) were thus incorporated prior to November 1, 2008.

The operator of an MMC Site may republish an MMC contained in the site under CC-BY-SA on the same site at any time before August 1, 2009, provided the MMC is eligible for relicensing.

Index

Symbols